+HN90 .M6 O43 1986

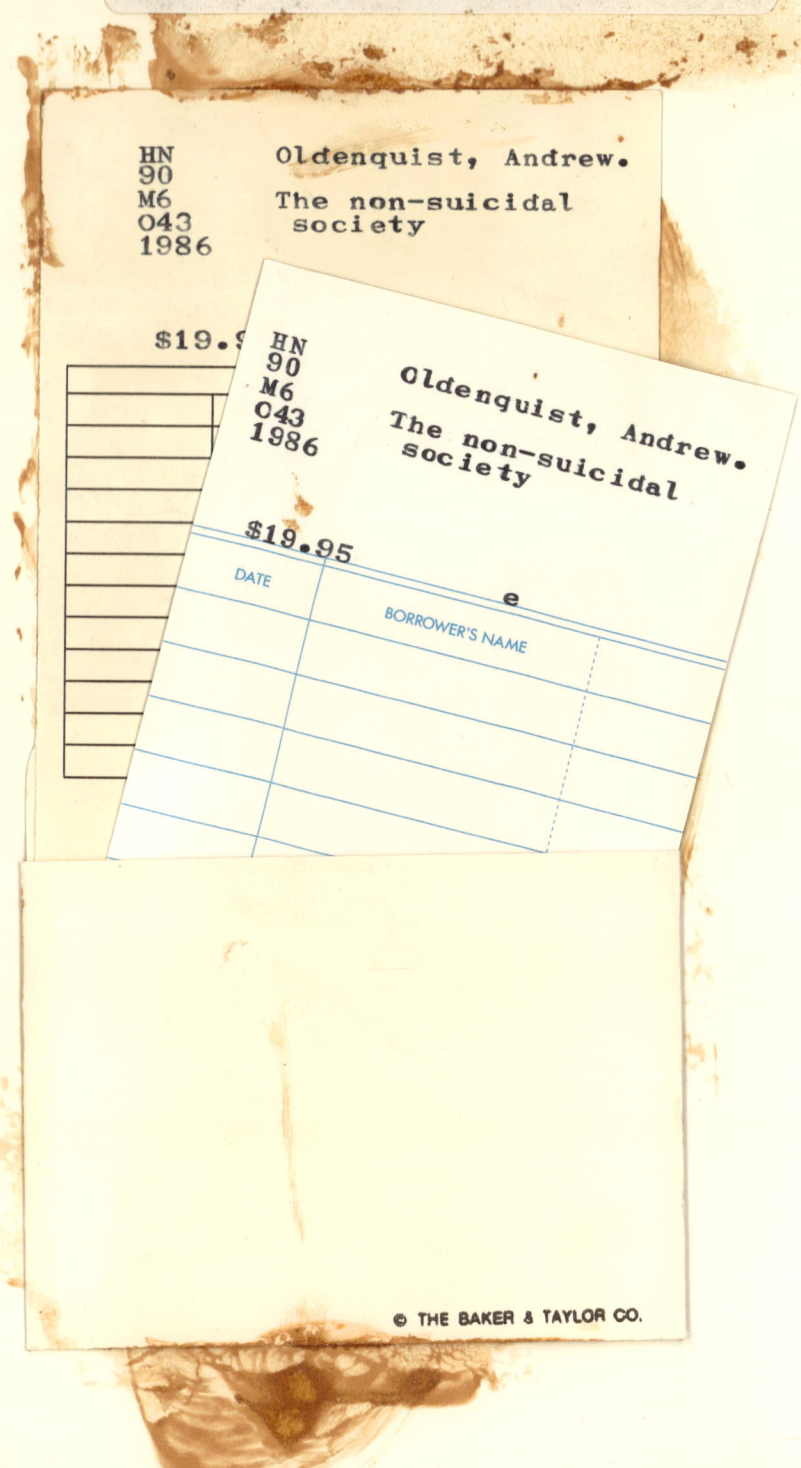

Y0-BKC-715

```
HN      Oldenquist, Andrew.
90
M6      The non-suicidal
O43        society
1986
```

$19.95

```
HN      Oldenquist, Andrew.
90
M6      The non-suicidal
O43        society
1986
```

$19.95

DATE | BORROWER'S NAME

© THE BAKER & TAYLOR CO.

THE
Non-Suicidal Society

THE
Non-Suicidal Society

Andrew Oldenquist

INDIANA UNIVERSITY PRESS

Bloomington and Indianapolis

32767

© 1986 by Andrew Oldenquist
All rights reserved

No part of this book may be reproduced or utilized in any form or by any means, electronic or mechanical, including photocopying and recording, or by any information storage and retrieval system, without permission in writing from the publisher. The Association of American University Presses' Resolution on Permissions constitutes the only exception to this prohibition.

Manufactured in the United States of America

Library of Congress Cataloging-in-Publication Data

Oldenquist, Andrew.
  The non-suicidal society.

  Bibliography: p.
  Includes index.
  1. United States—Moral conditions. 2. United States—Social conditions—1960–1980. 3. United States—Social conditions—1980–   . 4. Social ethics.
  I. Title.
  HN90.M6043   1986   306'.0973   85-45804
  ISBN 0-253-34107-8

1 2 3 4 5 90 89 88 87 86

FOR

Riek, Nina, and Mark

CONTENTS

PREFACE   xi

PART I
LEARNING FROM THE '60s and '70s

- ONE   *Introduction*   3
- TWO   *The Price of Perfect Individualism*   15
- THREE   *The Trashing of American Education*   30
- FOUR   *Moral Education without Moral Education*   45
- FIVE   *The Ethically Neutered Society*   57
- SIX   *Laconic Violence*   67
- SEVEN   *The Selling of Selfishness*   87

PART II
WHAT IT MEANS TO BE A SOCIAL ANIMAL

- EIGHT   *The Failure of Selfishness*   99
- NINE   *The Metaphysics of Self and Society*   113
- TEN   *The Ethics of Parts and Wholes*   127
- ELEVEN   *The Ethics of Evolution and the Evolution of Ethics*   141
- TWELVE   *Human Nature and the Social Contract*   153
- THIRTEEN   *Our Secret Pleistocene Inheritance*   166

viii / *Contents*

FOURTEEN	*Human Nature and Society*	180
FIFTEEN	*Race*	198
SIXTEEN	*Sanitized Revenge*	210
SEVENTEEN	*Why There Is an Ethics of Work*	225
EIGHTEEN	*Alienation and De-Alienation*	239
	NOTES	251
	INDEX	259

Illustrations

FIGURE 1	Adult and Youth Suicide Rates	8
FIGURE 2	The Scholastic Aptitude Test scores	31
FIGURE 3	Why Johnny Can't Add Anymore	38
FIGURE 4	Homicide Victims, by Race	68
FIGURE 5	Delinquency Rate	69
FIGURE 6	Prisoner's Dilemma: For Egoists and Altruists	101
FIGURE 7	Prisoner's Dilemma: Decay into State of Nature	102
FIGURE 8	Prisoner's Dilemma: Its Classical Form	103
FIGURE 9	Prisoner's Dilemma: For Large and Small Groups	106
FIGURE 10	Prisoner's Dilemma: For Summed Possible Worlds	108
FIGURE 11	Criminal:Victim::Altruist:Recipient	109
FIGURE 12	Group Egoism, Morality, and Self	121
FIGURE 13	Nested and Overlapping Group Loyalties	130
FIGURE 14	Selfish Genes vs. Selfish People	149
FIGURE 15	Out-of-Wedlock Birth Rates	202
FIGURE 16	The Movie Line	248

Preface

It is a perilous business writing about the history of ideas just a decade or two old. But American society went through a great trauma between the sixties and the early eighties. If there is reason to think ideas from those times prompted policies that contributed to the present state of education, crime, and urban life, there is no choice but to plunge in. For two decades schooling has been seen as failing in various ways, the quality of urban life is generally considered to have declined, and the elderly and the vulnerable have lived in heightened fear of violence and incivility.

The mid-'70s to the early '80s were the worst period. The headiness of the '60s was gone and the loss of respect for and involvement in social institutions, spawned by the war, the riots, Watergate, and the civil rights revolution had had time to incubate: There was no excitement anymore, just a gathering awareness of intolerable crime, failing schools, and blue collar blues. People turned inward and each person and each apartment became a fortress. The regard citizens had for the common good—including our schools, ceremonies, rituals, as well as patriotism, mutual civility, and mutual assistance—fell out of fashion. The ideas of the '60s gave us the practices of the '70s—the guilt-exorcism of the psychotherapists, the self-esteem fetishism and flight from standards of educators, the selling of selfishness by pop psychologists, and the criminologists' bland relabeling of crime and delinquency as "deviance." The practices of the '70s left us with problems for the '80s and '90s.

There is now a national will to put an end to this. But the will requires a way and it is my hope to make some small contribution to the fashioning of it—to the articulation of a rational, self-respecting, policy-oriented social philosophy as America finishes the twentieth and prepares for the twenty-first century. The basis of our problems, I shall try to show, was a temporary breakdown of Americans' conception of themselves as social creatures; it was a transitory narcosis of the multitude of filaments that link individual persons to their societies.

I wish to express my gratitude to the Department of Philosophy and College of Humanities at The Ohio State University for a sabbatical leave during which the final draft of this book was written. The department also was generous in providing me with research assistants. I am also indebted to Ohio State's Mershon Center, and to its director Charles Hermann, for a National Security Award in the summer of 1980 to write on loyalties. From that essay, which began as a modest defense of a communalistic conception of society and citizenship, the outline of a book quickly took form. I was greatly assisted, during the four years of writing the book, by the congeniality, intellectual stimulation, and generous support of the Mershon Center. The Ethics Resource Center in Washington, D.C., and its director, Gary Edwards, have been a source of encouragement, useful discussion, and funding for research on the phenomena of alienation.

I am grateful to the editors of the following magazines for permission to use material from articles I published: *The Public Interest*, for "'Indoctrination' and Societal Suicide," and "The Case for Revenge"; *The Harvard Educational Review*, for "Review Essay: Moral Education Without Moral Education"; *Character*, for "Tribal Morality" (co-authored with Michael Lynn); *The Journal of Philosophy*, for "Loyalties"; *American Education*, for "The Decline of American Education in the '60s and '70s."

A number of individuals have given generously of their time to comment on drafts of chapters. I am particularly grateful to Norman Care at Oberlin College for extensive, provocative, and helpful comments on a long early draft. Davydd J. Greenwood at Cornell University, William Lycan at the University of North Carolina at Chapel Hill, and Edward Wynne at the University of Illinois at Chicago also provided very helpful critical comments on early drafts.

My colleague Richard Garner has discussed with me at length a number of more recent draft chapters. Helpful comments have been made by other philosophical colleagues including Wallace Anderson, Daniel Farrell, Donald Hubin, Joel Kupperman, Bernard Rosen, Robert Turnbull, and by anthropologist Daniel Hughes, zoologists Paul Colinvaux and Edward O. Wilson, and political scientists Lawrence Herson, Charles Hermann, and James Q. Wilson. I owe a special debt of gratitude to Michael Lynn, who, while a psychology graduate student, was a tireless research assistant, remaining available even when I was out of funding; he has been a critic and supplier of good ideas, and a source of moral support. Other students, especially Douglas Chismar, Erdinc Sayan, Barbara Scholz, and Lidia Moreno helped with ideas and sheer labor. I must, finally, mention the indispensable support and patience of my wife and children, without which the will would have failed.

THE
Non-Suicidal
Society

PART I

Learning from the '60s and '70s

ONE

Introduction

> Less attention, I suppose, is paid to philosophy in the United States than in any other country of the civilized world. The Americans have no school of philosophy peculiar to themselves, and they pay very little attention to the rival European schools. Indeed they hardly know their names. Nevertheless, it is noticeable that the people of the United States almost all have a uniform method and rules for the conduct of intellectual inquiries. So, though they have not taken the trouble to define the rules, they have a philosophical method shared by all.
> —Alexis de Tocqueville

> The proper design of public policies requires a clear and sober understanding of the nature of man, and, above all, of the extent to which that nature can be changed.
> —James Q. Wilson

In Gorky Park one September morning in the autumn of 1979, an old man, poorly dressed, sat on a bench reading the paper when four teenagers wandered by and began throwing stones at a squirrel. He shouted at them, called them hooligans, and they stopped and slunk away; they said *nothing*, much less the string of obscenities such an interference would be likely to produce in America. Russians are taught to tend to each other, to get involved, and it can become a pain in the neck.

Outside a junior high school in Maine, a student who had been suspended tried to turn her dog on the teacher apparently responsible for the suspension. A number of students were at the scene. Some gave advice and encouragement to the teacher menaced by the dog, but no one criticized the dog's owner: Assistance to the victim was socially all right, but moral criticism was socially taboo and none of their business. Such responses, in Maine or Moscow, exemplify a small part of a society's social philosophy. The school incident is but one of countless ways we reveal our social assumptions, some so deep they are never articulated but just lived.

Americans are inclined to accept the idea, and our adversaries hardly demur, that what we believe in, religion aside, is conspicuously negative (anti-communism, anti-collectivism), and otherwise morally neutral (individualism, capitalism). Until now the articulation of a positive social philosophy for Americans has seemed a dispensable luxury, possibly because we thought that what plainly worked didn't need selling. Perhaps America's great size, wealth, and past invincibility have created a sense that it needs no special care and tending, that it is a juggernaut that runs on its own energy, its citizens needing more to cope with it than to love and nurture it. Given the difficulties our society faces today, that attitude may be difficult to maintain. In these years, it might even be conceived of as part of national defense to articulate a set of ideas that can be defended before the world and which is appropriate to our way of life without merely sanctifying it.

It is widely believed that for some time Americans, especially the poor and the elderly, have been less secure from violence; that public morality and civility have declined; that high school graduates are poorer at reading and math; that social self-destruction has been paralleled by personal self-destruction, particularly among the young; and that in general things have gotten bad. It is largely true, and data will be offered to show it. The incredible diversity of the bad trends that began in the early '60s and continued into the '80s—crime, suicide, divorce, out-of-wedlock births, declining Scholastic Aptitude Test scores, the high school dropout rate—are evidence that the causes are deep and not something such as unemployment, which cannot begin to explain the phenomena. It is a challenge to detectives in the field of social causation. What happened, to show up in such diverse ways in 1963? In 1981 some of the bad trends, especially certain kinds of crime, began a modest reversal. *Why*? And what about the appalling trends that have not reversed? Do we just thank our stars, or wail, and wait stupidly for the next thing to happen, like novices watching the stock market go up and down? We need to understand the causes, for in no other way can we control the quality of our lives in the future.

The response of some educators and social scientists was to deny that school achievement and crime had gotten worse. The response of the political Left is to attribute it to the "twilight of capitalism in the West." The response of the political Right is to blame government interference and bureaucracy.

These are shallow answers. The Left appeals to arguments derived from Marxist theory and explains our problems in terms of contradictions in a free market society and "laws of history": It is the internal rot of a doomed and expiring capitalist stage of society. This explanation is supported by neither empirical data nor cogent argument, nor are the detailed causal links provided that would connect a regulated free market economy with what actually happens in America in the 1980s. The Right blames big government, but again, no actual causal connections are provided between, say, government subsidies and guidelines for schools and increasing illiteracy and school vandalism. Big government is bigger in Sweden and the USSR and their problems with school vandalism and illiteracy are less than ours.

Christopher Lasch, in *The Culture of Narcissism*, has given elegant analytical descriptions of much that is wrong with recent American society.[1] He also suggested the cause: "Late Capitalism." This is like brilliantly describing a disease and then saying the Devil did it. If one doesn't know what causes our very real problems, one is tempted to reach out for a villain—late capitalism if one speaks from the Left, big government if one speaks from the Right. The problems American society faces in the last fifteen years of this century are beyond the explanatory capacities of these two kinds of devils. Our national problems regarding crime, bad schools, disintegrating families, and disintegrating individuals can be understood only by examining, at the deepest level, both human nature and the nature of the relation of individuals to the societies in which they live; and then seeing whether, in this light, the way we live, raise children, and treat each other is rational.

A suicidal society is one whose social ethics, family and community structure, procedures for rearing children, physical layout, educational and juvenile justice systems, are so counterproductive or ineffective as to produce unacceptable numbers of hostile, wretched, useless and dangerous citizens. In certain respects contemporary American society has for two decades been suicidal and is only now beginning to question some self-destructive policies. The causes of our problems are not inevitable historical forces but specific, correctable mistakes. They are not a matter of fate or an exhausted political system, but, in large part, a matter of bad theories which have guided policies and which need to be thrown out.

Policy mistakes are to a considerable extent *philosophical* ones, which oughtn't surprise anyone: The policies of juvenile justice officials, educators, city planners, and legislators reflect their ideals, principles, and views of human nature. They are crucially influenced by their beliefs about rights, responsibility, the good life and the just society, what makes us secure or anxious, what motivates us at deep levels, and the goals of education. These beliefs comprise a person's social philosophy. It is in this sense that we are all philosophers, however "practical" or "nuts-and-bolts" we may think we are—what is practical according to one person's facts, dreams, and principles being unfeasible or undesirable according to another's.

Part of the key to a viable modern society is to be found in the emotional, ethical, and institutional features of humanity's prehistoric past. There are, of course, dreadful aspects of prehistoric social life, but I shall not propose we adopt those. If we have a number of social policies that have not been working very well it is natural to seek a better underlying theory that implies better policies. The theory I shall suggest is that human beings are innately social, tribal creatures, and that attention to typical mechanisms by which tribes function suggests a number of hypotheses for reducing crime and suicide, improving schools, and improving the overall quality of urban life. Evolutionary biology provides a basis for educated guesses about what human social life was like for tens of thousands of generations. I shall hypothesize that in such environments, emotions and desires evolved that reinforce social living. Anthropology can help us identify cultural universals, ranging from incest taboo and a core of social morality to ritual and ceremony. To connect the evolutionary and the anthropological I hypothesize that 200,000-year-old hominid bands are not very different genetically from present-day stone-age tribes, especially in their emotional makeup. I also hypothesize that contemporary stone-age tribes are not biologically different at all, in any socially important respects, from present-day New Yorkers and Muscovites. This assumption of minimal genetic variation across present-day cultures and going considerably back in time, at least regarding traits relevant to our species' sociality, is a crucial part of my theory and it is not, I think, challenged by very many biologists.

Social scientists, educators, and philosophers will be brought on stage to present theories about human nature, ethics, and politics of the sorts that underlie our social policies, and then the criminologists and compilers of statistics consulted to see how we are doing. The argument proceeds by a number of what-you-see-is-just-what-you-should-expect-type explanations, together with suggestions for alternative policies that are implied by the critique of radical individualism, by the ways of tribes, and by what we see today. The experts I draw on in each field are those whose findings support my diagnoses and suggestions. Undoubtedly, other experts will disagree. But that is how broad theories are developed. The important question is not a matter of whose findings I have ignored, unless they become too numerous or are pivotal ones. Instead, the issues are: Are the predictions true? Is the overall theory plausible? Are the explanations of particular social phenomena persuasive?

Some of what I wish to say about societal suicide is relevant to the suicide of individuals. What weakens the social fabric contributes to the causes of individual suicide. Policies by which a society slowly kills itself make the individuals in the society, who depend on its viability for their own sense of identity and significance, more prone to commit suicide. In 1897 the great French sociologist Emile Durkheim argued that the rise of individualism accounted for the great increase in suicide in nineteenth-century Europe. More specifically, a person's immunity to suicide is a function of the degree to which he is enmeshed in society:

> Thus, the only remedy for the ill [of suicide] is to restore enough consistency to social groups for them to obtain a firmer grip on the individual, and for him to feel himself bound to them. He must feel himself more solidary with a collective existence which precedes him in time, which survives him, and which encompasses him at all points. If this occurs, he will no longer find the only aim of his conduct in himself, and, understanding that he is the instrument of a purpose greater than himself, he will see that he is not without significance. Life will resume meaning in his eyes, because it will recover its natural aim and orientation.[2]

Over the past two decades we have continually diminished the bonds of community and the range of demands, duties, and restrictions made on our citizens. Our social theorists said we should give people what they need, multiply their rights, and not demand anything without offering payment. If we look at the suicide chart, which is taken back to 1914, we see sharp declines in the overall rate of suicide during World War I, and throughout the Great Depression and most of World War II. Even the Korean War is correlated with a decline. The rate of suicide soared during the "roaring twenties" and began a steady ascent in 1958.

If Durkheim is right, the hyper-individualism and dissolution of social structure of the mid-1960s through the early 1980s should correlate not only with an increase in the overall suicide rate, but especially with youth suicide: Youth would be especially at risk because during their crucial years of socialization and entry into social institutions, society was demoted from an object of pride to one of ridicule, moral suspicion, and minimal importance to one's life. Unlike older people they lacked a rooting in society that was formed prior

8 / THE NON-SUICIDAL SOCIETY

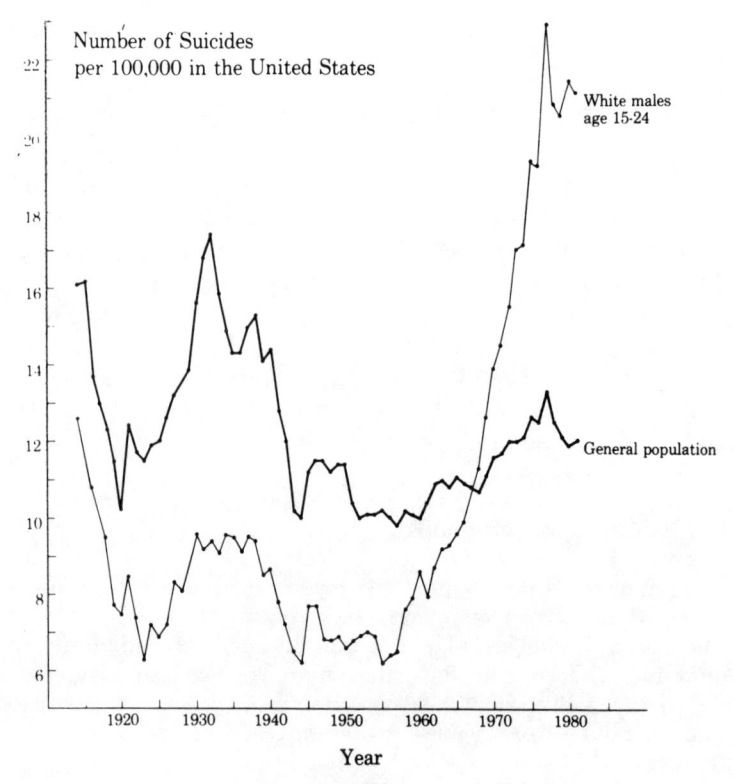

FIGURE 1. Adult and Youth Suicide Rates

The number of suicides per 100,000 since 1914, together with the number per 100,000 for white males aged 15 through 24. Suicide by young white males roughly paralleled adult suicide, at a lower level, until about 1958, and then shot up from 6.5 per 100,000 in that year to 21.1 per 100,000 in 1981. However, the suicide rate for black youth is half what it is for white youth, and the rate for young females lower than for any category of males.

to the '60s. This indeed is what we find. While the overall increase is bad enough, between 1957 and 1981 the annual rate of suicide among white males between the ages of 15 and 24 increased from a little more than one half the rate in the general population to almost double the overall rate. It has become an epidemic and most older teenagers seem to know of someone who has committed suicide. The educational philosopher Edward Wynne, following Durkheim, explains why the Great Depression lowered the suicide rate and why what we do today has increased it, especially among young people:

> Suicide is not so much the outcome of "pressure," but *pressure without social support*. Suicide does not automatically mean that a person has not

been loved or cared for. It probably does mean that he was not needed by others in an immediate, tangible fashion.... In this light, it is understandable that one of the highest suicide rates is that of middle-aged bachelors, and one of the lowest is that of married women with children; yet which of these two groups is subject to the greatest pressure? ... While it is nice to know we are loved, it is essential to know we are needed.... In effect, suicide is a measure of the extent to which society has succeeded in integrating its citizens and its institutions..... Less self-centered persons will withstand such pressures better, because they will be tied to social systems that provide them with demands as well as help.[3]

Group commitments and loyalties are the glue of human social life, more fundamental than either self-interest or moral principles. Group loyalty is tribal morality: From loyalty, as from love and friendship, I prize something because it is *my own*—my family, my territory, community, or company. Since what is mine can also be yours, and therefore *ours*, loyalty creates a social value: *our* community or company. By contrast the rational egoist's one ultimate value, the self, is isolating and intractably presocial. The common core of social morality which practically every society on the face of the earth tries to observe and teach its children—honesty, fairness, and keeping unwanted hands off other people's bodies and property—constitute the rules that preserve the society's collective good and enable its members to live together. A full-fledged society is a *moral community* because it has common values and accepted institutions that define the society as an object of group loyalty; social morality is the collection of rules designed to ensure its integrity and perpetuation.

We recently began envying the Japanese their efficient and loyal auto and electronics workers, and their low crime rates. About 4 percent of convicted Japanese criminals are imprisoned and the rest are taken care of in their communities. According to the *Wall Street Journal*, "Instead of formal punishment, the goal of Japanese prosecutors is to convince the defendant to repent and return to the fold. This can consist of confession and public apology, of restitution to victims, even, according to Mr. Shikita, of facial signs of remorse."[4] This has similarities with age-old tribal practices, with religious confession, and with Soviet treatment of minor criminals.

But we sigh with despair at the Japanese solution: What sincere remorse are we to expect from a mugger arrested for the fifth time? And to what "fold" are we to return him—Manhattan's 8th Avenue? We sigh because we know that the entire social infrastructure on which remorse, expiation, and re-acceptance depends is missing: There usually is no functioning moral community to which we can return a young urban criminal; and even if there were, there is no basis, deep inside the young criminal, for a positive, pro-social response.

Japanese and present-day tribal treatment of criminals both depend on personal, individualized decisions, where great trust and reliance are placed in the judgment of officials or village councils. (Americans frequently think individualized treatment requires informality because we mistakenly think formal, ritualized justice implies inflexible rules; this is a mistake that is reinforced by the story of Jesus and the Pharisees.) For a personalized system to work, members of the society have to trust each other to be fair; there has to be a single moral community to which all feel they equally belong. In America this sense of being a "moral community" is limited by our ethnic and religious diversity; it was truncated from the start by the isolation of American Indian cultures, by black slavery and its aftermath, and for all of us strained to the breaking point by the civil rights movement with its accusations, distrust, anger, and corrective legislation. A significant number of Americans do not trust their officials to base judgments on the observed character, remorse, and personal circumstances of employees, students, delinquents, or criminals: They will, it is charged (often on weak evidence), use this power against blacks, Hispanics, the poor, women, and homosexuals. A smaller number of Americans simply do not accept the moral authority of our judicial institutions: Young defendants go to sleep in court, or curse the judge, and Larry Flynt appears in court wearing an American flag as a diaper.

Where there isn't trust we legislate; we try, in printed laws, regulations, job descriptions, or grievance procedures, to anticipate every possible situation. This automatically depersonalizes our societal transactions, and at the same time creates inflexible rules—paper Pharisees with whom one cannot even argue. As I write, my college dean is packing hundreds of documents about rejected and accepted job applicants, subpoenaed by the U.S. Department of Labor because someone has sued charging sex discrimination. A conversation with the dean will no longer do. What counts is not judgment, but paper, and this means that the letter, not the spirit, is what guides our public life. To attend to the spirit of a rule is to remember its moral point; which requires that we give discretionary authority to deans, employers, teachers, police, juvenile justice authorities, and other officials; which implies we trust them; which we don't.

The less we trust each other to be fair and reasonable in hiring, promoting, managing, renting, admitting, grading, and sentencing, the more we insist on legislation and a mountain of regulations.

Rules, when there is no leeway for discretionary judgment, have their communal purpose blurred and retain about as much moral authority as the law of gravity. It is a matter of how far we have drifted, ritually and communally, from a tribal council. It is also a vicious circle because as citizens become alienated they rely more on impersonal, written regulations, which further alienates them. The legalistic, litigious society is a sign of the loss of mutual trust and also of the relativizing and sealing off of morality from public life, a topic we shall have occasion to pursue in detail later on. As Jethro Lieberman has said,

> Litigiousness is not a legal but a social phenomenon. It is born of a breakdown in community, a breakdown that exacerbates and is exacerbated by the growth of law. A society that is law-saturated inclines toward the belief that in the absence of declared law anything goes. In many ways, the courts have become the final repositories of social trust. . . . [5]

During the civil rights revolution and the Vietnam War mistrust was, for the intellectuals who took up these causes, mixed with abstract guilt and with a sense of righteous indignation that bordered on the voluptuous. The result was hatred of one's own institutions and the gradual elimination of the ritual and ceremony that testify to a society's respect for its institutions. During those years, writers and policy makers on education and criminal justice were ashamed to be proud of anything, they throught loyalty was a sin, and they only loved abstract principles. The mind-set of the times made them contemptuous of belonging to anything, and made them less able to understand what builds loyalty and sense-of-community than are street gangs and college social fraternities. They did not think of mainstream middle-class society as something of which we should feel proud to belong, and like libertarians they thought of an individual's relation to society as never more than a commercial, selfish one. At no other time in American history did we so completely forget that humans are social animals, and never were there so many influential people who simply did not believe in human nature.

A grand theme of scientists and philosophers of the past several centuries has been the gradual increase in our understanding of how man is part of nature. While thinking in this way naturally suggests that man *has* a nature, the idea of human nature has had a bad reputation in the middle decades of the twentieth century. That was the time to attack irresponsible claims that had been made (and some that were imagined to be made) in the service of politics and prejudice: People are "by nature" warlike, or competitive, or prejudiced against other races; and thus—as fuzzy and illogical a "thus" as there can be—we should accept, or expect, or even approve, war and prejudice. And if people have natures why not kinds of people?—another "thus," preceding such claims as that women are "by nature" hysterical, Jews grasping, blacks stupid, Asians cruel, the Irish drunkards, and so on.

At the same time, cautious claims about human nature, made on a more scientific footing, began to reappear, at first not always recognized for what they were. For example, in the late fifties, the linguist Noam Chomsky suggested that a capacity to learn grammatical structure was innate. The psychologist Lawrence Kohlberg, building on the work of the Swiss psychologist Jean Piaget, argued there was cross-cultural evidence of a natural tendency for children to develop through predictable stages in their thinking about morality and values. Beginning in the '50s and accelerating in the '60s and '70s biologists began talking about innate predispositions to aggression, territoriality, incest taboo, and, importantly, altruism.

Consequently, this is also a story of evolution. Social practices and institutions that tend to make us anxious or secure, hostile or cooperative, indifferent or committed, do so because of human nature, which is why a social philosophy needs a biologically and anthropologically plausible theory of human nature. We should expect our evolutionary legacy to include layer upon layer of predisposed emotional responses, from different times, needs, and dangers. I shall offer evidence that our well-being, security, even our sense of self-identity, depend on feeling that we belong to our societies, and on a multitude of other predispositions as well.

The 99 percent of human evolution that took place in hunting-gathering bands made us into tribal creatures, whose security and survival depended on group membership and a predisposed receptivity to socialization. For a million years or more, ostracism and exile meant death and those who did not accept the constraints and common undertakings of social life were unlikely to pass on their temperaments to the next generation. As the psychologist Robert Hogan puts it, isolated primates get eaten by leopards. For reasons such as these, students of prehistory pretty much agree that we became social, tribal creatures even before we became human creatures.

Is it not possible that clues to the content—even to some of the details—of innate human sociality can be discovered in what is very widespread among the tribes of the world? To raise one example now, the *personal* nature of social control is something we discover in accounts of primitive peoples, whether they be the Chenchus of South India, the Onge of the Andaman Islands, or the Iroquois of

New York State. Wrongdoers have to face the disapproval or contempt of people among whom they live and on whom they are absolutely dependent for esteem and acceptance. The ultimate rejection is banishment. But the basis of banishment, and of lesser punishments, is overt, public, and usually ritualized moral censure by one's clan or village. Their disapproval threatens the withdrawal of just about everything one needs: security, nourishment, companionship, a mate, acceptance, and respect.

Fear of personal censure and rejection by one's clan had tens of thousands of generations to become part of man's emotional inheritance. How is America at the end of the twentieth century to come to terms with this? We can begin by seeing that the mechanical, impersonal, and "non-stigmatizing" nature of our juvenile justice and educational system is as different from that of our tribal ancestors as it possibly can be. But we cannot abandon technological civilization and live again like Nagas or Chenchus, or their prehistoric ancestors; on the other hand there is growing evidence that it is as foolish to ignore our biological history as it is to ignore our much more recent political history. So what can we do?

Imaginative intelligence can create (and preserve) in urban and suburban America *surrogates for and analogues of the deep structures of tribal life*. Starving is not part of what I have in mind; nor is head hunting, dying of diseases, or nibbling on roots. Rather, we must try to make the smartest guesses we can about the ways in which our innate sociality operated in those less experimental days of long ago, and which today we can try to recapture in form or structure. The reason, again, is not a love of what is ancient, but a quest for what triggers innate emotional responses.

One might begin by reinstituting delinquency control that included the personal, temporary disgrace of delinquents among those with whom they live. In our urban planning we could include schemes for stimulating the growth of group loyalties and minimizing alienation. These include some of the standard social/economic measures of liberal reformers—the mitigation of poverty, chronic unemployment, and racial discrimination—but they also include, as we shall see, proposals that seldom are discussed by social planners. One reason why it is not crazy to talk about tribal surrogates in a big country such as America is that most of us, in addition to sharing our national "tribe," belong simultaneously to many very small social units nested within the nation. Of this I shall have much to say in subsequent chapters.

I am suggesting that many of our most distressing social problems—crime, youth suicide, delinquency and vandalism, the failure of public education, and an unsatisfactory quality of life—can be ameliorated by paying attention to clues to fundamental forms of social life that can be found in our tribal prehistory and corroborated in the streets of our cities today. Thus the book makes bold to offer partial cures. But the case for de-alienation strategies based on "community" and group identity is especially susceptible to a romanticizing corruption. Ferdinand Tönnies, the German sociologist who invented the contrasting notions of community (*Gemeinschaft*) and society (*Gesellschaft*), wrote wistfully of simple village life and medieval society. But we would not want to pay the price in poverty and despotism to resurrect a fancied golden age of homogeneous villages and medieval communalism. Even nineteenth-century American one-room schools, about which some people are sentimental, had their share of drunken, sadistic schoolmasters; and villages could be cruel to those who did not fit the mold.

Romanticism infects many of the twentieth-century American utopian societies, communes, or "intentional communities." They are for the most part isolated, poor, quarrelsome, grubby, and short. Even these societies, with their thirst for community and collectivism, couldn't loosen the grip of their individualistic roots: Their founders had economic and political ideas, but no conception of human nature, and no patience for ritual, tradition, or disciplined socialization. New York street gangs are more genuine tribes (and probably have a better survival rate), because their internal, structural features follow felt needs instead of half-baked theories. This book is about the grounds of social identity, social control, and alienation in present-day America, and the implications for crime, education, and the civility of our society. It is also a philosophical and scientific critique of an individualism that has gone too far. It is concerned with the 1980s and beyond, not the 1880s. In order to do this intelligently we must learn from the very ancient past, but without trying to recreate it.

In the chapters that follow diagnoses of some of the problems of American society will be offered and solutions suggested. I am not certain the solutions proposed are wholly on target. Even if they are, they surely are not the whole solution. Everyone with a new idea or a version of an old one must resist the temptation to peddle it as *the* answer to all our problems; and even if we resist, it is difficult in the course of developing an idea not to sound as though one meant it to explain everything.

TWO

The Price of Perfect Individualism

> All moral doctrines, all practical suggestions about how we ought to live, depend on some belief about what human nature is like. (This includes doctrines that we "have no nature," since that means that we are—naturally—quite plastic.) Very often these beliefs are wrong. When they are so, they are often evolutionarily implausible. Some understanding of ourselves as an animal species can therefore help us to avoid subscribing to them.
> —Mary Midgley

> The Left and the Right are dead.
> —Frithjof Bergmann

Individualism, in the form endorsed by a long line of British philosophers, is the theory that in a good society each citizen forms his own goals and life plans, organized society providing a background of services and protection. The society itself is only an instrument—something each individual values just insofar as it is useful. Usually when people make an ideology of individualism they also think egoism rules us; or if it does not, that it ought to rule us. Thomas Hobbes and Ayn Rand, living three centuries apart, represent, respectively, these positions. In the 1830s Tocqueville deplored the connection he saw between individualism and egoism:

> "Individualism" is a word recently coined to express a new idea. Our fathers only knew about egoism. Egoism is a passionate and exaggerated love of self which leads a man to think of all things in terms of himself and to prefer himself to all. Individualism is a calm and considered feeling which disposes each citizen to isolate himself from the mass of his fellows and withdraw into the circle of family and friends; with this little society formed to his taste, he gladly leaves the greater society to look after itself. Egoism springs from a blind instinct; individualism

> ... is due more to inadequate understanding than to perversity of heart. Egoism sterilizes the seeds of every virtue; individualism at first only dams the spring of public virtues, but in the long run it attacks and destroys all the others too and finally merges in egoism.[1]

Tocqueville's individualist is retiring, but captures the idea of indifference to a common good and society's institutions. To a more active individualist, organized society is a referee, hired to run a clean game by a horde of mostly egoistic atoms all competing for security, love, wealth, and power. Society is not a communal object of love and pride, it is not like family and clan; it is an instrument, a protection agency, it is just business. The things we share, such as our laws and social institutions, are never more than tools: What is mine alone, my happiness, is good-in-itself (for me), what is *ours* is a means to an end.

In contrast to these modern views, strong collective values, by which I mean a collectivist, communal mentality and not a collectivist economy, have characterized traditional societies from the very birth of our species: a thoroughgoing tribal morality that gives little scope to individualism has been the rule until very recent times. The basic cause of individualism is an easier life—diminished fear of starving, freezing, or being eaten by a big cat the minute one deviates from proven clan routines and goals and begins to forge a life plan by one's own lights. Specifically, it was the breakdown of feudalism and the loss of the security provided by class identity; it was the rise of commerce and trades and therefore of commoners with the money and freedom to move about in social and geographical space; and it was the Protestants' insistence on a less mediated relation of the individual to God. The genius who appeared when all these causes were in place, at just the right time to create individualism as a political theory, was Thomas Hobbes.

For Hobbes, organized society, the State, is something people invented. It is a sovereign or ruler to whom people have given the sword in exchange for peace. They see that however much the sovereign preys on them, this is preferable to living in a "state of nature" in which everyone preys on everyone, security is nonexistent, and life, Hobbes says, is "solitary, poor, nasty, brutish, and short."[2] It is from selfishness alone that the king agrees to rule, for he gets to live like a king, and from selfishness alone that the people agree to submit to him. Hobbes was criticized for his belief in universal selfishness, his deep distrust of human nature, and his conviction that security and order outweigh the inconveniences of submitting to the English kings. John Locke had this to say about Hobbes' sovereign:

> If . . . the state of nature is therefore not to be endured, I desire to know what kind of government that is, and how much better it is than the state

of nature, where one man, commanding a multitude, has the liberty to be judge in his own case, and may do to all his subjects whatever he pleases. . . .[3]

Locke and nearly all subsequent thinkers rejected Hobbes' defense of monarchs and his derivation of social morality from conventions backed by the sword. But they accepted his most important premise: that man is a social animal by convention, not by nature; that society is an invented thing each person accepts just so long as it lets him pursue his private goals better than he could in the state of nature.

Locke and John Stuart Mill replaced Hobbes' sovereign with majority rule, but they never questioned the premise that a person's relation to society is purely self-interested and commercial. Had these British philosophers spent one year closely observing the behavior, customs, and rituals of a stone-age tribe, or for that matter an English village, they could not possibly have believed the "useful convention" theory of organized society. The Lockean version of individualism crossed the Atlantic and inspired American revolutionaries, who were so taken with the idea of government as a *democratic* referee that the Federalists among them, at least, did not seriously explore the idea that society is more than a group of individuals with a referee.

Hobbes in the seventeenth century, and Jean Jacques Rousseau in the eighteenth, speculated about the origin of human society and what they offered us were social creation myths, much like the cosmological creation myths of earlier times: Instead of gods, cosmic eggs, and broad backed primal tortoises, they told us about solitary savages, the state of nature, and social contracts. Following in the tradition they established, subsequent Anglo-American social thinkers usually begin by assuming a human mind that is nonsocial, selfish, and rational, and then look for clever moves that will make this mixture yield social morality and civil society. This is rather like thinking that stirring a salad fast, the right way, might produce Beef Wellington. Group loyalty and sense of community are left out, either completely ignored or some pallid form of them assimilated to rational self-interest.

For individualists it is a convivial idea, and one they share with Marxists, that every aspect of our sociality comes from nurture, not nature. Unlike every other creature on the earth we could *decide* to be social animals. And after all, if we can invent social life itself, surely we can choose the forms it takes. The idea pleases existentialists, for whom each person makes his own nature, and also Marxists, who wish to remake man in the image of their ideology. These theories of the inventedness of society seem to depend on a certain amount of arrogant species-pride. Social revolutionaries often are outraged by the very idea of human nature, for anything but a limitlessly plastic human nature cramps their style: They can tinker with society and change people's values and personalities, but they cannot (so far) tinker with our genes. To admit there is a human nature is to admit that something besides politics and economics affects the success of our social schemes and experiments. If we evolved to be social creatures and were fully so when we were Neanderthals, the theory that humans are social by convention is another origin-myth, another cosmic egg story, and organic conceptions of how individuals relate to society become more plausible.

In 1972 the anthropologist Colin Turnbull published a book about a small Central African tribe called the Ik.[4] The Ik had been resettled in an arid, mountainous region by the Ugandan government so that their hunting land could become a national park. Turnbull describes a people devoid of almost all sociality. Though they live in small villages and go hunting and foraging together, they do so only for mutual protection and, as Turnbull relates, for the "pleasurable prospect of being able to enjoy someone else's misfortune." During his three years among the Ik, he did not once see any evidence of love or affection. Children are turned out of their parents' house at three years of age and if they make the mistake of returning are likely to be shut in alone and allowed to starve, as was one girl named Adupa. They recognized one positive value: a full belly.

The Ik had lost their culture as well as their land, for their traditions, stories, daily routines, economic transactions, rituals, and ceremonies took their point and meaning from their nomadic, hunting life. When their culture ceased to function they also lost their social morality, their concern for each other, their love of life itself. The Ik are amused by the death and suffering of others, selfishness and apathy are the rule, and they will not lift a finger to help one another. Food is stolen from the sick and aged, the bodies of the dead are unceremoniously heaved out. Children beat their grandparents, a father first shows amusement and then indifference as his ten-year-old son dies, unnecessarily, of an intestinal blockage. In the late 1970s, magazine articles held the Ik before us as objects of wonder, like Martians or walking disproof of all we thought we knew about human nature.

At the beginning of the 1980s a young New York murderer was photographed yawning in apparent boredom as he was led into the police station. In a poor neighborhood of my own city teenagers kicked in the front doors of houses and raped, robbed, and murdered the seventy- and eighty-year-old women inside. In 1983 the local paper made much of a seventeen-year-old arrested again and again for rape and robbery, and released as often by the juvenile authorities. Youthful robbers have shot their victims for no apparent reason, and in some neighborhoods people whose cars break down are likely to be casually and systematically looted and assaulted.

These people are our own, homegrown Ik, more dangerous certainly than the Ik of Uganda. They are white, black, Appalachian, Native American, urban and suburban, having in common with the Ugandan Ik only that they have somehow lost the essence of a social existence. For these people everything that makes the life of a human social animal secure and meaningful is missing—mutual civility, traditions, responsibility, internalized ethics, the idea of a common good, useful work, and a sense of group belonging. The cases I mentioned are especially dramatic, but many more suffer to a milder degree the disease that lies behind their behavior.

The Ik are not Martians; they do not confound our social human nature but testify to it. We want to be able to see what is common to them, to American urban criminals who do casual violence, to workers who care nothing for their work, and to suburban youngsters who are always angry or find nothing meaningful. What unites them is our old enemy alienation, where I mean the breakdown of community institutions and the severing of vital connections between individuals and their various communities, their "tribes." In the case of the Ik the tribe itself died on them: Almost completely gone were its rituals, routines, gods, traditions, communal goals, with the result that the individuals in the tribe found their lives incomplete and functionless, like bees who return to find their hive burned. Their culture became inoperative but their need for it remained; its disruption during resettlement apparently had the effect of dissolving their social identity and leaving them with an atomistic, egoistic individualism.

Turnbull sees in the story of the Ik the individualism of human nature and the fragility of society—the vindication of the Hobbesian doctrine that human sociality is a convention, something thought up and easily lost. This seems to me to be a mistake. What their tragedy testifies to is the fate of creatures who evolved to be innately social, and then lose (or in the case of some urban Americans, never achieve) a truly social existence, which for human beings is participation in a culture.

While the Ik were hungry, hunger alone no more explains their behavior than it does the behavior of American casual murderers. Many groups have faced starvation without losing their social identity and their humanity. The behavior of starving peasants and villagers around the world seldom approaches the dreadfulness of youthful urban American criminals. After leaving the Ik, Turnbull learned that the weather had improved and food had become relatively plentiful, for the year at least. He returned to see the effect of a full belly; but there was no effect. Neither the Ik, nor the young Americans who murder elderly people for ten dollars (or for nothing), can be explained by the shallow cliché, "this is what to expect when people are starving (or unemployed, or underemployed)." Better we should say that when your culture doesn't inculturate you, when none of the myriad filaments grow between you and your culture's values, needs, geography, routines, ceremonies, institutions—the culture's "form of life" as the philosopher Wittgenstein might say—or when, alternatively, your culture dies, leaving you connected up with nothing, the result is the disvalued life: frustrated, aimless and hostile young people who honor and value neither themselves nor those who become their victims.

Hence one of our vital questions concerns how individualistic we can become, and how much of the machinery of communal life we can jettison, without becoming Ik. Individualism is America's sacred cow; a collectivist mentality is a Soviet sacred cow. If I were a Soviet, I would be concerned with collectivism-gone-mad as it is found in the USSR, but I am not and my concern is with the individualism-gone-mad we find in the United States. Emigration policy illustrates in a small way these different ways of understanding the relation of an individual to society. Soviets who want to emigrate are condemned as ingrates and they are generally forbidden to leave. They are thought to betray obligations created by the education, care, and security the State provided them. Contrastingly, only in wartime do Americans criticize emigrants or expatriates and the U.S. government rarely acts to prevent citizens from leaving the country. It is, after all, hard for a nation of immigrants to morally condemn emigrants.

A native-born Soviet can be stripped of his citizenship, his university degrees—everything can be taken back—and he can be drummed out of the country as was Solzhenitsyn in 1974. Exile as punishment is archetypically tribal and collectivist; it rests on the prehistoric idea that the separation of a person from his society is devastating, perhaps even fatal. As practiced by the modern Soviet state it is a kind of tribal-moral posturing, for the act of expulsion is viewed with cynicism and the expellees are not eaten by sabertoothed cats but instead come to America and give lectures. Nevertheless the very act of casting out, because of its roots and associations, probably brings the Soviets moral credit, and is a useful counterstrategy when lots of people want to leave anyway. Contrastingly, the citizenship of a native-born American is alienable only by the citizen himself (if we include acts by which he is said to alienate himself, such as serving in a foreign army). Americans think of citizenship as a contract that binds the State more than the individual: The individual can terminate it and the State cannot, whereas for Russians it is, with some exceptions, the other way around.

This is part of what it means to be an individualist. In this sense I, too, am one. Individual liberties that maximize elbow room for trying out one's own formula for happiness are the reward our species received for intelligence, mastery of nature, and reduced pressure for conformity. But a viable society must simultaneously be collectivist. Radical individualism ignores needs that are as old as our reptile brains. It forgets that we are social animals by evolution and not by convention. We are not ants in an ant colony, nor are we solitary wandering beasts with no need for group affiliations. We are human beings, creatures with more complex requirements.

To many people who were caught up by the anti-institutional passions of the '60s and '70s, organized society is not even a referee but a potential oppressor with which we must cope. Coming out of those chaotic decades we were prone to view our relation to society as coldly, warily, and self-interestedly as our relation to a used car dealer. Given this mind-set, we enter into commercial transactions with society: We pay our taxes and expect equal value in return. There is no more place for gratitude or affection than in any commercial transaction. The social mechanism provides police, fire protection, and public parks, and our local taxes pay for them. Our freedoms and territorial integrity are protected by a national defense establishment, for which we pay mightily.

On this hyper-individualist view our society is like a store: We receive our services and pay our bills and then the account is quits, we owe it nothing, it owes us nothing. In a period in which one thinks that society is something to which one owes nothing but taxes, it is natural that military conscription and national service are rejected and replaced by a wholly voluntary military: It becomes less a matter of serving and closer to an ordinary job. The essence of the individualist ideology is that organized society is a purveyor of protections and services with which one has business transactions on the basis of enlightened self-interest.

If it is true that crisis often makes a nation's prevailing ideology hypertrophy, there is an interesting parallel between America and China: Each nation had an ideological "cultural revolution" in the '60s and '70s. China strove for the purest communism, the U.S. aimed at the most perfect individualism, and each created disorder and wrecked its educational system in the process. Thus the individualism which in America had always coexisted with sense-of-community, was catapulted into dominance by the civil rights and Vietnam crises, upsetting a balance between them, and capturing (in different ways) both Left and Right. I shall be arguing that our individualism has gone too far and now damages the quality of American life in a number of very concrete ways. I am not sanguine enough to think that individualism, of which huge numbers of people are mindlessly proud, can easily be turned into an object of suspicion. But if a case can be made that radical individualism rules out the group loyalties on which healthy societies depend, some doubts may be planted.

Before these arguments can be persuasive, one must demonstrate the independence of radical individualism from our economic system of regulated capitalism. It will help, I think, to distinguish between what we might call the "strict and philosophical" and the "loose and popular" senses of individualism. The former is the subject of much of what follows, the latter is identical with self-reliance, inner-directedness, and entrepreneurship.

It is no mystery why American intellectuals pay their respects to "community" *en passant* and move on as quickly as possible, even though it has always been an intimate part of the life of the American people. "Community" implies an "organic theory" of society, which gives American social thinkers unpleasant thoughts of Hegel and ant colonies. Thirty hippies living together in the California desert make a pleasant sentimental stew of community, *Gemeinschaft*, and collectivism, but bringing these concepts into mainstream political philosophy seems to lead us into the arms of Mussolini: An organic, collectivist theory of society combined with ultra-nationalism is perceived to be the recipe for fascism. An organic, collectivist theory combined with state ownership and central planning is held to be the recipe for communism. Small wonder the theory has a bad name; but if we are innately social creatures who become wretched and alienated when we try to live otherwise, we have deep needs to relate to our societies pretty much as an organic theory of society says we should. The "individualist-collectivist dilemma" arises from the need we have for both individualism and collectivism, together with the conventional wisdom that thinks of them as though they were matter and anti-matter.

On a simple level it is a matter of balance. A human society is a little like a swarm of particles orbiting one another in space. Group egoism or "community" is like gravity, pulling them all together into a clump, homogenizing them within a veritable black hole if unresisted by a contrary force. Individualism is like inertia: It keeps each particle in orbit, separate from one another; but unresisted by gravity, it would send each off by itself into cold space. The stability of the system, of individual particles comprising an interacting group, depends on the continued efficacy of both forces, inertia and gravity. So too, human society depends on the continued existence of individualist and communalist motives, of egoism and group egoism. If individualism is destroyed we become like an ant colony, a kind of social black hole; if group loyalty is lost we fragment, as in a burst centrifuge, and cease, in this second way, to be human beings. But the solution this analogy suggests is too simple, namely, that it is just a matter of maintaining a proper tension between these two forces. We shall see that the collectivist and the individualist aspects of a person, and of a society, are related in a fairly complex way that reflects our evolved human nature.

The reason why community and group egoism do not lead to Fascism or a "social black hole" is that each of us belongs to many "tribes" at once, often nested within one another, no one of which can be proved to have an *absolute* claim on our loyalties. These "tribes" are our neighborhoods, towns, nations, unions, companies, churches, fraternal organizations, and humanity itself: They include the multitude of "associations" which so impressed Tocqueville about the Americans.

Understood as an evolutionary product, one can better perceive the deeply conservative nature of "community," its distinctness from an interest group, and the difference between collectivism as community and collectivism as state ownership. If we are tribal creatures, community cannot, without abandoning what is important about it, be reduced to public spiritedness, egalitarianism, interest groups, or to some other idea familiar and innocuous to the Western individualist mind. We shall have to take group loyalties seriously and find some way of accommodating the idea of insiders and outsiders.

We are unlikely to take kindly to the word "collectivism," but it is the right word for calling attention to a sense of possession, belonging, and acknowledgment of obligations to a common good. It is a way of grasping what community in the "strict and philosophical sense" means before it gets sentimentalized and diluted. For example, community as collective mentality is very different from membership in an interest group, such as people might form to fight a proposed tax levy. You can become alienated from your community but not from an interest group. The reason is that the whole value of an interest group lies outside it, in what it is trying to achieve, such as the defeat of the tax. The interest group has an instrumental value that simply disappears if it fails to achieve its goal, and when that happens we suffer no loss of affiliation and belonging. It promises usefulness but does not claim our loyalty, although it can, over time, create camaraderie and evolve into a community. Another difference between interest groups and communities is that we do not always *choose* our communities—our families, schools, neighborhoods, or mother countries—they are arranged marriages, done before we were born, but we are still obliged to them for all that.

We need to inquire how these notions, individualism and community, relate to political and economic systems. Is there a chain, a deadly dialectic, that leads from capitalism to radical individualism to egoism to a suicidal society? Must capitalism create an individualism which, as Tocqueville said, "merges in egoism" and destroys community? We need to separate community from economics, if we can. I would not argue that a nation's economic/political system has no effect on how individualistic its citizens are. I do argue that the Left has no grounds for proprietary feelings about community, and that capitalism does not tie one to radical individualism. Indeed, the flourishing of local group loyalties within Japanese capitalism should by itself make us suspicious of such connections.

The Soviets preach socialism *and* group commitment, but the economic system and the social state of mind have no inherent connection. "Collectivism" in the sense of felt obligations to the good of shared enterprises and institutions probably is more suppressed than nourished by state ownership and central planning. Americans preach a free market economy *and* radical individualism, but the two have no inherent connection. The free market is not an important cause of socially destructive individualism, although it does encourage individualism in what I called the loose and popular sense.

Americans who reject the free market usually take from Marxism only economic collectivism, which allows them to retain their deep-seated individualism. Thus American leftists generally have been fondest of those parts of Marxism which experience has shown to be the greatest failures: state ownership and central planning. The communalist mentality and the organic theory of society are ignored or rejected. The USSR likewise rejects the free market, and even preaches community, but it is hard to think of a labor force with less commitment or collective identification with their work than Moscow service workers and store clerks. They stare into space, oblivious to the long lines, and mumble *"nyet"* without meeting your gaze. The women who work in *stolovayas* (inexpensive dining halls) take to heart the maxim of their liberation: "We serve food, not people."

Economic collectivism and collectivism as community are very different things. There is more non-economic collectivism in a thoroughly capitalistic Iowa town in which people have strong group loyalties toward their town, schools, organizations, churches, and other sub-societies, than there is on a Soviet collective farm where the workers have little concern for anything besides their families, friends, and their private garden plots. Not even the Marxist-Leninist idea of a "collective" has any necessary connection with public ownership, and therefore has no incompatibility with the free market. The hostess in a nearly empty Moscow restaurant generally seats one with strangers, including lovers who want only to be left alone, thus creating a table-collective. A Soviet educator was horrified at the sight of four American nursery school children at a table, each doing something different: They didn't form a collective. Neither case concerns *economic* collectivism. Conversely, as we have seen, collective ownership, and certainly state ownership, is no guarantee of a collective mentality. Ten egoists with joint title to a worn-out farm have collective ownership, but they do not make a "collective."

Capitalism, unlike modern Marxism and communism, is not a religion or a philosophy of life. It is a free market economy, taking forms which range from *laissez faire* to "Swedish socialism." In most of the world it mixes smoothly with a major religion—Christianity, Islam, or Hinduism—which it could never do if it were itself a major religion. A people's social morality and sense of purpose come from their religion, traditions, and ceremonies, not from capitalism, which has never pretended to organize the whole web and purpose of our lives. What it means to be a capitalist isn't anything like what it means to be a Roman Catholic or a Muslim or a Marxist. That is why the question "I'm a communist, are you a capitalist?" is rather like, "I'm a Christian, are you an engineer?" and slightly unfair. Capitalism is instead a force, like modern medicine or the industrial revolution, that wrought great change but did not tell us what is good and evil. Capitalism doesn't explain the meaning or purpose of life and therefore does not compete with systems which do, unless such a system includes an economics, as does Marxism.

Since Soviet economics is integral to their ideological system their laws protect its purity, whereas American laws aim to protect the interested parties and the public interest but rarely the purity of capitalism itself. For example, in major Soviet cities there are what are called "commission stores," one on the Garden Ring in Moscow selling stereo equipment and TVs. If you bring in an article the store will sell it for you, 7 percent going to the government. Soviet-made goods have fixed prices but the prices of foreign items—which was almost everything in this particular store in the autumn of 1979—are determined by local supply and demand. A nice-looking Kenwood stereo receiver which a journalist might have purchased abroad for about $500 was tagged at 1800 roubles, about $2,790, or 34.8 months' pay for the lobby guard at the University Hotel. This particular store and the sidewalk in front were jammed with men who were seeking private deals; a few looked at my fat briefcase and asked, "What do you have?"

The rules of the game were designed to prevent the formation of a market: You could bypass the store and legally sell your turntable or amplifier, provided you took your buyer home to do it. Thus this kind of capitalist act between consenting adults is legal, provided it is not committed on the street. Since you cannot advertise, the store is a place where buyers and sellers can find each other. If you take your buyer home to a virtual store—to shelves groaning with amplifiers—you commit a capitalist act whose motive is profit and whose legal description is the crime of speculation. By contrast, we do not outlaw "socialist acts." Unlike Marxism-Leninism, and to our great advantage, capitalism has variations that are defended on grounds of fairness or efficiency, but it does not have heretics or deviationists. There is nothing sacred about capitalism and those who think we ought to sacralize it are trying to make an ideology out of something which cannot (and ought not) bear the weight.

Consequently we should be on our guard against giving capitalism credit for moral rot and the decline of commitment. Capitalism is an economic system, it never was in the morality business, and what should control it are the ideals and social morality of the moral community. A potential for abuse and the need for moral control are to be found in *any* purely economic arrangement. The abuses which are most tempting within a system of central planning socialism are, to say the least, as dangerous as those which exist within a regulated free market economy.

Focusing on individualism and collectivism instead of economics reorders our political spectrum. We are used to a Left-to-Right continuum that goes: Marxist, liberal, conservative, libertarian; which makes perfect sense when it is understood in terms of the decreasing role of government in the economy. But when we understand collectivism as community instead of state ownership, through this different lens we see that conservatives have more in common with communists than with libertarians; and liberals have more in common with libertarians than with communists. Conservatives accept a collective good, a way of life worth conserving and passing on to the next generation. The deeply collectivistic idea that my society and subsocieties are *my tribes*, possessions that partially create my identity and to which I am personally responsible, is equally a conservative idea (the conservatism of tribal life is a commonplace among anthropologists). Conservatives wish to defend the collective good against the social fragmentation and insecurity of unlimited individual rights. So do communists, in countries in which they rule. Hence both support the vigorous enforcement of law and the indoctrination of the young in social morality. They do not share much else, but both emphasize collective values and are enemies of unrestricted individualism.

So too, American liberals and libertarians both believe in a self-interested, commercial relation between the self and society. For each, organized society is a convenience and government a hired service. To each, the society's common values, traditions, and collective good are more a threat than a precious inheritance because they can infringe on the rights of the individual. The continuity of both the American moderate Left—the "liberals"—and the libertarians with classical liberalism lies in their rejection of an organic conception of the relation of an individual to society, however much they might disagree about what quantity of government is best.

We have the technical and economic ability to experiment with how we raise and educate children, regulate sex, structure our economic system, cope with criminals, and space ourselves from each other in towns and buildings. Our Pleistocene ancestors couldn't "afford" mistaken social experiments; extreme conformism was their way and clan extinction the price they paid for mistakes. Their punishment was plain and tangible: starvation, predation, exposure. But in adapting and surviving they evolved a range of emotions, anxieties, satisfactions, and fears that fit how they lived: a life dependent on strong group loyalties within small-scale, close-knit, ritualized clan life. The social cement that made them a community was group-egoism, not egoism.

What price do *we* pay for social experiments, or can our technology and surplus food production let us off scot-free? That is, if an experiment does not ruin our economy or cost us our freedom, is it then costless? If, in the midst of political freedom and the world's greatest economic prosperity, we are dissatisfied, and have some of the world's highest rates of crime, youth suicide, and out-of-wedlock birth, we might at least consider the possibility that our problems are not just economic and political. We should be ready to explore the idea that the emotions our Pleistocene ancestors evolved come back to haunt us, that we are genetically predisposed to need to live (and be brought up) in certain ways, within certain limits, and that we feel insecure, aimless, and hostile when we are denied these limits or overstep them.

If this is so we possess a "secret Pleistocene inheritance" that we ignore at our peril. I shall offer evidence that it bonds us to small-group loyalties, shared values and rituals, and a number of very specific things we need to discuss such as how frequently you are recognized in your neighborhood. Most important, it created in children an emotional need for socialization in the ways of their culture—an inability to fully develop into human beings unless they are socialized into a culture; and in adults a need to be needed and to be personally accountable in the eyes of one's fellows.

Perhaps, when all of these things are denied us, we become Ik. Perhaps we can be relatively rich and be Ik, for, after all, Colin Turnbull made it clear that the terrible problems of the Ik were more emotional and spiritual than economic. Certainly, many children in our large city slums, and some in our suburbs, could not, if we tried, be reared in a way more antithetical to the development of sense of belonging, social morality, a work ethic, and a sense of usefulness and personal responsibility. It is equally certain that their aimless and casual predation, vandalism, and self-destructiveness—their laconic violence—cannot be explained as the acts of people who are fighting for something: for power, easy wealth, revolution, or just a full belly. People dedicated to some such goal would be more effective and their behavior, like that of traditional bandits or anarchists, would display a rational pattern. A youth who pushes a total stranger in front of a subway train is not a predator, revolutionary, anarchist, or even a terrorist; he is, more accurately, *nothing*: His nature was left uncompleted and he simply thrashes about, enraged at being nothing, like a butterfly whose metamorphosis went wrong and hatches with wings that remain crumpled.

We are by nature tribal, social, ritual-performing animals, and I shall suggest some reasons why many of our recent social and educational experiments probably frustrate our nature at the deepest emotional levels. When we get stung by our secret inheritance the social experimenters, who do not read science and think man is nothing but *homo politicus* or *homo economicus,* haven't the slightest understanding of what went wrong and can think of nothing but additional political and economic experiments.

I wish to show how individualism, if kept within reasonable bounds, and non-economic collectivism can exist together. Individualism finds expression partly in each person's unique assemblage of nested and overlapping communities, partly in the limited moral authority of each. Americans have a sense of national community, and we would be doomed without it, but the communal sentiment toward an object that immense is possible only if we have commitments to a great multitude of other, mostly small, communities. The solution to the individualist-collectivist dilemma partly depends on seeing that there is no necessary connection between collectivism as community and either economic collectivism or absolute political authority. It also depends on the more peculiarly American understanding of individualism not as moral isolation but as membership in a partly self-chosen, unique package of smallish moral communities. The detailed working out of this idea is the task of Chapters 9 and 10.

The human animal has a fundamental need for something more than individual advantage. Religions and philosophers have been saying this for a few thousand years, but perhaps it will be thought a surprising claim to come out of the twentieth century's revolution in biology: If you do not love something besides yourself, you will find it nearly impossible to love yourself. Why? Because it is our nature, not a product of convention or contract, to be social animals; we are genetically primed to be socialized and brought up belonging to and caring about the good of our families, clans, tribes, or countries. This social love or group egoism is as essential to the flourishing of a human being as is self-love or egoism. We shall have to see what evidence is available from anthropology, criminology, and the study of human evolution, for the thesis that frustrating our innate sociality, including the need of children for the socializing process itself, is a cause of alienation, crime, and the horrid casual violence that we witness in our cities.

THREE

The Trashing of American Education

> If it doesn't matter which course you take, can it matter how often you go to class? If schools radiate the sense that nothing in particular is vital to learning and to maturity, why should students discipline themselves either to attend regularly or to master their work? Student truancy is a rational response to the perceived devaluation of the work of the school.
> —Diane Ravitch

Since about 1963 American public schooling began a pattern of overall decline, with a few hopeful signs beginning to show up near the midpoint of the 1980s (e.g., Scholastic Aptitude Test scores, but not high school dropout rates). The educational decline, for reasons that have been a mystery, begins at about the same time as the bad trends in crime, suicide, and out-of-wedlock births. The raw data that have been most damning for education are Scholastic Aptitude Test scores, which declined nearly every year since 1963. Iowa Tests, administered to primary school children and not only to the college-bound, show a marked, though not quite so drastic, decline in math, reading comprehension, and writing during the same period. This indicates that the decline in SAT scores is at best only partly explained by the fact that since the '60s more people are going to college and more poor performers taking the test. It is not that educators ignored the decline. Yvonne L. Wharton compiled a list of 79 separate hypotheses that have been offered to explain the SAT decline;[1] the list seems to emphasize complaints of conservatives and would, perhaps, be considerably longer if it included more of the reasons offered by liberals.

By these measures of verbal and analytical ability, for nearly twenty years virtually every high school graduating class has been dumber than the preceding year's class. Since the late '70s universities have spent millions each year for remedial courses, and at my own university many freshman humanities texts used fifteen or twenty years ago cannot be used today because the students cannot read them: The vocabulary is too rich and the sentences too complex.

During the mid '70s the magnitude of the schools' failure began to penetrate the American consciousness and many who could afford it fled the public schools. Between 1970 and 1978, while public school enrollment declined, private school enrollment increased by 60 percent;[2] it increased in communities that do not bus for racial balance. Black enrollment in Catholic schools rose sharply in the big cities;[3] nationwide, nonwhites in private high schools increased from 3.3 percent in 1960 to nearly 8.0 percent in 1979.[4]

The flight to private and suburban schools by nearly all who could afford it was one of the major educational phenomena of the '70s: Most middle and upper middle-class people took the expensive suburban option; others stayed in the central city and paid tuition to a private school. Some fled to get away from blacks, some for safety and discipline, some so that their children might pray in school; the great

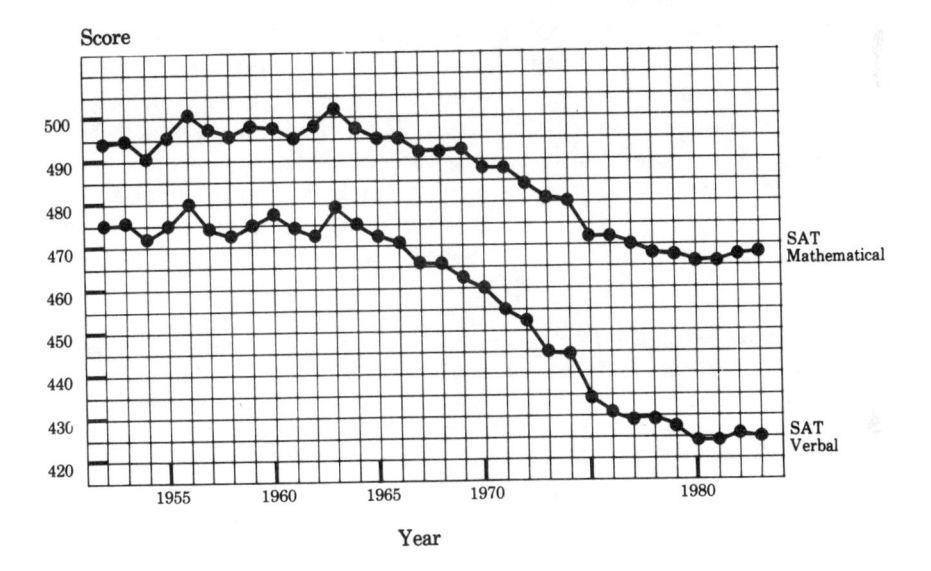

FIGURE 2. The Scholastic Aptitude Test

During the 20 years from 1963 to 1983, the mean score in verbal performance declined from 479 to 425. The mathematics score shows a smaller decline. One is tempted to surmise that whatever caused both declines is exacerbated by television in the case of reading skills. TV competes with reading much more than with math; and the widespread acquisition of TV sets in the fifties would start a cohort of seven-year-olds in 1954 on the road to poor reading test scores ten years later.

majority simply sought competent schools. The liberal intellectuals fled as much as any group, taking pains to explain to all who would listen that they made their decision for "educational reasons alone," before the federal judge imposed the local bussing plan. It was hard (for those who cared) to avoid looking like hypocrites, for the decline of the public schools and coercive school integration were simultaneous but largely independent phenomena.

A large influx of blacks from a slum might make a school worse, but the main causes of public school decline had nothing to do with race: The quality of nearly all schools declined, including all-white suburban schools (but from a much higher plane). The clearest evidence of massive flight from city schools by those who could afford it is the change in racial makeup, mainly reflecting the relative poverty and lack of education-consciousness of blacks: By 1980 the Detroit public schools were 12 percent white, the Atlanta schools 8 percent, those in Washington D.C., 4 percent.[5] The white populations of these cities, although diminished by suburban flight, are obviously larger than these school enrollment figures would indicate, the implication being that they, more than blacks, had their children in private schools. The issue, for most people, was not race but incompetent schools, but the two inevitably became intertwined: Poor families exacerbated the condition of schools already declining for other reasons, the poor were disproportionately black, and many people erroneously concluded that schools were all right if they didn't have blacks. Education journalist G. T. Sewall succinctly described the outcome:

> Middle-class flight's first cause is not racial antipathy but middle-class alarm at the standards in force at schools where most pupils come from disadvantaged backgrounds. Also, the apparent absence of serious scholastic standards in predominantly lower-class schools sends the signal to many taxpayers that minority students are incapable of meeting any. It is hard to imagine a more insidious spur to resurgent racial prejudice. . . . In many localities the most basic reversal during the last thirty years has been *desegregation by race* and *resegregation by class*. . . .[6]

Journalists, educators, and a sudden flood of commission reports proposed causes of why children cannot read and, more recently, assault their teachers, their schools, and each other: Too much TV, old-fashioned curricula, an increased youth population, the decline of the family, Vietnam, the elimination of school prayer, and government interference are among the causes that have been suggested. The proposed cures have been sometimes useless or harmful, sometimes plausible, often simplistic, and very American—new buildings, ever more money, new experimental curricula, better racial balance, and most recently, longer school hours, merit pay for teachers, and computers for everyone. The only thing certain is that for years after many of these "cures" were begun, public education continued its decline.

Nearly all the speculation about what went wrong neglected changes in our conception of the nature and purpose of education. This means the cause that was left out was not a gadget like television or an event such as the Vietnam War, it was an *idea*. It was really a set of ideas which came primarily from professors in the colleges and departments of education. Caught up in the American "cultural revolution" of the '60s and '70s, they taught future teachers to be suspicious of all social affiliations excepting the most local. They taught a radical individualism that borrowed the slogans of the Left but in reality had practically nothing in common with socialism: Their cause was individual rights, self-expression, and personal development. They preached the equal rights of individuals to respect, to reward, and to achievement; they stressed feelings and attitudes at the expense of knowledge and intellect, and children's autonomy over society's need for their socialization. They equated democracy with a thorough relativism according to which even suggesting that one person's performance, ability, or conduct was better than another's was demeaning, stigmatizing, and elitist. What is important is the effect these ideas had on class after class of new teachers and, especially, on the projects and experiments in the inner-city schools where the large federal grants went.

Simple logic tells us that if Tom says something is so, and Freda says it isn't so, one of them is wrong. Either that, or they are arguing about whether avocados taste good and there is no right or wrong of the matter. But the idea of calling someone "wrong," even about simple matters of fact, offended the sensibilities of the period. This was even more the case regarding ethics and morality, focused as the professors were on such ideas as "middle class values," "ghetto values," and "personal value systems," and many were led to treat ethics like avocados. In the next chapter we shall consider in detail the disappearance of ethics from public life and from the schools in particular.

The elitism implied by standards in science, ethics, or everyday affairs—the simple idea that some things are better than others and some people better than other people at doing something—is not the same as the elitism of fixed social classes or of experts looking down their noses at everyone else. But in the turmoil of the '60s and '70s educators did not see the difference between standards and arbitrary privilege. After all, privilege typically hides behind the maintenance of standards and there were millions of blacks, women, "disadvantaged," and handicapped people who had long been excluded by such rationalizations. By about 1970 logic had become the professors' enemy. In the education colleges reasoning was "playing head games"; the Law of Non-contradiction outraged them: It was elitist, indeed, downright un-American, because it ruled out the possibility of everyone's being right.

For educational policy it followed that academic standards had to be subjectified, made a matter of self expression, sincerity, and good will. Otherwise, there would be winners and losers, an elite, and self-esteem would suffer. Testing became an evil, grading of any kind a way of labeling children successes and failures. The year 1971 gave us the book *Wad-Ja-Get?—The Grading Game in America*. In the mid '70s a fifth-grade mathematics teacher told me that while she does give some tests she does not put grades on them, "because I would not want to stigmatize the children."

There is a connection between school teachers' reluctance to apply strict standards to their pupils and grade inflation in the colleges and universities. The decline in Scholastic Aptitude Test scores from the early '60s and into the '80s is paralleled by an increase in the average grades given by colleges. Typical is the University of California at Berkeley, where the undergraduate grade point average went from 2.5 in 1960 to 3.0 in 1974.[7] In a study of fifty leading universities and institutes of technology, Sidney Suslow found that between 1963 and 1974 the average undergraduate grade jumped from C+/B− to B, and the percentage of "A" grades awarded more than doubled, from 16 percent to 34 percent.[8] What could justify this? For it is clear that while the grades went up, average student performance declined, *and* the reading assignments and tests were made easier. The only answer is that respect for the system of grading students competitively on their actual accomplishments had been undermined.

Nationally, the leaders in grade inflation were the colleges of education, followed by the schools of social work. An evil that affected all departments of a university, in education departments grade inflation became a way to sabotage the very concept of grading. The University of Texas at Austin is stricter than many. In 1980 the average undergraduate grade given by its education college was 3.3, a B+, compared with 2.4 in business, 2.5 in engineering, 2.7 in liberal arts.[9] The college gave 45 percent A's in undergraduate courses, compared with 27 percent by engineering, 15 percent by business administration, and 24 percent by the natural sciences.[10]

When we turn to a large state university in a different part of the country the picture is similar. At Ohio State University in the spring of 1980, the average grade given by the College of Education was 3.45, compared with 2.3 in the College of Mathematics and Physical Sciences, 2.7 in the College of Humanities, and 2.6 in the College of Biological Sciences.[11]

The result was that class after class of future teachers went through school being told that everything they did was excellent, for they received nearly automatic A's in every education course they took, and then went forth into the schools and applied the same ideas to the nation's children: Everyone is doing just fine, everyone always passes. The education colleges' grades have been giveaways and bear little relation to acquired knowledge and skills; but the Scholastic Aptitude Test on which, several years later, the teachers' pupils perform poorly, is objective and measures knowledge and cognitive skills. Is it whimsical to see a connection between these phenomena? Of course, our effective teachers manage to unlearn this "hidden curriculum" of the education colleges.

Within the education colleges self-esteem became the chief good to be achieved by schooling and its perceived enemies were grading, competition, and standards of any sort that implied that someone might fail to meet them. These included ethical standards with their threats of guilt and shame. The single-minded fixation on self-esteem was another indication of the withdrawal from sociality: a retreat back to the self, to egoism and inner-directedness, and the innoculation of pupils against standards and responsibilities imposed from without by the community. The ultimate result of the unqualified praise of autonomy and self-fulfillment is that each individual pupil is taught to become a community unto himself, loyal only to himself.

The recipe for creating self-esteem emphasized "affective education" (i.e., programs concerned with emotions and feelings), which became a booming industry through the 1970s and, to a considerable extent, still is. "Cognitive education" (i.e., education) became an embarrassment. The aim, of course, was to humanize schooling and break with the picture that educators painted of martinet schoolmarms telling tender young psyches they are failures. By the end of the '70s, what actually went on out there in the trenches, in the classrooms, seemed to depend on which side you were on: The education professors still saw cowed pupils learning dead facts, and terrible assaults on pupil self-esteem. Their critics saw the abandonment of basics, discipline, homework, and in many schools even textbooks; and in the "open classroom" schools in particular, teachers left with little to do with their young pupils beyond trying to keep some order, playing with gerbils, going on field trips to McDonald's, and telling puzzled parents that their child will learn to read "when he is ready." In the large cities the evidence is that the truth lay with the critics.

Educators have not to my knowledge produced evidence that classes with strict academic standards and competition for grades have lower self-esteem, even among the bottom half of achievers, than classes in which everyone is told he or she is doing wonderfully and no one ever fails. The informal evidence is the opposite: Self-esteem results from competence and community, not from stroking. Losing sight of this was perhaps the most serious mistake of the professional educators. Diane Ravitch of Columbia Teachers College describes a study that supports the importance of challenging children. Ravitch asks,

> Should children encounter intellectual challenges? One answer to this question was developed by Jeanne Chall of Harvard University, in *An Analysis of Textbooks in Relation to Declining SAT scores.* Chall found that textbooks have been made easier over the years, presumably on the assumption that students would learn more if their tasks were less demanding. In fact, she found the opposite to be true. After an extensive review of textbooks used over a thirty-year period, Chall concluded "there seems to be rather compelling evidence that a positive relationship exists between the level of challenge of textbooks used by pupils and the scores they achieve on the SAT-verbal tests." She adds, the younger the child, the stronger the relationship between challenge and achievement.[12]

Children feel good about themselves when they sense they are actually learning things, acquiring skills, and participating with others in serious, structured activity. Of course, the *justification* of these things doesn't depend on children feeling good about them, but on the fact that their future satisfaction with themselves, and society's satisfaction with them, depends on the character and competencies they acquire. The eye of the times, however, was on the individual, on rights and equality, not on the demands a healthy tribe or society must make to preserve its moral vitality and common good.

The other side of the rejected coinage of traditional education concerned the nature of "cognitive" education itself. Here the new idea was that real education is learning how to think, to question, and to integrate experiences; it is not just learning "dead facts." Noble as this sounds, what it usually meant in practice is sneering at acquiring facts and substituting sessions devoted to discussion and self-expression. For it is not as though the professors had in mind "live" facts to replace dead ones; all factual knowledge is "dead" and its replacements are self-esteem pumping, "hands-on experiences," and self-expression. What was forgotten was that learning how to think—how to appraise, to reason, and to research facts—supplements and cannot replace learning lots of facts. Unfortunately the teachers who were supposed to teach children how to think were not themselves taught how to think, nor were *their* teachers (the education professors). No one in this chain was taught the necessary logic and scientific method, for that would require a rigorous and sometimes technical training that was contrary to the relativist and self-expressive spirit of the times.

Children respect facts, are proud of new ones they learn; this is also true of most great thinkers and scientists throughout history. It is true of ordinary good thinkers. It is absurd to be ashamed of teaching or learning lots of facts. But the greatest minds do something creative with facts that seems to transcend factual knowledge. The professors saw only this culmination and tried a short cut to wisdom and creativity. Perhaps they also forgot that just being able to name the beasts, or trees, or provinces, gives one power and control—the ability to reidentify things and communicate information about them, together with knowledge of the taxonomy or structure that lies behind any organized system of names.

The ideas of the '60s and '70s were uncongenial to the discipline, patience, and sense-of-wonder characteristic of science, and almost certainly contributed to the acute shortage of new science and mathematics teachers we face in the '80s. In 1971 the average college or department of education produced about 22 math teachers and 18 science teachers; in 1980 it was under five math teachers and six science teachers.[13] Ravitch summarized the changes of the past two decades that led to the general decline in achievement:

> The goal has been to make the schools less competitive; to de-emphasize achievement; to reduce the social distance between teacher and students; to encourage friendlier, more equal relationships between adults and children; to relax rules of behavior, dress codes, and academic requirements; and to diminish the school's role *in loco parentis*. The intention of these changes was to make the schools a friendlier place, a place that encourages self-fulfillment in a wide variety of interests, an institution characterized by cooperation rather than striving. The hope was that the school would become less forbidding, less demanding, and therefore more desirable from the student's view. . . . The results have begun to come in. . . . In some areas of educational policy, the unintended consequences have been close to disastrous.[14]

A key to the philosophical ideas behind these changes is not the formula for achieving self-esteem—all that bubble-minded stroking at

FIGURE 3. Why Johnny Can't Add Anymore
Cartoon by Mike Keefe, © by *The Denver Post*, 1982, and the Field Syndicate.

the expense of learning—but the goal itself. "Self-esteem" is the inward-oriented, ego-centered replacement for the "social adjustment" that was the educators' byword of earlier decades. To many observers it was, back then, disconcerting enough to see educators emphasize social adjustment at the expense of mastery of material. But it was at least a *social* goal of teaching children how to live among others as social creatures; by the early '70s we had lost even that. Radical individualists dropped the "social" in "social adjustment" and reconstructed the aim of education in terms of "self-image," "feeling good about oneself," and "self-esteem." They no longer sought to train children for life as members of a society; they taught them to view society as hostile terrain in which they must cope. This move from "social adjustment" to "happy self-image" as a goal of education is a perfect paradigm of individualism-gone-mad. Masquerading behind chic leftist rhetoric, it had in actuality practically nothing to do with socialism or Marxism but was a very American over-reaction to tumultuous radical eruptions, and later, an unpopular war: We retreated from common, collective values to the individual, from "us" to "me."

The educational ideas of the period had their greatest impact on minority students, because they appeared most in need of the professional educators' help, because they could not so easily escape to private and suburban schools, and because much of the big federal grant money was specially allocated for them. That youngsters from black slums need help educationally is statistically demonstrable in a number of ways; one way is to look at college performance figures. The attrition rates at state universities that enroll large numbers of ill-prepared students are frustrating to taxpayers, students, professors, and parents. The record is especially dismal for blacks. Consider the class of 1979 at Ohio State University. Of all students, black and white, who entered in the autumn of 1975, only 25 percent graduated after four years. The graduation rate for blacks after four years was 8.5 percent, and for black males, 4.9 percent, which is less than one in twenty. When we give students five years to graduate, the overall graduation rate is about 40 percent (obviously higher for whites alone) and under 21 percent for blacks.[15]

While Ohio State was worse off than most because it was an open admissions university, the graduation rates at state institutions across the country are lower for blacks than for whites. At some universities, while the overall graduation rate is still very low, the race difference is small—for example, at the University of Texas at Austin. Consider again the class of 1979: 37.5 percent of the whites who entered in autumn 1975 graduated after four years, compared with 34.3 for blacks and 27.5 for Hispanics. The dismissal rate at Texas, at the end of four years, was 8.4 percent for whites, 15.6 percent for Hispanics, and 21.9 percent for blacks.[16]

The assumption of the education professors was that when lower-economic-class black students enter college their main problems are psychological and societal—perhaps a defeatist attitude coupled with an uncaring and still partly racist academic environment—rather than more devastating shortcomings that have nothing especially to do with race: great ignorance of facts and of how to reason, very poor work and study habits, or poorly formed character. We are understandably loath to admit we are bringing up large numbers of children to be truly stupid, permanently so after a certain age, and worse, bringing up some to have characters so poor they are incapable of living lives useful to themselves or society. Consequently, the tendency has been to locate the problems of even the worst-off slum children exclusively in what is external, or superficial, or temporary—to describe the children in any way that does not imply that after age eight or nine, or even age fifteen, their inmost minds and characters are ruined.

A large part of the problem in the schools today is that teachers and administrators are less willing to force blacks than whites to do homework, perform up to standards, and behave civilly. We should also remember that poor blacks have been the primary guinea pigs for the educational experiments of the '60s and '70s, with the result that they and other poor children have been taught useless things, if anything at all, and their desperate need for self-discipline has been ignored.

For example, my black freshmen, more often than my white ones, neglect an assigned paper topic and "express themselves" on some vaguely related idea; that, apparently, is what they were permitted to do in high school. The capacity to accurately explain a passage is poorer in my black than in my white students: another aspect of education that apparently had become obsolete in inner-city schools. White college students make mistakes in papers or exams and ask (though not as often as 15 years ago) about the right way to do it. My black students, with the exception of those obviously from educated, middle-class backgrounds, seldom ask about the actual text or theory they were to explain; they don't seem to think it had anything to do with how their paper was graded. I don't mean they assume they were given poor grades because they were black, but rather, they appear simply unused to being penalized for failing to master specified material.

What we demand of school children in slums should be the same as what we demand in private and suburban schools: hard work, prompt and accurate performance, and a trained capacity to postpone gratifications. A school in a wealthy, educated neighborhood will have a larger college preparatory program than a school in a very poor neighborhood; but there can be no excuse for any difference in the effort that is demanded or in the habits we try to create. God knows, a school cannot do these things by itself: We now know that simply coming from a single-parent family—white or black, poor or wealthy—is correlated with poor school performance and with other problems, and that half of all black children are from single-parent families.

But the general approach of the public education establishment to school children in black slums has been timid and undemanding. More ominously, for a number of reasons it has rejected the indoctrination of character traits and work habits that *any* American needs in order to be a well-functioning, useful, and reasonably satisfied member of society. The thrust of educational ideology was that hard work and a work ethic, promptness and accuracy, and civility, cannot reasonably be imposed on children in black slums, that the circumstances and "value systems" of children in black slums call for a different kind of training.

What this comes to in practice is a system of social triage for a large minority of American children. Like military triage teams who set aside the wounded who look hopeless, the educators who practice social triage fail to insist on the same levels of performance, self-discipline, and hard work that they demand of "more advantaged" children. It is a "Catch 22": One of the most important ways the more advantaged children are more advantaged is that these things are demanded of them. Slum children are trained how to live in their slum, with a character, education, and speech appropriate for the slum, and nowhere else. This is a policy that is racist in effect, in spite of intentions that were the very opposite. On matters of race, "'60s think" was such an intellectual mess many educators felt obliged to conclude that black slums were nice; indeed, they thought, simultaneously, that (a) black slums are dreadful and socially and spiritually harmful to the people who live in them, (b) since all values are relative, the black slum lifestyle is just as good as any other, and (c) we ought to be ashamed of our white, middle-class lifestyle.

Confusion about race has infected the issue of tuition tax credits. It was objected that allowing parents vouchers or tax credits to help send their children to private schools was disadvantageous to blacks and the poor. However, the actual effect of making school taxes in part "user taxes," like bridge tolls, is that it better enables the poor to afford the private schools the middle class already can afford, and it especially would benefit poor blacks, for whom moving to the suburbs is less of an option.

If it is a burden on a middle-class family to pay twice—once for the public school it doesn't use and again for the private school—it is a greater burden on a poor family. If a public school system spends $2,400 per pupil, and a family is allowed to earmark $1,000 of that for a private school (say, a Catholic high school, which in my city currently charges about $1,700 a year for tuition), it is obvious that the greatest beneficiaries of such a policy would be the black poor. They have, after all, reasons at least as strong as the middle class for removing their children from inadequate and dangerous schools, and less money with which to do it. It should be added that one could never justify giving families more than a fraction of their school taxes for private schools, because the public school system remains obliged to teach the handicapped, the disturbed, and the delinquent, the cost of which everyone should share.

The objection that tax credits for private school tuition constitute state support for religion is partly met, I think, by understanding the fraction of school taxes that does not go to problem children, the retarded, and others, as a users tax. But one must add the proviso that no one can decide *not* to use it (e.g., get a refund if one is childless), but only choose what school to spend it in for one's child. Nonetheless, I suspect that the objection concerning religion is a red herring, at least for educators, and the real reason educators dislike tuition tax credits is that they fear the effects of a competitive market in education. They would lose their customers where their product is poor, and then they would be forced to make changes that run counter to ideas that have been dear to them.

There is considerable evidence that the educators' fears would be borne out. For example, a 1983 National Institute of Education survey revealed the following: 20 percent of Hispanic parents with children in public school said they very likely would transfer them to a private school if a $250 tax credit were available; 18 percent of black parents said the same; only 6 percent of white parents said this (whites are more satisfied with their schools, doubtless because more of them who would prefer to send their children to private or suburban schools already have done so). Eighteen percent of parents with incomes under $7,500 said they would transfer their children to a private school, fewer than 3 percent of parents with incomes over $25,000 said this. So much for the argument that tuition tax credits are of interest mainly to the white and the wealthy. These results are corroborated by a 1981 Gallup Poll that stated 23 percent of parents said they would switch to a private school if there was a tuition tax credit of $250-$500.

The poor performance of slum children, particularly black slum children, in school and college today has very little to do with money or facilities; it has much to do with *ideas*—philosophical ideas about human nature, the work ethic, responsibility, the good society, and the methods and purposes of education. Spending billions of additional dollars on buildings, gadgets, and special programs will not do a thing to improve the performance of inner-city black kids in school and in business if the philosophy of education remains the same. Our love affair with gadgets and gimmicks as solutions to problems of education is just another example of the great American quick-fix. In the past few years educators (and computer manufacturers) have diverted our attention from the deeper problems with the "need" for "computer literacy" and the promise of computers for everyone. I like computers and I am writing these very words with one; but what will it profit a slum child if he or she is led to a computer but cannot read what is on the monitor?

What is needed, within the limits of what schools can provide, is simple in idea, although certainly not politically simple: Tough, demanding teachers and school officials, with authority to put pressure on parents, and who will kick kids' behinds, metaphorically speaking, until they do their homework, do lots of it, do it accurately, do it on time, do it in correct English, and take criticism with civility. But *nobody*, black or white, will learn how to study, gain self-discipline, and acquire competencies, under the philosophy of education that rose to ascendency in the '60s and '70s and is largely with us still. It is the glory of that period that it produced our first public, national commitment to racial equality and sensitized us, as did no preceding decade, to the rights of women, the handicapped, and others. But every social revolution has its Terror, in this case a fixation on rights and the self that extended to rejecting the most basic socialization and civilizing of the young. The self was everthing, all the connectors between individuals and their society were cut, and a sense of belonging was lost.

Hyper-individualism leads to alienation and societal fragmentation in education as it does in other areas of society. The issue of Black English is an example. Black English is an argot spoken by many low-economic-class urban blacks, but not by black people brought up in middle- or upper-class families except as an affectation. It is isolating because those who speak only Black English cannot be well understood by outsiders, nor can they adequately communicate in the larger worlds of business, science, and government. It is, for just that reason, an inferior means of communication for Americans, unless their aim (or their teachers' aim) is that they spend their lives in black slums. The relevant question for educators is, why pay any attention to Black English? I don't mean, why even think of it, for knowing that at home a pupil speaks Vietnamese, Russian, Spanish, or an American slum vernacular may be worth knowing when we detect problems in the pupil's speech and reading. But why should teachers fail to correct it in class, and why should they pay fulsome compliments to it or use books written in it? In doing such things we make it easier for Cubans, Soviet Jews, and Vietnamese to fully join the ranks of Americans than for blacks who have been here three hundred years.

Insistence on bringing black slum children into the cultural and linguistic mainstream is as dependent on moral and cultural self-confidence as is expecting refugees and immigrants to learn the national language. And insistence on mastering the national language is as much a sign of the non-demoralized society as is insistence on a common core of social morality. Each requires the indoctrination of the young; the acquisition of each is a principal badge of societal membership, its neglect a badge of alienation. The learning of English by immigrants should be viewed as an important initiation rite: a tribal requirement, but less objectionable than scarring the face or walking on hot coals. As the Slavic linguist Kenneth Naylor said, "As long as you have a language, you are a people."

The educational philosophy I have been criticizing may be illustrated by a few recent examinations for the Ph.D. in Education. In one, a candidate was asked what he would do, as a teacher, if a pupil told him to shut up. He would, we were told, try to find out "whose problem it was"; it was, he said, most likely his problem, and he would let the pupil know he realized adults impose their wills on kids too much. He would, in effect, apologize to the pupil for the pupil's telling him to shut up. In another exam, a candidate for the Ph.D. degree defended the thesis that teachers must always connect their teaching with students' pre-existing interests. The candidate and his committee showed no concern that doing this, as a general practice, might interfere with students learning how to postpone gratifications.

The public schools are beginning to emerge from nearly two decades during which teachers and pupils have been taught that "values" and ethics are relative; that feeling good about oneself is the main goal of education; that a work ethic and even standard English are just white, middle-class values, the imposition of which on blacks, Hispanics, and the poor is a kind of cultural imperialism; that children will learn to read "when they are ready"; that grading, criticizing, or punishing pupils is wrong because it may stigmatize them and damage self-esteem; that self-expression and learning to question and criticize are more important than learning "dead facts"; that children have the right to decide what they will learn and that doing work on time and accurately is uptight and middle class.

They have learned what we have taught them. Where the above educational philosophy is perfectly implemented we have its perfect products: Students who can barely read, who "turn off" when an explanation gets difficult, who know nothing of science, their history, or their culture, and who are suckers for astrology, witchcraft, and similar nonsense; who believe everyone is always selfish and morality is hypocrisy; and who view their society as their enemy, are unable to persevere at onerous tasks, cannot accept authority or follow instructions, and insist on constant entertainment.

The causes of recent failings of public education, like our problems about crime, delinquency, and communities in general, concern what is in our power to change: It is not "Late Capitalism," "Laws of History," or other ideological nonsense that is making our children stupid and producing bad citizens, but mistaken policies regarding how young humans must be trained in order to be competent, civil, productive, and relatively satisfied members of their societies.

FOUR

Moral Education Without Moral Education

> Moral education is a primal necessity of social existence. The unrestrained passions of men are not only homicidal, but suicidal; and a community without a conscience would soon extinguish itself.
> —Horace Mann

> However divergent the moral systems of two given societies may be, the difference and consequently the mutual incomprehensibility seems to be never as complete as between two unrelated languages. Whereas the differences between such languages as English and Chinese precludes all communication, there are in the moral sphere no comparable barriers.... The two languages have no common features at all, neither in vocabulary nor grammatical structure; but the respective moral systems contain a number of common elements, such as the value placed on filial piety, charity, courtesy, and truthfulness.
> —Christoph von Fürer-Haimendorf

If we were anthropologists observing a tribe it would be the most natural thing in the world to expect them to teach their morality and culture to their children and, moreover, to think they had a perfect right to do so on the ground that cultural integrity and survival depend on it. Indeed, if we found that they had ceased to teach, through ritual and other institutional means, the values of their culture, we would take them to be on the way to cultural suicide. Like cultures whose values and traditions wither in the face of technological civilization, we would think them ruined, pitiable, alienated from their own way of life, and on the way out.

Most of us have similar attitudes toward the educational policies of nation states other than our own, though not for systems of propaganda that serve threatening and wicked ends such as Hitler's Germany. Few non-communists criticize Chinese communes for raising children to respect and internalize current ideals, even when we criticize the ideals themselves. We expect Japanese and Nigerian children to be educated to be, among other things, good Japanese and Nigerians. We find this a natural and reasonable expression of societal self-interest or group egoism, even when their moral teaching has national peculiarities that go beyond those basic traits of fairness, honesty, willingness to work, and disavowal of criminal violence that are necessary for any society to survive and perpetuate itself.

Some of the very people who would be the first to accept all this regarding other cultures are the first to deny it regarding their own American culture. How shall we understand them? Is it that our educators are so concerned with the rights of the individual that they think individuals can grow up and flourish without any training in social morality or commitment to a common good? Then why would they grant Japanese and Nigerian society the right to indoctrinate *their* citizens in their values and culture? Or is it guilt, shame, or political opposition to the *kinds* of values American society transmits to its citizens? It is surely something like the latter. American writers on education, crime, and racial problems are embarrassed to see their society do the things they find self-respecting and prudent in other societies. They can view a foreign culture as a whole, through the other end of the telescope, and it becomes obvious that without indoctrinating the young in its morality and ceremonies it dies. But at home professional educators have been leaders in denying their own society the right to transmit its values and basic social morality from generation to generation.

Moral education in the public schools, from the end of the '60s and into the '80s, is a story of the rise of two theories to immense popularity, commercial success, and influence on American public education. These are Values Clarification and the "moral stages" theory of Lawrence Kohlberg and his followers. The theories became programs for the schools and each taught, in a thousand courses and summer workshops for teachers, that nothing ought to be taught to school children as right or wrong, on the grounds that doing so is indoctrination.

The Values Clarificationists did not distinguish between what a person wanted and what was right or wrong. They clarified wants and preferences, which they called "values," by encouraging children and teenagers to rank their preferences in various ways and understand the consequences of acting on them. They published collections of simple word games and stories designed to help school children identify their "values," and led teachers and students to believe that better understanding one's personal wants was all there was to social morality and the obligations of a citizen. *Values and Teaching*, the Bible of Values Clarification, tells us that values are very personal and students should not be asked why they have the values they do, lest they be intimidated or come to think some values are better than others.[1] There are, we were told, no right answers to moral questions.

Lawrence Kohlberg, working since the fifties and heavily influenced by the Swiss psychologist Jean Piaget, argued that children progress through as many as three levels (and six stages) of moral development. These are:

The Pre-conventional Level
Stage 1. The punishment and obedience orientation.
Morality is avoidance of punishment and unquestioning deference to power.
Stage 2. The instrumental relativist orientation.
Right action is what gets you what you want, sometimes by trading favors.

The Conventional level
Stage 3. The "good boy—nice girl" orientation.
Morality is earning approval by conforming and being "nice."
Stage 4. The "law and order" orientation.
Morality is doing one's duty in the sense of respecting authority and the social order.

The Post-conventional or Principled Level
Stage 5. The social-contract orientation.
Morality is based on law, rights, and social utility.
Stage 6. The Universal ethical principle orientation.
Morality is a matter of self-chosen universal principles of justice.[2]

Kohlberg and his co-workers tested children in several countries over a number of years. He concluded that we all begin at Stage 1 and progress stage by stage, never skipping and never regressing (except college students, who regress back to pre-conventional self-centeredness but recover when they leave college). Kohlberg's theory suggests there are innate developmental tendencies, thus breaking with the social science orthodoxy that attributes all norms and social behavior to social conditioning. The application of the stage theory to moral education in the schools was obvious and irresistible: It was assumed that higher stages were better than lower ones (What else? Could children's morality be "higher" than adult, or higher be worse than lower?), with the immediate implication that the aim of moral education was stage advance. So they devised tests, gave them to school children, and labeled each child with a stage-of-moral-development number. The teacher would try to speed up the process of getting each pupil to move on to the next or higher stage by discussing made-up "moral dilemmas," the idea being that students are naturally attracted to moral reasons one stage higher than the one they are at. Here, for example, is Kohlberg's famous Heinz dilemma:

> In Europe, a woman was near death from a special kind of cancer. There was one drug that the doctors thought might save her. It was a form of radium that a druggist in the same town had recently discovered. . . . The druggist . . . paid $200 for the radium and charged $2,000 for a small dose of the drug. The sick woman's husband, Heinz, could only get together about $1,000, which is half of what it cost. He told the druggist that his wife was dying and asked him to sell it cheaper or let him pay later. But the druggist said, "No, I discovered the drug and I'm going to make money from it." So Heinz got desperate and broke into the man's store to steal the drug for his wife.

We should try to lay aside the childishness and medical illiteracy of the example, as well as the moral attitude toward business suggested by the example of a heartless, profiteering druggist. Children are asked, Should Heinz have stolen the drug? Why? The point is to see the *stage* an answer reveals. There is nothing in the method that tells you that a "yes" is better than a "no": The question, "Well, which is it, right or wrong, at stage so-and-so?" is never raised. For what made Kohlberg's system fit in so nicely with the relativism and indoctrination phobia of the '70s is that it could be marketed as a *process*, without moral content, and thus be immune to the charge of moral indoctrination.

On reflection it would seem that the obvious differences between selfish, conventionalist, and "universal principle" points of view would lead to different answers to a moral question, and that reasoning at the highest stage would yield the correct answer. But the '70s educators were so relativistic that everything was reduced to opinion: Any suggestion that a "value" might be mistaken or irrational was really just a case of a teacher "imposing her values on other people's kids," and therefore "indoctrination." The Kohlbergian scheme of moral education advocated a method but denied it gave answers. The problem with this is that the point of any method, including a method of moral reasoning, is to get results you cannot get as confidently without it. The best or "highest" method of moral reasoning ought to *answer* the question about the drug; if it cannot, why is reasoning at that stage better than reasoning at any other stage?

The desire by both Values Clarification and the Kohlbergians simultaneously to work out a method of moral reasoning and to pander to the relativism and egoism of the times necessarily resulted in incoherence. Each ended up saying they were morally neutral but that everyone else was moralizing and therefore indoctrinating. "Indoctrination" became the scare word educators used to tar their competition, but it probably is only in education circles that it is entirely a bad word. The military services and other institutions are proud of their systems of indoctrination and call them so. *Are* moral education programs indoctrinative if they teach that certain things are right and wrong? And if they are, is that bad? All teaching, indeed all social living, involves passing on, from generation to generation, the morality, manners, ceremonies—the way of life—of a culture. When we have been examining our own society from too close up it helps to lift our eyes from the local paper and read an anthropological study of a tribe, such as the Gonds, Nagas, or Iroquois, in order to see how much must be passed on for a society to live.

The popularity of Values Clarification was due in large part to the education professors' receptivity to a romantic, sentimental view of human nature. Whereas European medieval societies thought human nature inherently wicked and socialist societies believe it to be almost limitlessly malleable, American educators thought children naturally good, even naturally civilized, requiring only self-esteem and affectionate stroking to be good persons and good citizens. For Kohlbergians there was a "natural" and nearly inevitable march through the moral stages. For Values Clarificationists, a perfectly fine character already lay inside the child, needing only to be "clarified" to be set free. If one sufficiently romanticizes the doctrine that people are naturally good, moral education as most people understand the notion is unnecessary: The wants that are clarified, and our opinions about dilemmas, will be kind, honest, fair, and considerate.

Actually, the British experimental educator A. S. Neill, of Summerhill School fame, best expressed the essence of the '70s moral education movements:

> We set out to make a school in which we should allow children freedom to be themselves. To do this we had to renounce all discipline, all direction, all moral training. We have been called brave but it did not require courage, just a complete belief in the child as a good, not an evil, being. *If left to himself without adult suggestion of any kind he will develop as*

far as he is capable of developing. I believe that it is moral instruction that makes the child bad, not good.[3]

It is difficult even to conceive of a theory of raising the young that is more profoundly mistaken than this one. The absolutely terrible consequences of not socializing a social animal is a topic that will occupy much of this book. To begin with a small point, how many of us would do our work on time, and do it well, without the knowledge that scorn, less money, or non-tenure await us if we do not? Will we work very hard if promotion and admiration are guaranteed, and our bosses and supervisors simply smile and stroke us? Just as most of us will be lazy if allowed to be, most of us also have a considerable predisposition toward greed, dishonesty, unfairness, and other vices which are revealed when our important interests are at stake. This is why humans, but not angels, need morality. Insofar as we act ethically and responsibly most of the time, it is partly because we have been trained to do so, partly because we fear the consequences of not doing so, and partly because we acknowledge the authority of principles.

Values Clarificationists in particular applied the American moral ideal of pluralistic democracy to morality itself; thus they treated social morality like tastes in food and personal ideals, the diversity of which, within limits, *is* guaranteed by our democratic ideals. Translated into moral relativism in the classroom, this became the view that one moral opinion or policy was no better than any other. How unique this remarkable view is to a thin time-slice of American social history is revealed by anthropologists' studies of tribes. Throughout history and in every tribe and society that has been examined, social morality is a matter of defensible limits on freedom and self-expression, imposed by the culture on its members. It is not, as the Values Clarificationists used to advertise, a matter of finding "values" that make you "joyous and zestful."

Ethical relativism is the view that right and wrong are relative to opinion: An act is not right or wrong, period. It is right *for me,* if that is my opinion, or right for my culture, if my culture favors it; and the very same act will be wrong *for you* if you think it wrong. It is, essentially, the view that there is no difference between something being wrong and its being *thought* wrong. Relativism naturally invites substitution of talk about "values" for talk about morality. Morality implies interpersonal standards that can conflict with our desires and about which we can be mistaken, whereas values are thought of as subjective and biographical. For Values Clarificationists in particular, values are not demands or constraints, they are personal features individuals have, like pimples; they are not standards that express what is necessary for a society to survive or flourish, nor are they capable of rational appraisal. Relativism is a natural expression of hyper-individualism because it rejects the authority of a collective, social good over one's personal, private good.

Historically, a certain disdain and arrogance has lurked beneath the surface of ethical relativism: The values of people far away, and in general whatever one doesn't much personally care about, are called relative, a matter of "doing your thing," and right for whoever thinks them right; but one's own values are absolutely right. Values Clarificationists preached tolerance of other people's "values" about sex, lifestyle, and the absence of honesty or a work ethic in children from black slum neighborhoods far from their own. But there was no toleration of what especially roused their own passions, such as discrimination, indoctrination, and authoritarianism. The anthropological relativists of forty years ago made the same moves—for example, Melville Herskovits' claim that whatever any culture or society *thought* was good *was* good, for *it*, and whatever it disapproved was bad, for it. From this Herskovits concluded that toleration of diverse values was an absolute good (while neglecting to check to see if his own society approved of toleration).[4] If Values Clarificationists really think there is no such thing as a justified moral belief, they cannot argue that it matters in the slightest whether one indoctrinates children, abuses them, or whatever. They can only say, "We feel this way; other people do not."

A more recent anthropologist suggested it may have taken Hitler to shake the cultural relativism of his profession:

> While [Western intellectuals] had argued quite happily that in the setting of the one or other primitive tribal society, head-hunting or slave-raiding fulfilled useful social functions, they found it rather more difficult to adopt a similarly detached attitude towards the violation of what seems basic human rights openly practiced by the governments of powerful European states.[5]

More like a traditional tribe, and less like the tribe of American moral educators, are the staff and students at Leningradski School Number 40 in the northwestern part of Moscow. It is a modern show school, with good athletic and other physical facilities. When I came to observe the school I signed a fat guest book already filled with the effusions of countless foreign delegations.

They use, as does probably every Soviet school, uniform manuals of "communist education," which are teachers' guides for bringing up children in a collectivist spirit. One manual that became available in

Moscow in 1979, *The ABC's of Moral Education*, had a printing of 400,000 copies, which is immense by Soviet standards and implies nationwide use. Here is a translation from that book of most of the "Moral Rules for Schoolchildren" in the first three forms (ages seven to ten):[6]

Rules of Comradeship

1. Help your comrade; if you can do something, teach him how to do it; if he is in trouble, help him as much as you can.
2. Share with your comrades; . . . .
3. Stop a comrade if he is doing something bad. To be good friends means to speak only the truth to each other; if a friend is not in the right in some matter, tell him so.
4. Don't quarrel with your comrades; . . . if you have acted badly, don't be ashamed to admit it and correct it.
5. Be able to accept assistance, advice, and comments from other children.

Rules of Fair Play and Competition

1. Observe the rules of the game and of competition: don't try to win and gain first place by dishonest means. If the struggle is not honest, victory is uninteresting.
2. Don't gloat when others lose.
3. It is disappointing when you lose, but don't lose heart and don't be angry with the winner.

Rules of Courtesy

1. Be courteous. Courtesy is knowing how to conduct yourself in such a way that you are acceptable to others.
2. Always be friendly; greet someone when you meet; thank someone for help and attention; when leaving, don't forget to say goodbye.
3. Give your seat to the elderly, the ill, and the tired on a streetcar, a bus, a train, or a park bench; try not to do this ostentatiously, and don't wait until you are asked to give up your place.
4. If someone has fallen, help him up. Help the old, the weak, the blind to cross the street. And do this sincerely, from the heart, amiably, not sullenly.
5. Never be late. Always arrive at the appointed hours, to the minute; be mindful of other people's time.
6. Don't make others worry about you. When you leave the house, say where you are going and when you will be back. And don't be late.
7. Don't be naughty. Your naughtiness may spoil others' moods and cause them concern.

These rules, and the fact that most Russians are reasonably civil and considerate, might initially surprise those used to thinking of the Soviets only in terms of foreign policy or KGB methods of internal control. Paul Hollander expressed the difference well when he said that "The Soviet system itself, no matter how manipulative, hypocritical, or deceptive it has been, has not instilled in the population the *values* of manipulation and deception."[7]

Neither should we forget that, as *Pravda* said, "the Soviet teacher is a soldier on the ideological front. . . ."[8] The Moscow teachers in Leningradski Number 40 are as open as they are dedicated about the kind of character they attempt to form in their students: earnest and serious, cooperative and helpful, service oriented, happiest in group rather than individual activities. The students were polite and very orderly in class; they practiced ball throwing and 1950s dance steps in perfect synchrony.

At the end of my visit to this school there were tea and candies with the administrators and senior teachers, all intelligent and obviously committed middle-aged women. They beamed with pleasure when I praised them for the serious atmosphere of learning, and the emphasis on courtesy, considerateness, cooperation, and public service. "In fact," I said, "your school reminds me more of the Roman Catholic school my own children attend than it does American public schools." Their smiles froze and all of the hundred icons of Lenin hanging in the rooms and corridors gave me dirty looks. Contrite, I praised again, even pointing out that I had come to like school uniforms (the Russian children wore dark blue with white trim), and again they beamed. "But you must understand," I concluded, "I am more conservative about education than are most Americans," and once more their smiles turned to ice.

Soviet moral education is woven into the structures and routines of the school rather than taught in special sessions, and is not significantly different from what Urie Bronfenbrenner described in his classic 1970 study, *Two Worlds of Childhood*.[9] Individualism now is discussed more openly (their problems with it naturally being the opposite of ours). They teach attitudes we would not want children to internalize such as class consciousness, class animosity, and a sense of guilt or unease at doing things on one's own outside of a group. But the Russians' commitment to the idea of directive moral education is highly conservative. This commitment presupposes there is something to conserve—a common morality—and that it is worth conserving and passing on to the new generation.

In their commitment to directive moral education in the schools the Soviet approach is superior to ours. They go all out to teach definite moral principles to children. We should do that too, although our principles would not be identical with but overlap the Russian list. This implies that we, too, have a common core of social morality—in other words, that we are a moral community, and that this core should be conserved with the help of the public schools.

American democracy makes this position more difficult for us than for the Soviets. The Soviet rulers need only decide on a moral code and set out to transform the people, whereas we must not only justify the morality we teach, but find it already existing in the consciousness, or close to the surface of consciousness, of the American people. We cannot, without gross paternalism and the risk of developing contempt for one's wards that invariably accompanies paternalism, use the apparatus of the state to produce a wholly new moral consciousness.

At the most fundamental level, American democracy, subject to minimal constitutional limits, is committed to giving the people what they want, not what is good for them. This ranges from the mindless vulgarity of daytime television to social morality in the schools. What may be the one great American exception is the abolition of the *morality* of slavery and, more recently, an official commitment to racial equality which almost certainly was a minority opinion in America until just a few decades ago. Soviet political elitism gives the people what it thinks is good for them, not what they want—including long TV panel discussions of the prospects for the next Siberian grain harvest. Each of us hopes, in vain naturally, that what the people want and what is good for them will coincide.

It is important to distinguish the moral core that sustains a moral community from the controversial issues that bewilder adults. The moral core is nearly the same in every tribe and society on the face of the earth because it is the minimum required for human cooperative living. This core morality is honesty, fairness, incest aversion, and keeping unwanted hands off other people's bodies and property. We can add personal virtues such as courage, diligence, and self-respect, and for our society a value that is not universal: respect for the democratic process.

Morally sophisticated citizens should be capable of factually informed, careful reasoning about controversial issues such as abortion, capital punishment, and racial quotas. But teenagers can benefit from reasoning about dilemmas only if they have already accepted and internalized a basic core of principles. For example, one has to accept and take very seriously a principle about honesty before one will agonize over exceptions to it. If students are taught dilemmas before or in place of principles, they will think morality is nothing but dilemmas; and if they discuss exceptions to principles without first having made the principles part of their character, the exceptions, meeting no resistance, will come all too easily. To put it another way, there is no point in carefully examining exceptions to moral principles with students who don't have any principles in the first place.

There are a number of reasons for wanting principled citizens and officials, one being that if they are principled they can be relied upon. Yet moral education programs for the public schools generally ignored principles for dilemmas and controversies, partly because these are what interest the adults who devised the programs, and partly because educators feared coming out of the closet and actually taking a moral stand on something. The result is they treated children as though they already had principles and were now ready to consider qualifications.

The social problems that most distress all of us and which threaten the very existence of our society—and I mean our high rates of juvenile crime, casual deadly violence, and moral cynicism—result from the absence in people of the most simple, basic core of social morality. These problems do not arise from an inability to cope with sophisticated dilemmas, such as whether to steal a drug to save the life of one's dying spouse, but are due to people who have no inhibitions whatever regarding theft; their cause is not ignorance of whether a physician should lie to a patient with cancer, it is people who lie whenever it suits them; not an inability to reason out how far pregnancy must progress before abortion is murder, but people who murder elderly women in elevators for ten dollars; and not confusion about whether affirmative action without quotas is acceptable, but downright simple bigotry.

Moral education without justified moral content will be perceived as a pointless game. What we owe children is strong direction in the actual acquisition of morality, not just chatter about "values." But what do we say to the relativists? Is there an answer to those who ask, "Who is to say what is right and wrong?" I suggested that the social morality most people must acquire and heed most of the time, if a society is to be viable, includes honesty, fairness, and keeping unwanted hands off other people's bodies and property. Examples of personal virtues individuals need are courage, the ability to postpone gratifications, and willingness to work for what one wants but lacks.

Their proof does not require any refined logic or philosophical subtlety: What are a child's chances to grow up to live well and happily without courage? To lack this quality completely means that one is frightened and intimidated by nearly everything—by examinations, competitors, police officers, officials, job interviews, various dangers, tough decisions, big opportunities, an attractive man or woman one wants to meet—in sum, by the things one must cope with fairly well in order to live well. To the extent one lacks courage one is inclined to back off, run away, quit, or perform in a way that fails to win the confidence of others.

Turning to the case for social morality, it is in everyone's interest that children grow up to be honest, fair, and averse to violence, because we live in the same society as these children and we do not want them to prey on us when they grow up. Children who grow up dishonest, unfair, or violent, make life more dangerous, insecure, expensive, and unpleasant for those around them. Clearly the best way society can protect itself is to bring up children so that they are not dishonest and unfair. It is also in the children's interest, for with honesty and fairness they are more likely to live well and happily. And if they are dishonest and unfair, it is a *better bet* that they will be distrusted, disliked, insecure, fired from jobs, and go to prison. In the absence of certainties, rationality requires that we act on the best bet; hence we have every reason to do what we can to make children honest, fair, willing to work, and averse to criminal violence, and to do so for our own benefit, for their long-term benefit, and for everyone's benefit. I realize this may seem like arguing that grass is green, but what justifies the obvious is not always obvious and there are people who maintain that nothing is true or false, or right or wrong, but thinking makes it so.

FIVE

The Ethically Neutered Society

> The ancient and Christian theories of government held that statecraft should be soulcraft; indeed, that government cannot avoid concerning itself with virtue.... The modern "night watchman" theory of government is that it exists only to protect persons and property. It can be ubiquitous and omniprovident regarding material things, but must be neutral regarding values. It can concern itself with nurturing soybeans, but not virtue.
> —George Will

> But, surely, the most needed innovation in the American classroom is the involvement of pupils in responsible tasks on behalf of others within the classroom, the school, the neighborhood, and the community.
> —Urie Bronfenbrenner

In the corridor of a Midwest high school in 1982, a 15-year-old boy stabbed another boy in the heart. On television that night the school superintendent said he felt a sense of failure, that this was his worst afternoon since he took the job, and that he regretted that the students had not been taught another way to settle their conflicts. The superintendent did not say they should be taught it is *wrong* to stab someone, or to commit murder. He and countless other school officials have learned never to mention ethics or morality in public, not to decry even a murder in the vocabulary of morality. He spoke of alternative strategies—better conflict resolution techniques—but not a word about the fact that this boy, at least, had not learned that stabbing someone is wrong.

In general, officials fear criticism if they say publicly that the school or parents need to do a better job of teaching morality. They can say something is illegal, against the rules, or unpopular, but never that it is *wrong*; saying so is unprofessional, emotional, and certainly not good for one's career. Sometimes we use euphemisms for the right and wrong of things, calling them "inappropriate," "controversial," or "in bad taste," but that is as far as we go.

We have become a nation of closet moralists: While we may speak out publicly in the flat, neuter language of the law, strong moral responses are locked up and kept in the family or among friends. The moral dimension of even the most heinous crime, betrayal, or swindle is confined to the privacy of family, where we can thump the dinner table and be indignant. But talking about right and wrong "officially" or in public opens one to criticism—it is a loss of coolness and control, like taking sides in a quarrel where one does better to remain aloof. Consequently, we have nothing to say to the vandal or the subway thug; we just stare at him. He already knows his action is illegal, and public criticism is seen as pointless interference and socially out of fashion.

The stabbing case has another dimension because both boys were black. Our closet morality is reinforced by the Super Guilt Syndrome that characterizes white officials: How dare we, with our 300-year history of slaveholding and racism, presume to preach morality to black people, or morally criticize young blacks in public? Suppose a different incident: In school a white boy shoves a black boy and calls him a stupid nigger. Assume there was slight provocation. Now would the officials say only that better methods of conflict resolution are needed (assuming they did not hide the fact that a racial incident occurred)? Only when white guilt is involved do officials dare to say there is a moral issue, in this case on the sound basis that racial abuse is unfair. One can find no other exceptions among school officials to the de-moralization of the public education environment. Yet there seems to be little doubt that if we should teach students and remind the public that racial slurs are wrong, we have all the more reason to do so over stabbing and murder, which are much worse.

Plato 2400 years ago asked whether virtue can be taught, and shortly afterward Aristotle gave the right answer: Yes, of course, if we understand it as in large part a matter of *training* the young to internalize principles, so that the powerful force of habit will be on the side of moral behavior. Aristotle's answer is important today because delinquency by adults and teenagers results in large part from failure in the socialization of children. The schools cannot wash their hands of the issue: They share responsibility with families and churches for the socialization of the young and they are themselves seriously harmed by its failure. The National Education Association estimated that in 1979 110,000 teachers were assaulted in school. In 1978 the National Institute of Education published a study entitled *Violent Schools, Safe*

Schools, in which it reported that 9.5 percent of urban junior high school students said they were robbed within the past month (it was 7.5 for suburban schools, 7.1 for rural schools).[1] Also, 8.2 percent of the urban youngsters reported being assaulted within the past month.

A citizenry's internalization of basic principles of social morality is more essential to the existence of a society than is the provision of police protection or the levying of taxes. Our ancestors endured for hundreds of thousands of years without police and taxes but not without social morality. To say that a society is a moral community means that it has a shared morality that regulates interpersonal contacts in a way that is predictable and mutually acceptable: We know what to expect, or at least what not to expect, from the stranger coming down the street or from one we must ask assistance. Perhaps the most significant respect in which the quality of life in large American cities has declined is loss of confidence in predicting the behavior of strangers. In cities we move among strangers and encounter strangers all the time; if we cannot count on basic civility and safety we have lost what is minimally necessary for a human society.

The predictable civility we require extends to the respect due strangers and acquaintances in virtue of the offices they hold. The rending of the social fabric is hastened when young people are taught the slogan that "respect must be earned." In a civilized society this simply is not and cannot be true, for if every police officer, schoolteacher, elderly person, official, or priest must count on loutish, or at best, casual and overfamiliar behavior from new people they meet, their roles in society will be impossible. It is, again, a matter of whether one has a communitarian or individualistic conception of society. The former outlook accords office- and role-holders the respect due those offices and roles, initially without regard to who occupies them. One can *lose* the respect one starts with by disgraceful or incompetent behavior, but one does not start from zero. Individualists who only acknowledge relationships the individual creates, and reject obligations that derive from social institutions, are much more likely to be receptive to the dogma that respect must be earned.

The respect given elders in tribal and traditional society is not something that is earned, nor could such societies function if it had to be. Schoolteachers cannot function—and as a matter of fact often do not function—in an environment in which youth have no respect for teachers or for adults in general. In such a setting the teacher can try to "earn" respect, from an initial situation of statuslessness at best and surly contempt at worst: The situation rewards teachers who can be hip, macho, physically intimidating, or who can win a battle of wits and "put down" their pupils. Teachers have enough crosses to bear already without having to play these games.

Internalized morality operates in the absence of police or threatened social disapproval far more effectively than cynics believe—one need only think of the countless usually minor occasions on which, in the absence of social threats, one keeps one's word, refrains from theft, and acts fairly. But a child does not become principled by magic or by heredity, nor is it possible to transmit moral principles to children by talking about insoluble dilemmas or personal preferences. They must be made so by the society's institutionalized civilizing agencies—families, churches, public opinion, and schools.

Learning a principle of social morality is very different from learning a fact. This is an important difference between morals and science that can be easily illustrated. I can read in a book or be told by someone I trust that cobras are deadly, and instantly I have the belief, full and complete, and I respond appropriately: I will not pick one up, if I meet one in the family room I will be terrified, and so on. But if I read in a book or am told by someone I trust that dishonesty is wrong, I may in some sense believe the words, but it needn't follow at all that I have that moral belief. It doesn't follow that I will avoid dishonesty as I avoid cobras. What the intellect learns about cobras hooks up with a pre-existing fear of death to produce the belief and the appropriate behavior, but really to believe dishonesty is wrong requires work on the emotions and habits, not just intellectual work. A well-brought-up person *feels* badly at the thought of dishonesty or theft and has to have an awfully good reason, or very strong temptation, before he will go ahead and do it. This is part of what it means to have a moral belief as distinct from a mere readiness to assent to words. The philosopher Joel Kupperman puts the point as follows:

> To learn a simple moral rule is not just an intellectual exercise: it is to acquire a habit of not behaving in a certain way, a reluctance to behave in that way, and a strong tendency to feel psychic pain at having acted in that way. It is to acquire an inhibition. . . . Such a person will be, as we say, a poor liar, awkward and troubled about breaking promises. . . .[2]

Aristotle made the same point by saying that a morally educated person finds virtue to be (relatively) pleasant and vice (relatively) disagreeable. To think robbery is morally wrong is to be against it, to hate it, and to be inclined to hate those who commit it; and if one is sorely tempted to do a wrong, really thinking it *is* wrong implies having a strong contrary feeling: that is Aristotle's point. It doesn't mean you won't rob, it only means you will be less likely to, other things being equal, if you think it is wrong.

It is time, I think, for someone to spare a kind word for hatred. Moral sentimentalists will pout and wag their fingers, but are not vicious crime, gross bigotry and injustice, and all great evils, appropriate objects of hatred? If someone tells you murder and race discrimination are wrong, but he is perfectly dispassionate about the matter and amiably has murderers and bigots to tea, will you not doubt his sincerity? The great evils in the world—the ones people do to one another and not natural evils such as earthquake and famine—are things we fear and hate, and we hate those who do these things. To say hatred is always wrong is simply a mistake. It was right to hate Hitler. It is right to hate brutal criminals, unless we have reason to think them truly mad or simple-minded. It is right to hate evil.

If children are introduced to moral principles by a cool discussion in which a teacher says, "in our culture dishonesty is disapproved," they will note that as a dry, sociological fact, much as, "in the Bongo Islands it is wicked to eat jub-jub berries." American educators and public officials intellectualize morality at the same time as they relativize it: We stay as far as possible from the emotional component of moral principles and moral education, the effect of which is to abandon moral talk altogether and substitute talk about resolving conflicts. Thus we feign moral neutrality, for it is flight from the open emotional expressions that genuine morality requires which, as much as anything, makes us into closet moralists.

If teachers (or parents, or juvenile justice officials) confronting a brazen lie or a gross and hurtful act of unfairness became indignant, shouted, and trembled with anger—and said *why* they reacted this way—it would serve as an instrument of moral education better than a thousand calm-voiced, morally neutral discussions of dilemmas where all the "yes's" and "no's" have equal rights. For children know anger is real, and the teacher's anger would help them to understand that morality is part of the real world. Anyone who *really* believes that what someone did is immoral—say, a lie that destroys the career of a rival—hates or intensely dislikes it, fears it, and is angry at similar instances. The things we sincerely believe are wrong are things we truly do not want to happen, and therefore it is perfectly natural that we become angry and indignant when they do.

Because morality involves the emotions as much as the intellect, children will be confused if we "play it cool," are "laid back," and never get excited about moral issues. For they are already learning to approve and disapprove of things outside the school in language which is inherently emotional, whether it be conventional moral language or invective that plays the same role.

Teachers, parents, and juvenile authorities who are "objective" in the face of real issues of social morality will find themselves substituting either of two different things for morality. On the one hand, they may replace talk about what is right and wrong with talk about people's "values systems" and the fact that rape and theft happen to be disapproved in our culture. This is the path that turns morality into sociology and moral principles into personal "values"—my values, your values, and Charlie Manson's values. On the other hand, they may decide that it is all right to let go and get just plain, *non*-morally mad at theft in the classroom or an incident of race discrimination. The idea is that getting emotional is all right so long as you don't try to justify it: It is just personal, autobiographical anger, forgivable in anyone, whereas justification and the use of moral language would imply claims on other people's emotions. This is the path that replaces "It's wrong" with "I don't like it."

Each of these moves—the flight to sociology and the flight to personal feelings—is a method of escape from having to face morality itself and commit oneself, in front of innocent little children (or delinquent teenagers), to the principle that dishonesty is *wrong*. Each is also a form of decadence. Consider the tribe whose deep sense of right and wrong and cultural vitality wither in the face of a modern civilization that ignores the tribe's moral code or, worse, considers it quaint. The etiology of what happens has to do with what Immanuel Kant called lost innocence and which, he says, naturally leads to relativism and moral cynicism. The existence of a unitary society—however much it may be internally subdivided—depends on its members' awareness of having a core of deeply and confidently held common moral values together with customs and ceremonies which bear witness to them—in other words, *on their being a moral community*. Within the moral community they may dispute, but with confidence that at the deepest levels they are still one people.

The dependence of the meaningfulness of our individual lives on the integrity of our group morality was expressed by the British anthropologist Raymond Firth when he defined morality as "that system of rules and standards which give significance to the activity of individuals in relation to one another in society."[3] Not just restraint and suppression but significance, which is what to expect of innately social creatures whose social roles partly constitute their being.

The cultural breakdown of some American Indian tribes resulted when they saw their gods, traditions, and values overwhelmed by surrounding European culture, their ceremonies and dances become dead things that are trotted out Tuesdays and Saturdays for tourists. Their culture died on them, as did that of the Ik, but much more slowly. They ceased to be a moral community, and the further result often was drinking and listless poverty. Ruth Benedict said it as well as anyone, commenting on the remarks of a California Indian chief:

> "In the beginning," he said, "God gave to every people a cup, a cup of clay, and from this cup they drank their life. . . . Our cup is broken now. It has passed away." Our cup is broken. Those things that have given significance to the life of his people, the domestic rituals of eating, the obligations of the economic system, the succession of ceremonials in the villages, possession in the bear dance, their standards of right and wrong—these were gone, and with them the shape and meaning of life. . . . He did not mean that there was any question of the extinction of his people. But he had in mind the loss of something that had value equal to that of life itself, the whole fabric of his people's standards and beliefs.[4]

Moral diversity at a deep level, or even what falsely appears to be so, destroys innocence by destroying the givenness of the basic principles that define the moral community. When this innocence is lost, a natural dialectic takes over, whose first step is the shift from "the gods forbid so-and-so" to "*our* gods forbid so-and-so". The next step is, "we have our value system, but all those other societies (and sub-societies) have different ones." Reflection on this leads us to downgrade moral principles from objective claims to reports about how we feel: These are the "values" many moral educators think is the proper subject of moral education. The final step is withdrawal of serious commitment to any principles of morality: Now we are alienated from the morality even of our own community, and become like a field anthropologist who sits on a hill and watches with perfect detachment as two tribes slug it out. One has achieved objectivity; one is an observer, classifier, and clarifier of "values," ready to say to a teacher who is upset at theft by a child from an urban slum, "but you see, he (or she) may simply have been brought up to have a different value system from yours." When we have reached this stage, our cup is broken.

What to do in the face of moral heterogeneity is a serious and genuine problem and it is obvious that the answer cannot be the enforcement of innocence. Innocence once gone is gone forever, as much for American society as it is for an island tribe. But the decadence lost innocence threatens is as potentially deadly to our society as it is to the tribe. Objective, noncommital discussion of our own moral principles, conducted as though one were discussing the mores of a distant tribe about which one cares nothing, will lead young people to sense that it is not *morality* that is being discussed and, perhaps, to view their own moral community as though it were that distant tribe.

Psychologists, therapists, criminologists, and nervous public officials have all made their contributions to the moral neutering of American society. One consequence is the failure of young people and potential delinquents to understand at the earliest age that crime is fundamentally a moral fault. While jurists have discussed at length recent moves to *decriminalize immorality,* by legalizing prostitution, gambling, and other so-called victimless crimes, the *demoralization of crime* is the more significant aspect of this disengagement that has taken place over the past two or three decades. The point of criminal law, from its earliest forms in tribal or clan councils, is to prohibit what is wrong and hurtful, either to individuals or to the security of the clan by the violation of taboos. Anthropologists confirm that a moral basis for criminalization and the personal accountability of criminals are features of traditional societies, including the most primitive, the world over:

> The principle of public recognition of socially desirable conduct is extremely widespread. Rewards no less than punishments represent a society's reaction to the conduct of individuals, and implied in both is the recognition of man's status as a free agent. Even primitive peoples distinguish very clearly between the actions of those they consider sane and the conduct of the mentally deranged who are not held responsible for their deeds. . . . Without some consensus on the rightness or wrongness of different types of behavior no human society could avoid a decline into total chaos, because the actions of the individual members of the society would be entirely unpredictable, and normal social cooperation would hence become impossible.[5]

The most famous case of moral passivity was the New York murder in 1961 of Kitty Genovese in front of 38 witnesses who did nothing—a murder that generated numerous scholarly articles and experiments and made the careers of a number of social psychologists. One can see the "Genovese syndrome" taking shape in elementary school classrooms: If a student is committing a minor infraction, classmates watch and giggle; if the infraction is serious they sit and watch with their mouths open, leaving any intervention or protest to an authority. At the most a student might inform a teacher, but do nothing at the scene. The school environment has become demoralized and legalistic, a microcosm and partial cause of our legalistic larger society. But the moral neutralization of the classroom takes place only from the school's side, students themselves filling the vacuum with their own, often antisocial, approvals and disapprovals.

It need not be this way. Peer-reinforcement techniques and compulsory service activities are two de-alienation strategies (among several to be considered) that help a school rebuild an atmosphere of moral purpose and combat closet morality. Schools are microsocieties which we manipulate and experiment with in innumerable ways, the good and bad results being important not only for schools but as clues to what works and doesn't work in the larger society. Urie Bronfenbrenner's comparative study of Soviet and American education led him to the following comments on peer influence:

> The peer group need not necessarily act as an impetus to antisocial behavior. Among Soviet youngsters, it has just the opposite effect. Why? The answer is obvious enough. The Soviet peer group is given explicit training for exerting desired influence on its members, whereas the American peer group is not. Putting it another way, the Soviet peer group is heavily—perhaps too heavily—influenced by the adult society. In contrast, the American peer group is relatively autonomous, cut off from the adult world—a particularly salient example of segregation by age.[6]

Bronfenbrenner conducted experiments which showed that Soviet twelve-year-olds are as deterred from misbehavior when they believed only that their peers would learn of it as when they believed adults would be told; and that they are much more disposed than Westerners to talk to a misbehaving peer themselves rather than report it to adults. In particular, fewer than one percent said "it was none of their business."[7]

It is easy to be critical of Russians minding each others' business, but if American socialization had been a little more intervention-minded, perhaps the unresponsive spectators to the attack on Kitty Genovese would have responded. It is not impossible to socialize American schoolchildren to express public and collective disapproval of obvious breaches of moral norms by other students. They can be taught to get involved and publicly criticize the unethical actions of others. While subtler methods doubtless can be devised, teachers and administrators can begin simply by telling students to say, "Hey, cut it out, you'll hurt him (or break it, or start a fire, or prevent the rest of us from getting any work done, etc.)."

What is most important is the effect on adult behavior. What begins as a habit of peer intervention in school might well contribute to an adult "uproar reaction" to street crime. If A started beating up B, or forcing C into a car over her screams for help, and everyone in sight flew into an uproar, running over, shouting, and demanding to know what is going on, A would very likely be intimidated. The importance of group uproar, in addition to the relative physical security it provides those who intervene in, say, an attempted subway car robbery, has less to do with the criminal's fear of apprehension than with his aversion to loud, collective disapproval and criticism from his community. We can call this response the "uproar effect," a kind of rejection anxiety, and later I shall speculate on the evolution of such emotions in hominid bands, in terms of fear of exile and the phenomenon of mobbing the predator.

Tending to one's peers can be positive as well as critical. Compulsory service activities strengthen group affiliations, for the most effective way to make young people feel they "belong" to a school or community is to make demands on them and demonstrate they are needed. In addition, service to younger children, to the elderly and poor in the community, and to adults in general, makes members of these groups familiar and therefore more likely to be viewed as part of one's "tribe." Bronfenbrenner, writing at the end of the sixties, is remarkably prescient:

> As we read the evidence, both from our own research and that of others, we cannot escape the conclusion that, if the current trend persists, if the institutions of our society continue to remove parents, other adults, and older youth from active participation in the lives of children, and if the resulting vacuum is filled by the age-segregated peer group, *we can anticipate increased alienation, indifference, antagonism, and violence on the part of the younger generation in all segments of our society—middle-class children as well as the disadvantaged.*
>
> Nor is service to the very young the only . . . goal relevant to children in our society. There are also the very old. In segregating them in their own housing projects and, indeed, in whole communities, we have deprived both them and the younger generation of an essential human experience. We need to find ways in which children can once again have contact with old people, to assist and comfort them, and, in return, gain the benefits to character development which accrue from these experiences. For it is not only the disadvantaged or the old who gain from such humane actions. . . . American middle-class society and its children . . . are by no means free from a variety of social and emotional ills, prominent among which are problems of apathy, alienation, and antisocial behavior; and it is participation in service to others that provides the most promising antidote for these social maladies.[8]

It is difficult to believe that youths who, when young, regularly participate in service activities for the aged, and keep company with them, would later find it morally or psychologically possible to prey upon the old, in the ways that are so cruel and notorious in our large cities.

SIX

Laconic Violence

> Predatory crime does not merely victimize individuals, it impedes and, in the extreme case, even prevents the formation and maintenance of community. By disrupting the delicate nexus of ties, formal and informal, by which we are linked with our neighbors, crime atomizes society and makes of its members mere individual calculators estimating their own advantage, especially their own chances for survival amidst their fellows. Common undertakings become difficult or impossible, except for those motivated by a shared desire for protection.
> —James Q. Wilson

> Law is the witness and external deposit of our moral life.
> —Justice Holmes

As we have seen, something happened to America about 1963; a large number of unhappy trends, ranging from crime rates to out-of-wedlock birth, suicide, and aptitude test declines, and having little apparent connection with each other, all began about that time. Between 1960 and 1982 the rate of death by homicide increased dramatically. The robbery and delinquency rates increased even more rapidly and the steepest increase of all was in the number of rapes per 100,000 women.

Crime rates were quite low in the 1950s, comparing favorably with those of many European countries. Indeed, in all respects—divorce, delinquency, crime, student achievement, suicide—the "complacent generation" of the 1950s, those dull Eisenhower years, were our golden age, the best we've had since the Civil War. According to the F.B.I. Uniform Crime Reports, violent crime more than tripled between 1960 and 1979. Surveys of victimization—how many people say they were victims as distinct from police data—indicate a smaller increase. But there is no doubt that violence has increased

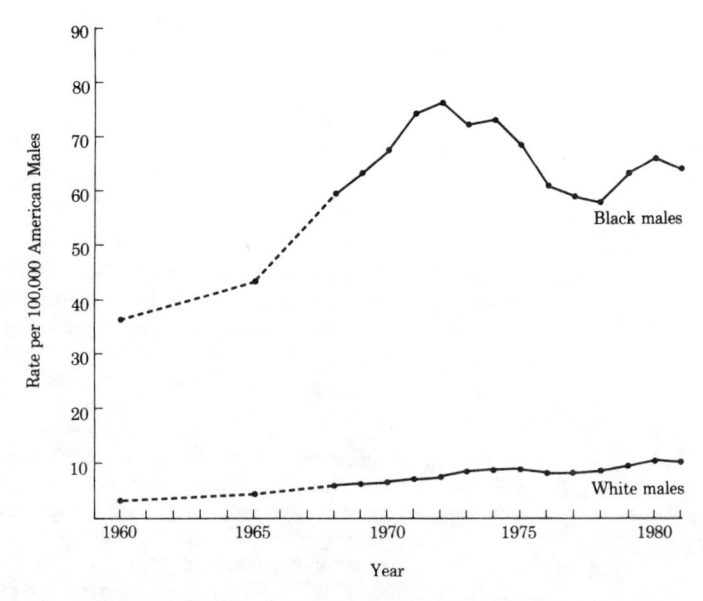

FIGURE 4. Homicide Rate per 100,000 American Males, by Race

The number of male homicide victims per 100,000 in the United States, by race for all ages. While the white rate is rising rapidly, for urban blacks it is vastly higher. When we restrict the rate to blacks murdered by blacks among males aged 15 to 24, the latest report of the National Center for Health Statistics gives it as 73 per 100,000 (compared with 12.5 per 100,000 for white males in that age group). The murder of blacks by blacks has become a national tragedy: Black-on-black homicide is now the leading cause of death for young black American males.

tremendously, especially spur of the moment, casual and apparently inexplicable violence: Life, to many, seems to have little value, and anything and nothing can be grounds for murder.

Homicide is now the leading cause of death among young black males in a number of cities, replacing accidents, for long the leading killer of young males of both races, while suicide is now second to accidents as the leading cause of death among young whites. We have lower overall suicide rates than Japan and a number of European countries, but in the matter of violent crime we lead the industrialized nations. The Russians do not publish crime statistics and from time to time announce they have no crime. While I have had a briefcase stolen in Moscow, have seen police arresting tough-looking young men on Gorky Street, and observed prostitutes operating not three hundred yards from Lenin's tomb, no one would claim that crimes against individuals are nearly as frequent in Russian as in American cities.

The crucial problem is to *understand* good and bad trends, so that we may manipulate them where possible. Many kinds of crime began decreasing about 1981, but even if the rates of youth crime decline sharply for several years, they would, after that, still be dreadful. In 1981, youths under 21 committed 60 percent of the burglaries, 57 percent of the auto thefts, 49 percent of the robberies, 27 percent of the murders, 31 percent of the rapes. The increase in the youth population is imperfectly correlated with the youth crime rise, for the youth population increase ended in the '70s while the rate continued to rise dramatically. Youth crime is only weakly connected with unemployment. It results in part from increased family breakdown, lack of consistent regulation of children, lack of sense of belonging within a moral community, a moral blackout in the social institutions youths encounter, and a kind of social triage that is practiced on the children of the poor, particularly children in black slums.

James Q. Wilson made the interesting and controversial claim that the search for the root causes of crime, while intellectually stimulating, is of little help in developing policies for actually reducing

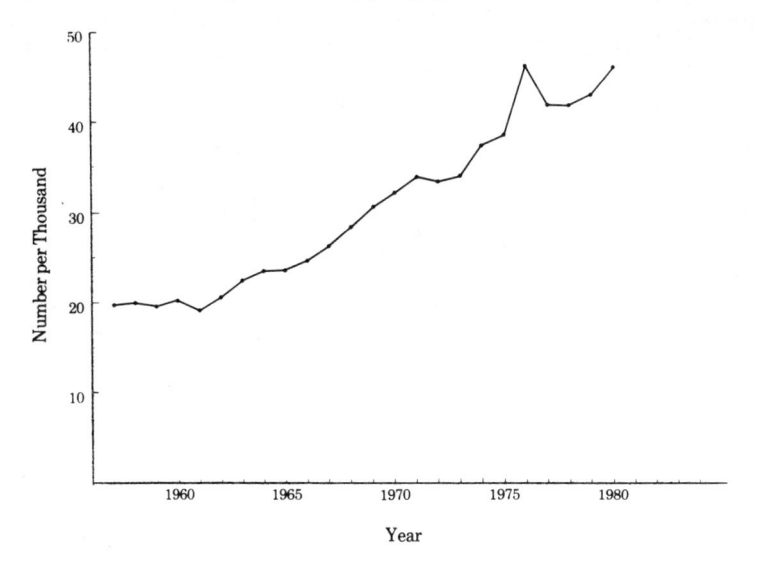

FIGURE 5.
Delinquency Rates per 1,000 Youths, Ages 10–17

The delinquency rate per 1,000 in the United States, for youths aged 10 to 17. These figures exclude traffic cases.

Data from *U.S. Statistical Abstracts* and *Historical Statistics of the U.S.*

crime. While the state might reduce discrimination and unemployment, it can, for example, do little about loveless or unethical families without violating our constitutional rights. But the state can, he says, attempt to make criminal penalties swifter and more certain for those who are convicted, and this (unlike just giving longer sentences) does seem to reduce the crime rate.

> Sociological theories of crime, widely known and intensely discussed in the 1960's, have certain features in common. All seek to explain the "causes" of delinquency, or at least its persistence. All make attitude formation a key variable. All stressed that these attitudes are shaped and supported by intimate groups—the family and close friends. All were serious, intelligent efforts at constructing social theories. . . . *But none could supply a plausible basis for the advocacy of public policy.*
>
> But to understand is not to change. . . . Though intellectually rewarding, from a practical point of view it is a mistake to think about crime in terms of its "causes" and then to search for ways to alleviate those causes. We must think instead of what it is feasible for a government or a community to do. . . .[1]

Is it not possible that the recent theories have simply been inadequate ones, unable to generate feasible policy implications? The central argument of this book implies we should be less pessimistic than Wilson about finding and manipulating root causes of delinquency. This greater optimism derives from an evolutionary theory of innate human sociality, for which evidence will be adduced. The question is whether criminologists have left out relevant variables that derive more from the life sciences than the social sciences. There is no question that Wilson is partly correct: Police and legislators cannot, by any direct action at least, make parents more ethical or more competent. But lawmakers and criminal justice professionals can, for example, affect the formality of the procedures delinquent youths confront, and whether or not there is a public moral atmosphere to the procedures, or they are localized instead of far away and impersonal. On a slightly longer view, a new generation of educators and justice professionals with more communalistic ideas about personal accountability, education in the slums, eliminating age segregation, and about a number of other matters, can have a significant effect.

Wilson is also right about the moral and voluntary aspects of crime. What I mean is that to a young criminal the straight, bourgeois life probably has become intolerably boring. Stealing, risking capture, and even arrest and brief imprisonment are exciting, a way to live fast. By comparison, the payoffs of a modest job are so far in the future, and often so unremarkable even then, and the routine so dull alongside crime, that the law-abiding life holds no attraction. This does not excuse criminals. But it partly explains the inadequacy of economic calculation to account for crime. On the usual account the criminal weighs the gain (in loot or revenge) against the risk of capture and imprisonment. But for some people, while the idea of prison remains negative, the risk itself may be positive because it is exciting, at least compared with the assembly line. It is possible that some of the emotional satisfactions men in particular find in hunting are found in predatory crime—stalking a quarry, danger, excitement, and physical violence.

Conceding all this, there is still much we can do that depends on discovering causes. I shall hazard a theory of human nature by defending the hypothesis that we are quite literally tribal creatures, our sense of ease dependent on analogues in modern society of the forms our innate sociality took during hundreds of millennia of difficult Pleistocene life. Stated very generally, I shall argue that delinquency causally depends on such matters as the following: How much a person identifies with a community, as measured by group loyalty or alienation; the degree to which sense of identity and self-worth depend on having social roles; sufficient early, emotional immersion in a society so that a person grows up having something to lose; whether one is held personally accountable to one's community and subjected, when appropriate, to moral criticism; juvenile justice procedures local and personal enough to bring disgrace on the delinquent; the presence or absence of solemnity and formal ceremony in judicial proceedings, and of ceremony and ritual in one's total environment; socialization in a core of social morality and personal virtues, and in habits of peer intervention and public service; the effects of age segregation, class segregation, and race segregation, on coming to view others as "not of one's tribe" and hence fair game. Causes of crime and delinquency that concern factors such as these can, to varying degrees, be manipulated by public policy.

One way to understand the breakdown of community is in terms of concrete harm to individuals. We can list them: You will feel insecure, *be* insecure, not have familiar and supportive people around you, and see signs of disorder which imply the presence of disorderly, threatening, and unpredictable people. Wilson rightly says it is very much in our interest to prevent the breakdown of community in this visible, concrete sense.

This is to talk about threats and needs, but it leaves out what lures and attracts us to social cooperation rather than what frightens us into it. There are more subjective aspects of group commitment that directly motivate people to pro-social behavior. Because our goal is the resuscitation of American urban society, so that it may regain a level of safety and civility it once had, we need to understand what causes a direct interest in the flourishing of our neighborhoods and larger societies. We need to fathom what inclines people to love their community and want to be proud of it, not just what makes them find it useful. For this reason society requires, and always has required, what Wilson called, with a hint of impatience, "the ancient, the instinctual and the tribal," so that people will act from love and loyalty when self-interest invites them to be crafty.

People who feel strongly that a community is *theirs* are less likely than outsiders or the alienated to vandalize it. Gang members are less likely to prey on fellow members; and close, clearly defined communities organized around a common good, such as the Amish and Mormons, have low crime rates. The reasons why people do or do not identify with a community have to do with objective, public, social institutions and practices, not just inner and relatively inaccessible causes such as loveless and unethical families. And even the reasons why families are loveless and unethical have a lot to do with these same social institutions and practices.[2] Hence it is far from plain that *these* causes—the causes of sense-of-belonging and its absence—defy conscious manipulation by educators, legislators, corrections people, and community organizations.

A number of American sociologists writing in the late '60s and the '70s had rather different reasons for thinking that root causes of crime are important and discoverable. In 1977 Denis Szabo classified writers on juvenile delinquency as defenders of the "consensual" or the "conflictual" models of delinquency.[3] The consensual model aimed at reforms that better enable people to function within existing social structures. As Szabo describes it, the model concedes that human nature and individual differences among people rule out a perfect society and the complete elimination of delinquency. The conflictual model, on the other hand, tells us the root cause of delinquency and implies a fairly straightforward solution. Delinquency is an expression of class conflict between capitalist exploiters and their victims, that is, the underclass who, on this model, are now called "deviants" rather than delinquents. The laws of juvenile justice have "no purpose other than to dispose of a class enemy." Michael Philipson says,

> Power is the essence of the conflictual perspective: it is a confrontation of value systems, of world views, of hope for a new society and stubborn defense of the status quo. . . . In the light of these considerations, it seems clear that nothing in the deviant act itself qualifies it as deviant; it is in the eyes of others that it becomes so.[4]

What is remarkable is that Philipson is talking about rapists and murderers, among others. James Q. Wilson pointed out, regarding this sort of view, that "The theory that crime is an expression of the political rage of the dispossessed, rebelling under the iron heel of capitalist tyranny, leaves one wondering why virtually every nation in the world, capitalist, socialist, and communist, has experienced in recent years rapidly increasing crime rates."[5]

There is a passage in an Emma Latham murder mystery, set in the textile industry in Puerto Rico, in which a police officer inquires about the identity of the murderer. He asks a young radical worker who immediately begins a speech, saying that the victim was killed by certain "forces" in reaction to other "forces." The policeman listens patiently for a moment and asks, "Do you know who shot him?" But the young radical isn't interested in who shot him, he is interested in "forces." To his mind, we might speculate, the person who shot the victim is at most marginally relevant to the killing; he has in mind a larger stage in which the actors are not individual human beings, but forces.

What is wrong with this picture is that an essential characteristic of a moral community is the willingness of its members to hold fellow members personally responsible for what they do. A crime is a personal transaction between a criminal and his victim; the transaction is an unfair, exploitative one, marked by a gross violation of the rights, property, person, or dignity of the victim. The exploitative party in this transaction is another human being, not "forces," and a society that does not acknowledge this is a suicidal one because its members are no longer moral agents and do not comprise a moral community.

The chief difficulty of the conflictual view is its irrelevance to the problem of crime. Its disciples, we can presume, are not against the strict enforcement of the criminal law in, say, Cuba, China, Cambodia, the USSR, or whichever non-capitalist society has caught their fancy. It is strange they were taken seriously as criminologists since their interest appears to lie in defending Marxist political philosophy rather than reducing crime. If the revolution triumphs they will, if they are like Marxists in Marxist countries, be staunch defenders of law and order.

In the USSR the question of the "root causes" of crime has a certain awkwardness. The Marxist-Leninist view of the social causes is much the same as the conflictual theory of the American sociologists, but since the Soviets hold that class conflict and exploitation are nonexistent under socialism it follows that there is no crime in the USSR, which is what Soviet officials announce from time to time.

Neither are the Soviets amenable to genetic or evolutionary explanations of human behavior, including criminal behavior. Heredity has long been their enemy because the biological natures of living things could be resistant to their political goals. Lysenkoism, the doctrine that acquired characteristics of food plants can be passed on by heredity (and which for twenty-five years ruined the science of genetics in the Soviet Union), and the Soviets' current unhappiness with evolutionary hypotheses about human society derive from the same source: the prideful, optimistic dogma that the natures of living things are almost limitlessly malleable.

There is another possible root cause of crime: Some people choose to be criminals out of greed, selfishness, weakness, and disregard for the harm they do to others. But the Soviets reject this as a significant cause, else they would not be able to say that when socialism evolves into communism crime will completely disappear. American criminologists also tended to reject it.

In *theory* the Soviets ascribe crime, what little of it they admit, to vestiges of the past, including inadequately educated parents and the occasional poor job of morally educating children. Less formally and in individual cases they attribute crime to personal failings such as greed, passion, and temptation, just as do most Americans.

Hooliganism is the crime the Soviets are most willing to talk about, indeed, enjoy talking about, partly because it is trivial compared with serious American crime and partly because it is widespread and difficult to ignore. Hooliganism accounts for about 25 percent of Soviet criminal convictions and is defined as violation of the public peace and order and disrespect for Soviet society. About 90 percent of the hooliganism convictions involve drunkenness. (On Lomonosov Prospect near Moscow University a few staggering, sentimental, but non-belligerent working-class drunks could be observed almost any late afternoon.) There is a fair amount of broken glass in Moscow each morning, patiently being swept up by middle-aged women, most of it from bus shelter panels kicked out during the night, but some of it is from store windows or the doors of public buildings. The concept is elastic; Russians will shout "Hooligans!" at groups of teenagers who harass vendors or otherwise make pests of themselves, and a young Russian academic told me about the "hooligans" who went into the Moscow zoo and killed a family of kangaroos. When asked about causes, Soviet pedagogues and social philosophers offer American sounding generalities: "Too rapid urbanization," "we are moving too rapidly into the future," and "improper home life." In spite of publicity in the West about executions for serious political and economic crimes, Russian prison terms are shorter than terms for comparable crimes in the U.S. In Russia it is rare for someone to be sentenced to more than fifteen years.

The three-judge panels in Moscow municipal courts that judge hooligans and petty thieves are more concerned than American judges with the moral dimensions of the offense and the personal circumstances of the defendant. As George Feiffer describes these courts, judges ask the guilty party to explain how he went wrong and harmed both himself and society.[6] They lecture him, expect him to be ashamed, and tell him he is personally responsible for undertaking corrective measures. Their sensible approach bears little relation to the theoretical accounts Soviet writers give of the ultimate causes of crime. Actual court practice implies confidence that the society is sufficiently just and orderly to warrant holding criminals personally responsible and that minor criminals, at least, can be *reached* by moral criticism: that they will hang their heads in shame rather than curse the judge or yawn in boredom.

Whether or not Russians reasonably may demand contrition from criminals, it is plain that a large number of American corrections professionals lack this moral confidence. A number of ideas, distinct from the Marxist position described earlier, have prompted American corrections officials to adopt a non-moralistic approach to the processing of delinquents. Not the least of these is the idea that society and not the individual is responsible for crime. This really says *no one* is responsible since society is made up of individuals each of whom, on this view, is a pawn of society. And as soon as we push the causes of crime beyond poverty and discrimination to the differentia that explain why only a minority of the poor are criminals, we find causes that apply to rich and poor alike. For example, studies of the families of criminals show them to be generally similar in being permissive, not setting consistent limits to behavior, and rejecting the child in various ways. Attributing crime to society is a way of jettisoning the idea of responsibility altogether, for society is not a person and cannot be morally responsible for anything: it can only be a cause.

The irony is, Soviet ideology teaches that the economic and class system is entirely responsible for crime, but Soviet judges moralize and hold criminals personally responsible. American ideology preaches individual responsibility, but American criminal justice professionals treat criminals as no more responsible than bacteria. We would each be more consistent if we exchanged ideologies, or better yet, exchanged practices. In the U.S. we hide the moral basis of the criminal law so that, in the eyes of the criminal, it becomes a pure mechanical process. Social determinism and ethical relativism come together in the idea that it is unscientific and subjective to bring values into a judicial proceeding. The most damaging consequence of our closet morality for the law is the draining of its ethical point, degrading it from what Justice Holmes called "the external deposit of our moral life" to mysterious and arbitrary rules.

Our history creates another reason, perhaps, ultimately, the most important one, why we immerse delinquents in blameless, value-free, antiseptic procedure: It is guilt over our history of slavery and racism, the idea being that we have no right to ask black victims of racism to be good citizens. Or at least, when they are bad citizens we have no right to blame or criticize them, and we certainly have no right to lecture them or demand contrition. This is one of many ways in which race skews our whole social and ethical life, doing more than anything else to destroy moral self-confidence in social transactions. For this attitude, where it exists, infects our attitude toward all criminals who have corresponding deprivations, including white criminals from wealthy backgrounds who very often have been abused or emotionally deprived. The result of these various causes is that criminals in general are treated as though they were not personally responsible for their acts, and the tragedy is that young criminals come to believe it.

Consider the attitude of cool values neutrality practiced by professionals in juvenile justice, corrections, and rehabilitation (but much less, it should be noted, by the police). The unforgivable, indeed, unprofessional sin in dealing with a juvenile robber or vandal is to express disapproval of him or his act, or to preach or moralize. Perhaps one might respond, "He has been preached at and scolded too much already," but I wonder if that is very often true. He is a client, like a client in any business transaction: We say, "I am sorry, Mr. Jones, but, you see, the law requires that if you do so-and-so, you be incarcerated." Suppose that Jones is processed in this way from start to finish, from arrest and prosecution to release and post-release supervision, no one ever confronting him as a wrongdoer but, at most, pitying him as a victim of society.

James Q. Wilson has described this de-moralization of the criminal process:

> To destigmatize crime would be to lift from it the weight of moral judgment and to make crime simply a particular occupation or avocation which society has chosen to reward less (or perhaps more!) than other pursuits. If there is no stigma attached to an activity, then society has no business making it a crime. Indeed, before the invention of the prison in the late eighteenth and early nineteenth centuries, the stigma attached

> to criminals was the major deterrent to and principal form of protection from criminal activity. The purpose of the criminal justice system is not to expose would-be criminals to a lottery in which they either win or lose, but to expose them in addition and more importantly to the solemn condemnation of the community should they yield to temptation. Anyone familiar with the police stations, jails, and courts of some of our larger cities is keenly aware that accused persons caught up in the system are exposed to very little that involves either judgment or solemnity. They are instead processed through a bureaucratic maze in which a bargain is offered and a haggle ensues at every turn. . . .[7]

This very likely has two kinds of cumulative effects on a delinquent youth. First, as he perceives it, it teaches him that not even the corrections professionals believe there is anything wrong with him or even with what he did: They are committed to the procedures, which their careers require, but not to any morality that underlies and gives a point to the law. For no one is mad at him. They just process him, and the conclusion he draws is one of complete cynicism, the law being a mindless threat, like the threat of disease or accident, which through bad luck snared him.

Second, "objective" and morally neutral officials depersonalize and threaten the very self-identity of youthful criminals. Heroes, good citizens, and successful business people get credited with what they do in the sense that their actions are attributed to *them* as responsible moral agents, as human beings and members of a moral community. But the youthful criminal is deprived of credit for what he does: He is treated like a manipulated thing, not a responsible moral agent, which means he has been demoted from a human being to an intervening variable—a mere intermediate link in an impersonal causal chain which begins with an idolatrous prime mover called "Society" and ends with the criminal's victim. So the delinquent, who would like to get credit for *something*, cannot even get credit for mugging somebody.

I wish to consider side by side two actual crimes and what happened afterwards. The first is an attempted rape which took place in 1949 in India, among members of a non-Hindu tribe called the Gonds; the second is an assault in New Jersey in 1975. In the first case, a young married Gond woman had left her father's house to fetch water from a stream. As she filled the jug, a young man, who had come to the house and conversed for awhile with her father, came up behind her, seized her by her breasts, and pulled her to the ground. He said, "Why do you object? Your husband is far away, he will not hear about this." They exchanged blows, she broke away and ran back to the house and told her father. The young man confessed his guilt and was brought before the village council. He was ordered to bow down before the girl and the assembled villagers and ask her pardon. He was made to stand still with his hands at his side while she struck him as many blows as he had struck her. It was decreed that they "blacken his face with soot and lead him round the village to the beating of a drum, announcing that any man trying to rape a girl would suffer the same fate."[8] Finally, he was ordered to pay five rupees for a rite to remove the pollution caused when the girl's father struck him with his sandal.

An engineer in New Jersey tells what transpired after his child was assaulted and severely beaten on the street. Three young toughs, boys not more than sixteen years old, were quickly arrested, and as in the preceding case there was no problem of identification. Everyone concerned—victim, assailants, and parents—was made to assemble in juvenile court. If now a Martian criminologist were to hover invisibly over the scene he would be very puzzled indeed. There would be no way he could tell the victim from the assailants or even that there *was* a victim or assailants. They were all seated together and the judge had them step forward in a single group, whereupon he conversed about their "problem." There was no difference in his tone or manner toward victim or assailants, no accusations, sharp looks, or admonitions; no way, to our Martian on the ceiling, to distinguish them from a group of friends planning an office party. That one of the persons present was wronged and others did the wrong was a totally absent fact. The judicial procedure had no connection with the reality of what had been done. When it was over, the victim and his father were driven home in a police cruiser and the assailants were driven home in an unmarked police car in order, the victim's father was told, "not to stigmatize them."

We know how bewildered the victim's family was and we don't care what the Martian thinks; but what were the assailants likely to think? For one thing, there was bound to be resentment at the time wasted having to appear in court, for nothing came of it. They also learned, in the universal language of tone, demeanor, and actions, that the court was embarrassed to even suggest that they might have done something wrong (why else the unmarked car, they reflect). But they were also treated like dogs. One doesn't blame dogs. They learned that they were in no way part of the community that the people in the court represented, for they were not held responsible for what they did. *They* know, better than the court, that he who harms or betrays the group he belongs to is punished. They know this because they have their gang, or at least, street peers they run with, and they know that a society one belongs to does not tolerate certain things. In this respect their street community is healthier than the one the court represents. They are told, in all the ways that speak stronger than words, that they don't belong, that they are not even a rival tribe but simply do not count as human beings, and that therefore they can do anything they want. Fellow human beings are held responsible for the harm they do unless they are infants or otherwise incompetent.

Add to this that they want to belong to the larger society (at least as one school of sociologists insists) and be acknowledged and credited by it for what they do. The pathetic, poor, nasty little tribe they have created on the street they know to be just that and no more. Their rejection is total and absolute, for while we might forget to reward members of our tribe we could hardly forget to punish them when they hurt or betray us. As regards their relations with mainstream society, they have nothing to lose. Rage and "to hell with them" seems their natural response and next time they may not just assault one of "them," they may push someone in front of a subway train. Perhaps the court *does* think of them as representing a totally alien moral community: It has given up on them and therefore is practicing social triage on a fairly large, mostly black and Hispanic, minority of American youth. If this were the court's attitude it would be difficult to justify bringing delinquent youths before it in the first place and subjecting them to irrelevant, time-wasting procedures.

It is said that in a Chinese commune, if Wang takes Chou's hoe, he is set down in a circle and lectured, complete with wagging fingers and all the reasons *why* what he did was a bad thing. While I have my doubts that exactly this procedure would work in Manhattan, it is obvious that what *is* done in Manhattan doesn't work very well. We should consider the possibility that values neutrality and impersonality by officials and teachers is one of the causes of delinquency. The familiar claim that people are fully human only in a society implies a need to be accepted as a member of a moral community, which means accorded rights and personal accountability to the society, and not treated like a virus or a tiger that ravages villages. Treating delinquents as mere causal agents exacerbates their sense of alienation, of being unable to identify with a community or society as *their own*. But to accept them is to judge them by the standards of our community; to judge them is to criticize them and hold them accountable; and to do that is to express the anger, indignation, and demand for repentance one does not waste on dogs, viruses, or intervening variables. I suspect many criminals choose crime because they like it and are insulted by talk about how they are pawns of various "forces."

Nagas are members of a group of tribes in North East India who, at least until recently, were head-hunters. Nagas liked to hunt heads, they prized the trophies, and they would sometimes buy a trussed-up slave to get a head without going to the trouble of hunting one. If a Naga chopped off your head, it wasn't personal; he just wanted a head and yours was available. The Indian authorities have, over the years, expressed their disapproval, and if the Nagas are still naughty it probably is only in the more remote areas.

Nagas live in large, fortified villages, accept frequent war as part of life, and, as one might expect, have "an intensified awareness of the contrast between in-groups and out-groups." Inside their villages could be found security and mutual aid, and it was unthinkable to take a fellow villager's head; outside was insecurity, enemies, and heads. Ferocious as Nagas might be to outsiders, within their villages there is a rule of law in the form of village councils with acknowledged authority to impose sanctions. The range of punishments is a familiar one in close-knit societies lacking jails and juvenile detention centers. A murderer is fined severely by the village council and beaten by his victim's kinsmen; usually he also leaves the village for fear of further retaliation by his victim's relatives. "A habitual thief is fined again and again, and when he has no more property the fines are realized from his brothers or . . . clansmen. In the end his clansmen, tired of paying his fines, will force him to leave the village."[9] The anthropologist C. von Fürer-Haimendorf tells us that in a Naga village ruled by a chief, where punishments were more severe apparently because the criminal's kin had less power to intervene, three men were executed in years just prior to 1962. Since it was taboo to use weapons against a fellow villager they were tied up and drowned in a river, one for habitual theft, one for killing fellow villagers' cattle, the third for torturing his own daughter because of objections to a love affair.

The Chenchus are a tribe of food-gatherers dwelling in the Indian state of Andhra Pradesh. In Chenchu society they could not, even if they had wanted, turn over delinquents to anonymous and impersonal officials.

> Unlike the member of an advanced society, a Chenchu cannot have casual and superficial relations with a large number of persons. . . . He has either to be admitted into the web of extremely close and multi-sided relations of a small local group or be virtually excluded from any social interaction. Hence the sanction of public opinion and the resultant approval or disapproval are normally sufficient to coerce individuals into conformity. . . .[10]

Among the pygmies of the Andaman Islands, and indeed nearly everywhere in the primitive world, the case is similar:

> The Andamanese cannot afford to arouse the permanent resentment or contempt of his own local group, for this group is the land-owning unit, within the territory of which he is entitled to hunt and collect. He can join another land-owning group only if its members are willing to accept him, and a notoriously troublesome and lawless man is unlikely to be welcome to another group. Hence there is a strong incentive to get on with kinsmen and neighbors. . . .[11]

Fürer-Haimendorf says,

> What conclusions can we draw from these observations among some of the most primitive societies of Southern Asia? Common to all these tribes on the level of food-gatherers—the level in which the whole of humanity remained for the greater part of its history—is the absence of any institutionalized authority capable of enforcing laws or punishing offenders. This non-existence of legal sanctions does not imply, however, the inability of the members of these societies to make moral judgments. Whoever has lived with Chenchus, Andamanese or Semang knows from experience that they distinguish clearly between "right" and "wrong" conduct, and that public disapproval of behavior regarded as undesirable and blameworthy acts as a restraint on potential offenders against tribal customs.[12]

The lesson for crime and delinquency control is that everyone should be embedded in society in such a way that he has something to lose. To anticipate the argument of the next several chapters: Evolution made us innately social creatures, hence belonging to social groups is man's natural condition and the loss of sense of possession and identity with a social group is our greatest loss. Unlike ants, however, our social structures are not hard-wired by our genes but are mediated by culture; and there's the rub: In prosperous cultures we can ruin all sense of social membership by foolish policies and experiments and create people who have nothing to lose. Therefore we need to examine, side by side, the present and our ancient past, for clues to what does and does not work. The ant's social safety net is his genetic program, which lets him do no wrong, ours is our brain, which lets us soar to great heights and, once we get beyond a subsistence culture, commit great follies.

What emerges from the pattern of social control in tribe after tribe is the insistence on an orderly and predictable social environment. A tribe member is sensitive and responsive to peer criticism and his behavior in social encounters is predictable. Intrinsic to the idea of living among one's own kind is the idea of knowing what to expect from them and being able to move among them with security and without unpleasant surprises. When American city dwellers are questioned about what makes them ill at ease and afraid in their own neighborhoods it is precisely this lack of visible signs of order and predictability that is most frequently mentioned. Criminologists Wesley Skogan and Michael Maxfield described this fear in the following terms.

> There is an ample supply of anecdotal and media accounts of the debilitating impact of crime on the quality of life. People of all races and regions are reputed to stay behind locked doors, to avoid using public transportation, to shun shopping downtown, to decline to go out on the town for entertainment, and to avoid involvement with strangers, even when they are in need of help. While these consequences for daily living are only indirect indicators of the effect of crime upon the quality of life in America, they reflect its impact upon some of the most fundamental human values, including freedom of movement and affiliation with others, freedom from fear and anxiety, and the quest for community based on mutual trust and dependence.[13]

They add that among the urban elderly fully 75 percent indicate they are afraid to walk the streets at night. All over the primitive world, the boundaries of a non-nomadic society are those points beyond which you cannot walk with assurance. The anthropologists testify to the near universality of this boundary, and the criminologists to its collapse, in parts of our cities, to the confines of one's apartment. Thus, for some of us, society has gone full circle, from a time not too long ago when we thought the whole world might be our neighborhood, back to a condition like that of the primitive Daflas, for whom a single long-house was civilization, and beyond its entrance the war of all against all.

> The range within which a man can move assuredly in the legitimate assumption that those he encounters will normally act according to an accepted system of rules varies greatly from tribe to tribe. The Dafla can feel secure only within the narrow limits of his own long-house and perhaps within the long-houses of near agnatic kinsmen and ceremonial friends, whereas the Naga has an equal sense of security within the confines of his fortified village. For both the potentially hostile world begins very close to their homes, for outside their long-house or village they move among people whose conduct is not subject to any common legal authority and is hence ultimately unpredictable. An entirely different atmosphere prevails among some of the tribal populations of Peninsular India. For the Raj Gonds, a people of settled plough cultivators, for instance, the range of security and predictable behavior extends at least ideally through the length and breadth of the tribal

territory, for all Raj Gonds, however widely dispersed in space, are conscious of a unity inherent in a social framework which allocates to every Gond a precise place in society.[14]

In parts of big cities such as Miami, if your car breaks down you are likely to be casually but thoroughly looted, dragged from the car, and possibly killed, with no more chance for fellow-feeling or empathy than if you were a Dafla dropped from the sky amidst a Naga hunting party. Fears scarcely less dramatic possess countless urban citizens, both black and white and especially the weak and elderly, every time they go out at night or past a certain intersection. Fear in one's own streets, forcing people to shrink what they think of as safe territory until it becomes no more than a bolted apartment smaller than a Dafla long-house, is a terrible thing, depriving them of the fundamental benefits of civilization. The immediate cause of this fear and insecurity is a breakdown in expectations: there is no longer a predictable pattern of greetings, civilities, formalities, and possible assistance from one's fellow citizens.

> What these concerns have in common, and thus what constitutes the "urban problem" for a large percentage (perhaps a majority) of urban citizens, is a sense of the failure of community. By "community" I do not mean, as some do, a metaphysical entity or abstract collectivity with which people "need" to affiliate. . . . When I speak of the concern for "community," I refer to a desire for the observance of standards of right and seemly conduct in the public places in which one lives and moves, those standards to be consistent with—and supportive of—the values and life styles of the particular individual. Around one's home, the places where one shops, and the corridors through which one walks there is for each of us a public space wherein our sense of security, self-esteem, and propriety is either reassured or jeopardized by the people and events we encounter. . . . And it is the breakdown of neighborhood controls (neighborhood self-government, if you will) that accounts for the principal concerns of many urban citizens.[15]

Skogan and Maxfield discussed the effects on our fears and the quality of our lives of perceiving the local social order to be in disarray. They describe four aspects of this, which they call the "signs of crime":

> [The] signs of crime—in our terminology, potential "problems"—serve as early-warning signals of impending danger because people have learned to associate them with things they fear. For example, in our field investigations we learned that an abandoned building is a source of considerable distress to residents of a community. People believe that

tramps will break into empty buildings to escape the cold and sleep; then "drug dealers" will ply their trade in them, marketing among youths in the area. Criminals of various sorts are thought to base their operations there, making it dangerous even to walk near an abandoned structure. At the very least vandals will deface an empty building, and perhaps loot it. Finally, abandoned buildings become targets for casual arson. . . .

Unsupervised teenagers also are seen as potential sources of disruption, harassment, and crime. . . . A large proportion of victimizations recalled by the elderly involved nonphysical, verbal harassment by teenagers.

Signs that drug use is frequent is a source of fear for neighbors because people believe that addicts are driven to crime to pay for drugs, and that they are crazed and irrational in their behavior when they are on the prowl. . . .

Finally, graffiti and visible vandalism are physical signs of the breakdown of social control. The aerosol paint dispenser is simply the latest twist in the urban arms spiral, a counter to the adoption of Lexan plastic school windows which are virtually unbreakable.[16]

We have always thought of crime as motivated by the traditional deadly sins—anger, greed, lust, and the rest—and sometimes by need. These motives do not explain the apparently irrational destruction and the casual deadly violence which in recent years have become a significant part of the American criminal scene. For example, some people fight, even to the death, to avoid apprehension on a completely trivial charge, turning petty theft or a traffic violation into murder or their own deaths. We are shocked not only by the disproportionate violence and the total rejection of society's authority, but also by the abruptness and casualness with which some people throw away their own lives. The authority of society is resisted as one resists an alien invading army, and at the same time the criminal's own life and future appears to mean nothing to him. This phenomenon suggests a connection between his sense of belonging in society, and hence the authority he grants it over him, and the value or significance he places on his own life. It suggests that to the extent a person is not socialized into a society and has no feeling that "X is *my* community," he suffers a corresponding diminution of self-worth.

Members of bandit bands are in one respect like these ruined people: They resist society's authority as one resists an alien invader. But they do not casually throw away their own lives. When it is necessary they defend their freedom and make strategic retreats, unlike the person who will not be taken alive for a speeding ticket. Traditional bandits, along with American organized criminals, have their own tribes that give meaning and significance to their lives. Very different are young people who place no value on society or on other peoples' lives and also place no great value on their own; they are no more self-regarding than they are other-regarding.

They may vigorously seek pleasure and avoid pain, but this is compatible with the absence of self-interest or self-esteem. Self-interest requires thinking of oneself as a *continuing being,* as a whole life whose flourishing is to be valued, protected, and planned for. A person can respond to the pleasant and painful stimuli of the moment, like a bug, and completely lack self-interest; indeed, he may not even have a concept of the self. This phenomenon raises fundamental questions about the nature of the self and the nature of its dependence on social institutions, which must be answered before we can understand the problem of laconic violence well enough to propose intelligent remedial policies. These questions form the subject matter of Chapter 9.

In New York City there have been some cases in which apparent strangers have been shoved off subway platforms in front of approaching trains. Across the country there are cases in which teenagers on overpasses drop concrete blocks on cars on the highway below; and cases where young people break into obviously poor homes and rape and murder the seventy- and eighty-year-old women who live there. It has happened that burglars, after completing their burgling, smash everything in the house and defecate on the center of the kitchen table; and sometimes robbers shoot their victims after the robbery is done, almost as an afterthought. Muggers and embezzlers are predators on society, but the people who do these things are not predators. No calculations based on gain can explain their behavior. It is said that these acts are expressions of rage and anger, and that seems plausible. But rage and anger at what? At being poor or not having a job? Why then are such acts almost unknown in other times and places where people are poorer and unemployment is higher? There has to be a better answer.

It is tempting to say that people who shove strangers off subway platforms have simply not been socialized; they are in the "state of nature," like wild animals. This insults the wild animals. No wolf or eagle would do a thing like that. Predatory animals kill for food, and even my cat, who lives on catfood but kills countless birds and chipmunks without eating them, can be thought of as exhibiting a genetic program that has survived thousands of cans of catfood and which enables its species to survive in the wild. The cat enjoys doing what it is genetically programmed to enjoy doing.

Pushing strangers in front of a subway train or putting cyanide in bottles of medicine on store shelves is a specifically *human* reaction, possible only in a social animal whose genetic program primes individuals for upbringing as members of a society. And that is the problem. Young developing humans who are *not* molded and disciplined to life as members of a society are thwarted and frustrated on the level of their genes; it is a denial as fundamental as the denial of food or warmth. Those who believe human beings became social animals by convention or by a "social contract" will not understand this. It is not just that the subway murderers are unsocialized, hence devoid of effective internal constraints on self interest. They probably are unsocialized or inadequately socialized, but this by itself is not an explanation. I want to suggest that it is not so much the *state* of being unsocialized that might explain their behavior, as it is their not having gone through the *process of socialization*: They are innately social animals who have not been initiated into society by the imposition of its rituals, goals, rules, and routines, and their response is murderous rage and frustration, directed against the society which has left them incomplete. As young children they waited to be taken through a long procedure of submitting to shared rules, tasks, limits, ritual, and initiation, and they waited in vain.

We should note that young people, however deprived of tradition, social morality, personal virtues, a work ethic, career goals, and a stable family, are in a sense still members of society: They can get jobs, go to school, use the public services, and claim the rights of a citizen. But they have been at best partly socialized and will not function well. *What frustrates us as animals genetically predisposed for life in society is not the denial of the material benefits of society but the denial, when we are young, of the socializing process, and later, of ongoing social roles and interactions.* They are responding as hostile, ruined creatures for not, when they were young, indoctrinating them with the shared values and social morality that make people members of a society and a moral community. They have been left incomplete, at a time when their whole being was primed to receive socialization into a group.

SEVEN

The Selling of Selfishness

> According to the tradition, Gyges was a shepherd in the service of the king of Lydia; there was a great storm, and an earthquake made an opening in the earth at the place where he was feeding his flock. Amazed at the sight, he descended into the opening, where, among other marvels, he beheld a hollow brazen horse, having doors, at which he stooping and looking in saw a dead body of stature, as appeared to him, more than human, and having nothing on but a gold ring; this he took from the finger of the dead and reascended. Now the shepherds met together, according to custom, that they might send their monthly report about the flocks to the king; into their assembly he came having the ring on his finger, and as he was sitting among them he chanced to turn the collet of the ring inside his hand, when instantly he became invisible to the rest of the company and they began to speak of him as if he were no longer present. He was astonished at this, and again touching the ring he turned the collet outwards and reappeared; he made several trials of the ring, and always with the same result—when he turned the collet inwards he became invisible, when outwards he reappeared. Whereupon he contrived to be chosen one of the messengers who were sent to the court; where as soon as he arrived he seduced the queen, and with her help conspired against the king and slew him, and took the kingdom.
> —Plato

> O Duty,
> Why hast thou not the visage of a sweetie or a cutie?
> —Ogden Nash

Egoists quietly go about the business of being egoists, on the ground that it is imprudent to lay their cards on the table. A remarkable exception is the Russian émigrée Ayn

Rand. Barely a teenager during the Bolshevik revolution, she attended Leningrad University and in 1926 came to America, where she managed to articulate the purest individualism with an eloquence that influenced more Americans than has any philosopher since John Dewey. Her writings are stern, moralistic, and totally devoid of humor—not unlike a Cotton Mather or Jonathan Edwards in tone—but preach "the virtue of selfishness" and the wickedness of altruism and self-sacrifice. She is despised by professional philosophers (her enormous book royalties and popular appeal may have something to do with this), ignored by social scientists. But the selfishness she advocates has long been assumed by the majority of psychologists, preached by two decades of professional educators, been made the aim of psychotherapy, and quietly agreed to by many business people. She is simply too blunt for them. She rubs their noses in the Hobbesian individualism they already profess in their scholarly jargon, and they reject her for it; only the artless and honest students like her bluntness and her dreadful habit of pushing doctrines to their logical conclusions.

This last she does with intelligent fanaticism, giving us, for examination, a simple, polished portrait of the ideal society that a world of rational, selfish, individualistic atoms would create. In Ayn Rand's utopia rational people are perfectly self-interested. In the communists' utopia people are perfectly collectivistic. Neither believes people are like this now, each saying, with Rousseau, that existing society is corrupt and prevents us from reaching our potential. Both utopian capitalism (for what else, she thinks, can accommodate perfect individualism?) and utopian communism assume that in the perfect state the garbage collector will not envy the orchestra conductor, for each will see that the job each has is exactly what, rationally, it ought to be.

Altruism, Ayn Rand says, is self-sacrifice, which is always wrong because your ultimate value is your own happiness. All other values are instrumental values and wrong instruments if they do not serve your happiness. It is not so much that Rand thinks self-sacrifice is wicked—she is too close to Nietzsche, and the ancient Greeks, to make much of *that* concept. Rather, she thinks self-sacrifice is foolish, irrational, and renders one contemptible; and moreover, it is the hallmark of totalitarian and decadent societies. Socialists and Christians preach that the essence of morality is *giving to others* (whether or not they deserve it) and denying oneself, and this, she says, produces resentment in both parties to an intrinsically unhealthy transaction. She says,

> Observe what this beneficiary-criterion does to a man's life. The first thing he learns is that morality is his enemy: he has nothing to gain from

it, he can only lose; . . . the grey, debilitating pall of an incomprehensible duty is all that he can expect. He may hope that others might occasionally sacrifice themselves for his benefit, as he grudgingly sacrifices himself for theirs, but he knows that the relationship will be mutual resentment, not pleasure—and that, morally, their pursuit of values will be like an exchange of unwanted, unchosen, Christmas presents, which neither is morally permitted to buy for himself. Apart from such times as he manages to perform some act of self-sacrifice, he possesses no moral significance.[1]

There surely is some truth in her moral psychology; we all know people hag-ridden by what they believe are their obligations, or who seem to think their own interests count less than those of other people. Of the latter we sometimes say, "You ought to be more selfish," and recommend them to the psychotherapists, who guiltlessly exorcise their guilt at $100 an hour.

If we set aside Nietzsche, who is difficult to classify, Ayn Rand makes the strongest and most complex case for rational selfishness of any modern writer. She is important because she has pushed Hobbesian, egoistic individualism to its logical limits, and has done so with high novelistic flair, with romanticism without sentimentality, and considerable attention to the psychology of moral (and immoral) transactions. What she finds is the minimal state as the basis for the good society. Society has no reality beyond the individuals in it, each pursuing that individual's own good, and the state is no more than a small number of hired services, more than the anarchists tolerate and somewhat fewer than are recommended by Milton Friedman.

Let us ask, then, of the purest individualism ever proposed, how we are to maintain the social morality a non-suicidal society requires. Won't rational egoists prey on one another? Why are the handsome, steely-eyed heroes and heroines of Ayn Rand's novels so upright, so honest, so righteous, just, and humorless, in a word, such sticks, such Protestants? Why are they not piranhas? *Will* rational egoists be decent to each other?

On this fundamental issue Ayn Rand's romanticism cannot compete with Thomas Hobbes's realism. They are both egoists. But Hobbes sees, with perfect lucidity, that a society of egoists will be moral only if the sovereign is given a sword with which to make them so. In the absence of the sovereign's sword egoists will cut each other's throats. It is clear why Hobbes thought there could be no morality or justice in the absence of positive law backed by force; for he is dealing with egoists:

> . . .And of the voluntary acts of every man, the object is some *good to himself.* . . . Justice, equity, . . . in sum, *doing to others, as we would be*

done to, of themselves, without the terror of some power, to cause them to be observed, are contrary to our natural passions, that carry us to partiality, pride, revenge, and the like. And covenants, without the sword, are but words.[2]

Rand, however, thinks that rational egoists will be honest, fair, non-violent, and non-exploitative *because* they are rational egoists, without any need to fear the sword. There is only one good explanation. She is not really an egoist, she only thinks she is. She is as much a moralistic ideologue as Marx.

Consider why she thinks a perfect individualist will be honest. It is, she says, just a matter of rationality. Telling someone the money is in your pocket, when you know it isn't in your pocket, is to "fake reality"; it is to let your verbal behavior be inconsistent with the true nature of the world, and this is irrational. This line might make some sense if we were speaking of self-deception. But if I deceive you to benefit myself there is no inconsistency in *me*, though I may be inducing in *you* a certain inconsistency with reality. It is a strange view, not unlike that of the eighteenth-century British moralist Wollaston, who said all evil was lying, a kind of misrepresentation of reality: An adulterous act "says" to the passing observer that the couple are husband and wife, when they are not; to which the Scottish philosopher David Hume replied that the couple need only draw the shades for their adultery to "say" nothing to passersby and thus be perfectly innocent. Present-day honesty-fetishists seem to have hold of the same "insight," managing to think they are as innocent as lambs so long as they are honest and aboveboard about their betrayals, adulteries, exploitation, and selfishness. And what of the pathological truth tellers who can create as much misery as pathological liars?

Why shouldn't I exploit you out of rational selfishness? Rand's answer is that rationality requires me to see that if my happiness is my ultimate good, each person's happiness is that person's ultimate good. She goes so far as to say that each rational egoist is an end in himself, not to be exploited, deceived, or done violence. (This, by the way, is pure Kant, although she rails at Kant whenever she mentions him because he draws a different conclusion about egoism.)

But if each person ought to pursue what most benefits him, what do we say when our interests conflict? Must I believe that I ought to do you in (when my good requires it) *and also believe* that you ought to do me in when your good requires it (because I also believe you ought to pursue your good)? If two egoists are in a one-egoist lifeboat, with the customary sharks circling around them, am I not as much required to believe you ought to throw me overboard as I am required to believe I ought to throw you overboard? Does the ethics of universalized selfishness then require that we both be eaten by sharks? Seeing the inconsistency that looms when an egoist asserts that other people should be egoists too, Rand heroically opts for the view that "there are no conflicts of interest among rational egoists." This avoids the inconsistency, but at the cost of being preposterous.

I have pursued this argument in some detail in order to illustrate the mental acrobatics of people who attempt to turn morality into smart selfishness. What emerges is that she is a moralist, no more an egoist than Immanuel Kant. That is the secret to understanding Ayn Rand: She erroneously *thinks* she thinks selfishness is the basis of all virtue. Her writings are filled with characters of rigid rectitude and sense of honor; they contain demands for retributive punishment devoid of all utility. Everywhere she expresses the purest moral contempt for deceivers, cowards, and parasites, and a conception of rationality that is both an end in itself and inconsistent with calculative selfishness. This is all put in the service of a political ideology most of us find inhumane and a sense of personal responsibility that brooks no excuses.

Ayn Rand's dilemma is the eternal one for social philosophy: How do we reconcile self-interest with the moral restraints needed to maintain safety and civility? Civilization requires that we be honest, fair, not hurt other people, and respect the common good. We can *begin* with social morality, and ask, "How can we be sure that a moral person will be happy?" Or we can begin at the other pole, with self-interest, and ask, "How can we be sure that a rational egoist will not hurt, cheat, or do violence to other people?" It makes no difference at which end we start. The mainstream Western tradition, from Plato on, begins with morality and tries to prove it is the sure and the only recipe for happiness; all too often divine machinery is required to pull this off—a heaven for Job and hell or purgatory for gangsters who live to happy old age. Ayn Rand begins with the rational pursuit of happiness and tries to deduce from it the honesty, fairness, and rejection of predatory violence she accepts as much as the traditional moralist. The moralist starts with A, and says it really implies B; Ayn Rand begins with B and says it really implies A. Each tries to show that happiness and virtue are one, starting from different ends.

It will not work, no matter where one starts. None of the arguments from either end are convincing. The evidence is that social morality must restrain freedom and self-interest if society is to be even minimally safe and satisfying. How, then, do you as an individual view your relation to society? How *should* you if the relationship is to be a healthy one? Is society your enemy, its flowering requiring your sacrifice, and vice versa? Is it perhaps merely your competitor? Or is society instead a paid provider of goods and services like a store? Is it a neutral environment, perhaps providing a referee to enforce the rules?

By the end of the 1970s the nation seemed to many observers to luxuriate in self-centeredness, to express a vulgarization of Ayn Rand's message, or possibly only a more consistent version of it.

Consider the menu of books on the "psychology" shelves of a local bookstore in 1981. There were eight books on child care, sixteen on body care, and seventeen guides for overcoming shyness, tension, and stress. There were twenty-one manuals and inspirational books on sex; most of these were just sex books, their prurience garbed in a pseudo-scientific or documentary format to justify their presence in respectable bookstores. Psychologists Robert Hogan and David Schroeder have pointed out that these books are the pornography of the middle class, designed for people who are embarrassed by "adult" bookstores.[3]

Most numerous were twenty-eight selfishness manuals, all offering guidance on how individuals should understand their relationship to the society in which they live. Here are some of the titles:

> *Your Perfect Right: A Guide to Assertive Behavior*
> *The Invisible War: Self-Interests at Work*
> *How to Get Whatever You Want Out of Life*
> *The New TNT: Miraculous Power Within You*
> *The Magic Power of Self Image Psychology*
> *How to Be Your Own Best Friend*
> *When I say No, I feel Guilty*
> *Winning Through Intimidation*
> *The Art of Selfishness*
> *Own Your Own Life*
> *Your Own True Love*
> *Looking Out for #1*
> *Born to Win*
> *Self Love*
> *Egograms*

In *The New TNT* Harold Sherman offers the following:

When you demonstrate a sincere interest in the activities or ambitions or problems of any man or woman or child, you can command their attention as well as their appreciation. Find and concentrate upon the outstanding self-interest of any individual and you have an increasing influence over him or her. . . . Self-interest is the most powerful interest there is—and when I am appealing to another's self-interest, I am most apt to influence him in my favor.[4]

According to Mr. Sherman, you are to demonstrate a "sincere" interest in the problems of an adult or child in order to gain influence over him.

Those of us who wonder whether enough Americans are meeting their responsibilities as parents, breadwinners, workers, and citizens, might ponder David Seabury's advice in his durable *The Art of Selfishness:*

> If no one could blame you for refusing the uncomfortable duty, for giving up the wearisome tasks, or for leaving someone you did not love, you would not hesitate. Only because you cannot face social blame and the pride of a conscience trained to its patterns are you hindered from exerting your free will and your instinctive good sense. . . . I have examined thousands of human beings during years of clinical psychology. In my experience the greatest single cause of moral delinquency is the Golden Rule in the hands of rigidly good people.[5]

Running through most of these books is the idea that there is a quick and simple secret to success, a psychological gimmick that will bring you affection, sex, the esteem of others, and power over them. They are books for failures, for mice who would be supermen, and who want to be respected, obeyed, and caressed without having to possess the character that makes one worthy of respect, obedience, or caresses. They parallel, in the realm of psychology and the spirit, the books whose gimmick for financial success is optimism, selling from your home, or buying a Cadillac for image before making your first detergent sale.

If everyone were to try to follow the advice in these books our society could not exist. A life wholly dedicated to dissimulation or manipulation can only exist within an environment in which *the rest of us* most of the time believe what we are earnestly told, act on principle and from group loyalties, and try to do our fair share. This is a fancy way of saying there cannot be parasites without a host. The parasitic nature of the life advocated by the selfishness manuals is plain enough. The manipulator must be carried on a sea of people who themselves do not lead that kind of life. The advice of the selfishness manuals is like a pyramid club or chain letter scheme in which only those who get in early are able to profit; hence it cannot sincerely be recommended as a policy for everyone. If one's ultimate values are purely selfish, other values being just instrumental, then it will be better to *appear* honest, fair, and non-exploitive than to *be* honest, fair, and non-exploitive. What will benefit you is the reputation, and not the fact, of commitment to social morality. Thus the emphasis, in the late '70s selfishness literature, on public relations, appearances, and images: "Every winner has a winning image. In frank, familiar terms, . . . author and business success Robert Shook shows you how to get yours. How to systematically create an image designed to make people like you, believe you, and do what you say—the most powerful and most positive image for yourself and your business."[6] This would require a change in elementary education: Young children would not, for example, be taught to tell the truth; they would be taught to "make people believe them." But then if it were universally adopted it would no longer pay off because we would all know what everyone was up to. Blunter but in the same spirit is the following:

> For what men say is that, if I am really just and am not also thought just, profit there is none, but the pain and loss on the other hand are unmistakable. But if, though unjust, I acquire the reputation of justice, a heavenly life is promised to me. Since then, as philosophers prove, appearance tyrannizes over truth and is lord of happiness, to appearance I must devote myself. I will describe around me a picture and shadow of virtue to be the vestibule and exterior of my house; behind I will trail the subtle and crafty fox. . . .[7]

This is Adeimantus, in his challenge to Socrates in Plato's *Republic*.

We could imagine different pop psychology books, reflecting a different ideal of an individual's relation to society. They might have such titles as, *How to Stop Brooding About Yourself; Commitment—the Cure for Loneliness and Boredom; Twenty-five Ways Your Community Needs Your Help*. The great inconvenience of democracy is that reformers and idealists must confront the appetite of the public and somehow persuade it, push the right buttons, tickle it into a new direction. The Soviets can, if they wish, empty all the bookstores in the USSR overnight and present the public with a totally new menu in the morning. The thought of this kind of power can lead reformers, if they are sufficiently passionate about the need for reform, to embrace totalitarianism. The literature of the "me generation" had to burn itself out and become associated with growing public revulsion at a way of life, before it began to disappear from the bookstores.

The turn of the hyper-individualist screw at the start of the '80s gave us the literature of survival. There are books on how to invest for the apocalypse and books that assume the apocalypse is already upon us. Left-wing survivalists in the *Mother Earth News* taught us to be independent of utilities companies and how to build a solar doghouse. In the 1980 Christmas catalog of Desert Publications, right-wing survivalists advertised books on how to kill your neighbors and illustrated homemade silencers and a candy cane dagger.

Perhaps most survivalists are Hobbesians who suspect that the sovereign is losing his grip, that economic collapse, Russians, or what Charlie Manson called "helter skelter" are around the corner. It is of no consequence whether they are liberals or libertarians, their common individualism dictates a common response: If the relation of the individual to society is a purely commercial one that has begun to go sour, the logical step is to pull out, to emigrate, or to build a fortress. If the social mechanism falters and citizens don't love it enough to try to save it, what can one expect but candy cane daggers and solar doghouses? Nevertheless, people who pull out of the larger society do not lose their tribal needs. They just form another society, sometimes a cranky little tribe that is the adult equivalent of a teenage gang. When mainstream society spins off a great many hostile mini-tribes, it is a sign that the larger society is more alienating than it can afford to be.

The *degree* of our preoccupation with self-interest is an aberration of the past 15 or 20 years: The flood of these books, and related fads and movements, came, and then it receded. But the belief that self-interest is the only engine that moves us has been one of our more prevalent delusions since the early days of the Republic. The trick is to discover, if one can, how a safe and civil society could run on intelligent selfishness.

PART II
What It Means To Be a Social Animal

EIGHT

The Failure of Selfishness

> The Americans . . . enjoy explaining almost every act of their lives on the principle of self-interest properly understood. It gives them pleasure to point out how an enlightened self-love continually leads them to help one another and disposes them freely to give part of their time and wealth for the good of the state. I think that in this way they often do themselves less than justice, for sometimes in the United States, as elsewhere, one sees people carried away by the disinterested, spontaneous impulses natural to man. But the Americans are hardly prepared to admit that they do give way to emotions of this sort. They prefer to give the credit to their philosophy rather than to themselves.
> —*Alexis de Tocqueville*

It is one of our most pervasive beliefs that, even conceding occasional spontaneous altruism, selfishness works as a basis for the good society: If each of us brightens our own corner—our business, family, and friends—we will prosper greatly and society will flourish. And insofar as we desist from preying on our neighbors *it is only because each of us sees that he is thereby best off.* This is the classic individualist view that runs back through Ayn Rand and John Stewart Mill to Thomas Hobbes. It is the premise of social Darwinians who think interfering with the survival of the fittest in the competition for wealth will ruin us. It is the view of contemporary philosophers who think that by a clever analysis of language they will be able to deduce morality from smart selfishness. It is the dogma, only recently questioned, of two generations of social scientists and psychotherapists. And it is a view which the evidence overwhelmingly indicates is false.

What is false is that selfishness, even rational, calm self-interest, *works:* I am not saying self-interest is bad or wicked, I am saying it *fails* as a basis for a community of people who can trust each other, solve communal problems, defend themselves, and prosper. Establishing this negative claim is the first step in showing the organic nature of human society and the importance of the tribal, group-egoistic side of human nature.

Some psychologists, of course, question the doctrine that the good society can rest on a citizenry that always acts from rational selfishness. Donald Campbell raised the question in a controversial and influential article:

> It is certainly my impression, after 40 years of reading psychology, that psychologists almost invariably side with self-gratification over traditional restraint. . . . In propagating such a background perspective in the teaching of perhaps 90% of college undergraduates (and increasing proportions of high school and elementary school pupils), psychology may be contributing to the undermining of the retention of what may be extremely valuable socio-evolutionary inhibitory systems which we do not yet fully understand.[1]

Imagine a society or world comprised of just two people who can be either "egoists" or "altruists." By altruists I mean people willing to make small-to-moderate sacrifices of self-interest when they think morality requires it, and on condition other people do likewise. I don't mean people who sacrifice their lives or their whole future happiness, or who in general put the good of others ahead of their own. Defined in this modest way there are lots of altruists walking around; and egoists too, that is, people who will not do anything unless they first believe it is in their interest. How would imaginary two-person societies which are all egoist, all altruist, and egoist/altruist mixtures get ranked relative to one another? And how would we rank the individuals who live in these societies? Social philosophers, sociobiologists, and game theorists all seem to agree on the rankings.

In Figure 6 we see that in the two-altruist world A and B each get a "good," the second best score, and that in the two-egoist world each gets a "bad." The Good/Good society is one of mutual cooperation, of doing one's fair share, and mutual restraint on self-interest. The Bad/Bad egoists' world can be thought of as the state of nature, the world of dog-eat-dog. Of course, diagramming it this way doesn't *prove* anything: It *illustrates* the idea that the best society depends on mutual trust and doing one's share, and not just on rational selfishness. But let us examine the four "worlds" of Figure 6.

An altruist paired with an egoist is obviously at a great disadvantage. He is willing to do his share and help the egoist when he needs

	B is an Altruist	**B is an Egoist**
A is an Altruist	Good / **Good**	Worst / **Best**
A is an Egoist	Best / **Worst**	Bad / **Bad**

FIGURE 6.
Prisoner's Dilemma: For Egoists and Altruists

Here are diagrammed four possible two-person worlds. In each world one's life gets a score, A's to the left of the slash, B's to the right. For example, in the world where A is an altruist and B an egoist, A gets a "worst" and B gets a "best."

help. The egoist says "Thanks," helps only himself, and exploits the altruist whenever he finds it profitable. So in the two mixed worlds the egoist gets a "best" and the altruist a "worst."

The first thing that is peculiar about this is that in the "Good/Good" world of mutual concession and restraint, A and B, while well off and equally so, are not best off. Why don't they get "bests"? The reason is that A can easily imagine a world in which he will be still better off. It is the world in which *he* acts only out of rational selfishness and the other person makes concessions and does his share. If he is in the Good/Good world he can say to himself, "It is surely in my interest to move down to the next box, the Best/Worst world where *I* am the best off." If A is motivated only by rational selfishness, his reasoning is irrefutable. For while he knows he benefits in the world of mutual restraint, and is better off than in the state of nature (the Bad/Bad world of mutual egoism), he also knows he is *still better off* if he cheats when it is rational to do so. He reasons that if the other person cheats he would be crazy not to cheat too, and if the other person does *not* cheat but does his share, he gains a special advantage if he cheats.

A's logic may be irrefutable but it is also (as readers no doubt have noticed) very theoretical: First, it assumes a world of just two persons and, second, assumes (in the Best/Worst world) that B either doesn't know what A is up to or else is a perfectly Christ-like altruist, ready to turn the other cheek every time. However, if rational selfishness dictates that A should try to be the only piranha in the fish tank it dictates the same to B. If it dawns on each that it pays best to be an

102 / THE NON-SUICIDAL SOCIETY

	B is an Altruist	B is an Egoist
A is an Altruist	Good/**Good**	Worst/**Best**
A is an Egoist	Best/**Worst**	Bad/**Bad**

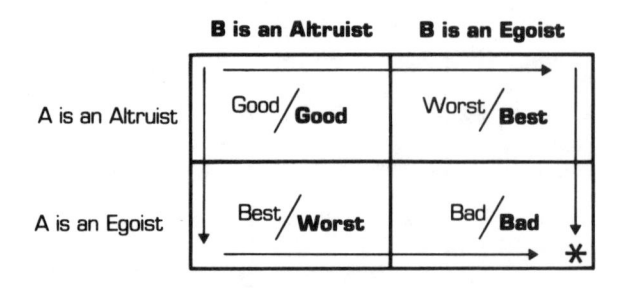

FIGURE 7.
Prisoner's Dilemma: Decay into State of Nature

The arrows indicate the decay of all societies into the state of nature, which is stable, when each party in the Good/Good world decides to improve his score to a "best" by becoming an egoist.

egoist and let the other person obey the rules, the Good/Good world and the mixed worlds become like unstable isotopes: A natural decay process takes place where each person tries to be "best" in the Best/Worst or Worst/Best world and so both end up in the Bad/Bad world of mutual selfishness, which is stable.

The fact that rational self-interest says "Be an egoist!," even though everyone is worse off when they follow that policy, is a consequence of a famous paradox in game theory called Prisoner's Dilemma. In Prisoner's Dilemma, you and your friend are arrested by the police and interrogated in separate cells (we will assume you are both innocent). You are told the following: If you *both claim innocence*, both of you will be locked up for two years, but if you claim innocence and your friend contritely confesses, you get four years and he goes free. If you *both confess*, you each get locked up for three years, but if you confess and your friend claims innocence, you go free and he gets four years.

The reasoning behind confessing is as follows and parallels the reasoning for always acting egoistically. First, suppose the other person maintained innocence; if *you* confess you go free and if you don't you get two years. So in this case it is better to confess. Now suppose that he confessed; if *you* confess you get three years and if you don't you get four years. So again it is better to confess. Well, he either confessed or he didn't, and in each case it was better for you to confess. Yet, it is *also* perfectly clear that you are both better off if you both maintain innocence than if you both confess!

Now the behavior of A and B in the above situations is very primitive, more primitive than the behavior of one-celled organisms:

There is no feedback—egoists are always egoists and altruists always altruists regardless of how the other person behaves. Or else, as in Prisoner's Dilemma, each encounter was assumed to be with a new fellow prisoner, allowing no opportunity to learn from the other's behavior. These are also, of course, two-person encounters, unlike the real world in which you meet many people, some only once and others again and again.

We have seen that exploitation is the best policy when you meet the other person just once, like a stranger you meet in a city you are just passing through, or a bad tourist restaurant that only needs to get each customer once in order to prosper. It is equally the most profitable policy when how the other person acts is always the same. In fact, from a game theoretic point of view there is no difference between encountering someone just once and encountering him many times if his behavior is always the same, or random, or otherwise is unaffected by your behavior. What this means for social theory is that exploitation is the most profitable policy if the people you interact with cannot or will not punish you for what you do.

But what if you meet your partner again and again and you can base your behavior on how you remember he acted last time? Then would cooperation be in your best interest? For this slightly more realistic two-person situation, in which you meet each other repeatedly and can react to past encounters, Robert Axelrod at the University of Michigan designed a series of computer simulations that constitute a breakthrough in demonstrating the rationality of coopera-

	He Claims Innocence	He Confesses
You Claim Innocence	2/**2**	4/**0**
You Confess	0/**4**	3/**3**

FIGURE 8. Prisoner's Dilemma: Its Classical Form

Prisoner's Dilemma. Your score is on the left, the other person's on the right, and this time the scores are numbers of years in prison. The dilemma is that you are both better off if you maintain innocence, but rational self-interest says to each of you, "Confess!"

tion.[2] In two-person interactions where you either cooperate or defect (analogous to acting altruistically or egoistically, maintaining innocence or confessing) there are a number of different strategies you can adopt, where the aim of your strategy is to gain the most points by coming out "best" or "good," as in the previous examples. Examples of strategies are, "I will always cooperate," "I will cooperate until he defects, and then punish him by defecting forever," "I will cooperate unless he defects twice in a row, in which case I will defect twice in a row," and so on. Computer programs can be written for an indefinitely large number of strategies, points given to each player in each encounter, and each strategy pitted numerous times against each of the competing strategies. This is precisely what Axelrod did. He solicited entries for two computer tournaments of Prisoner's Dilemma strategies, the ultimate aim being, of course, to see whether the strategies that accumulated the most points would be selfish, exploitive ones or cooperative ones.

The program that won was a cooperative one and the simplest of all those submitted. Called Tit-for-Tat, its strategy was to cooperate on the first encounter with a given player, and thereafter do exactly what the other player did: if he defects, defect, if he cooperates, cooperate. Axelrod describes the salient features of Tit-for-Tat as, (1) "Nice," that is, always begin by cooperating, (2) "Provocable," which means immediately answering defection with defection, (3) "Forgiving," that is, going back to cooperation as soon as the other player does, and (4) "Clear," not being so complex that your moves seem random or unresponsive to what the other player does.

The computer simulations suggest that free-riding and exploitation, however tricky, will not be in your interest in the long run (well, at least if you are dealing with people who behave like these computer programs). They suggest that non-retaliatory policies of turn-the-other-cheek likewise will not be in your long-run interest. The significance of this for understanding human nature lies in its similarity to a model of the biological evolution of cooperation that Robert Trivers described in 1971, called reciprocal altruism, and which we shall come to in Chapter Eleven.

These results are important because they constitute at least some evidence for the evolution of cooperative tendencies in members of hunting-gathering clans. Axelrod's studies are evidence that Tit-for-Tat-type behavior would be biologically selected for in the small groups in which our hominid and early human ancestors lived. But they do not show that rational selfishness dictates fair and cooperative behavior in the actual world today. This is because, first, rational self-interest still dictates "defection" when you believe you will see someone only once, or for the last time (perhaps because you plan to kill him). Second, the computer simulations of two-person meetings are very simplified. They assume you always remember what the other person did the last time, and that you have the power to do unto him as he did unto you. No incentive is provided for the strong and the clever to be cooperative and non-exploitive toward the weak and the slow-witted. So it is not clear that the results of these studies give us, today, *self-interested* reasons to be consistent good citizens; for there are too many opportunities to be selectively exploitive and predatory, especially when one can act in secret, or against the weak, or against people we will not meet again.

Finally, discovering self-interested grounds for one-on-one cooperation with familiar people does not in any obvious way explain group loyalty, the felt obligation to serve and protect one's clan or community. For we not only want to know if people are disposed toward cooperative *behavior*, we need to identify, if possible, the kinds of pro-social *motives* to which social planners and policy makers can usefully appeal. There is both evolutionary and anthropological evidence that cooperation depends on group egoism and altruism as well as rational self-interest.

It is one thing to hypothesize behavior back in Pleistocene times; it takes more nerve to speculate about what motivated people then. So even if the urge to follow a "nice" policy evolved (Tit-for-Tat, for example) back in our Pleistocene cave clan days, it doesn't follow that the motive is self-interest. What evolved might be just an urge to cooperate with cooperators, long before we had the ability to see the connection between acting on the urge and our long-term self-interest. After all, if American social scientists cannot agree on what motivates us, and we need computers to suggest to us what kinds of policies pay, my grandparents n-times removed, who were naked hominid cannibals with brains half the size of ours, hardly can be expected to figure out these things. Evolution gave them, as it did the lower animals, the right urges, not explanations.

Besides the fact that we see some people only once and others every day, and the fact that some of those we meet are powerless, there is another difference between the real world and Prisoner's Dilemma. The scores altruists get when they live with egoists depend on how many of each there are. One consistent altruist (the promiscuous altruist) put together with one or more consistent egoists clearly gets a "worst." If one person in ten is an egoist we might score the altruist-cooperators as "bads" instead of "worsts." If one in several hundred is an egoist, the altruist cooperators may score "goods," just as in the original two-person example: This is no more than the idea of

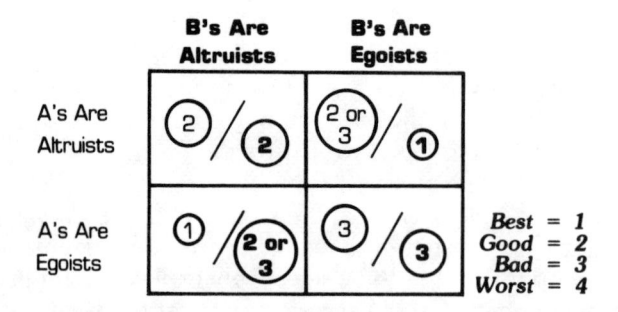

	B's Are Altruists	B's Are Egoists
A's Are Altruists	2 / 2	2 or 3 / 1
A's Are Egoists	1 / 2 or 3	3 / 3

Best = 1
Good = 2
Bad = 3
Worst = 4

FIGURE 9.
Prisoner's Dilemma: For Large and Small Groups

In the real world, as opposed to artificial two-person worlds, how well off the cooperators are depends on the ratio of cooperators to free riders (here, large circles stand for large populations). It also depends on whether the cooperators are promiscuous cooperators or instead are inclined to refuse cooperation with non-cooperators, as in Tit-for-Tat.

the tolerance level of a society, of how many free riders, parasites, or criminals it can tolerate before the quality of life for everyone significantly declines.

The crucial question, which a society's leaders, educators, and law enforcement officials must come to understand, is, Why not cheat, Why not be a free rider? Is it rational not to cheat, away from the world of computers who never lie, never run away, and never forget? We might try the following answer: B can say, "Everyone is better off in a world of mutual cooperation and restraint than in a world of dog-eat-dog; *I* want to be better off and since the cooperative world can survive only if most people cooperate, I should do my share." The trouble is, this argument appeals to morality and fairness, not self-interest. It is a sketch of a good argument why B *should* do his share, not why it is in his *best interest* to do it. This is the main fallacy of those who think they can base a cooperative, civil society on egoist individualism. They think that because everybody benefits in a society that follows rules and restrains self-interest, rational self-interest advises everybody to follow rules and restrain self-interest. But we have seen that it doesn't follow at all. What rational self-interest tells us is to let *other* people follow the rules while letting oneself be a free rider, thus getting the double advantage of egoism in one's own behavior and social morality in other people's behavior. Perhaps we couldn't get away with this if we were computers playing Tit-for-Tat; but then, they never can get away with anything: They don't know how to degauss or unplug each other.

In the eighteenth century David Hume gave a classic statement of the argument for the egoist origin of cooperative behavior:

> 'Tis certain, that no affection of the human mind has both a sufficient force, and a proper direction to counter-balance the love of gain, and render men fit members of society, by making them abstain from the possessions of others. Benevolence to strangers is too weak for this purpose.... There is no passion, therefore, capable of controlling the [self-]interested affection, but the very affection itself, by an alteration of its direction. Now this alteration must necessarily take place upon the least reflection; since 'tis evident, that the passion is much better satisfy'd by its restraint, than by its liberty....[3]

The air of paradox in the idea of restricting self-interest by self-interest disappears if Hume merely means that, in general, restraint and cooperation pay. But Hume's argument doesn't explain why it benefits me to be cooperative, kind, and honest apart from the particular cases in which I see it pays.

There is one remarkable feature of the box-diagrams. When we assign numbers to the scores A and B get (best = 1, good = 2, bad = 3, worst = 4), and add up their scores in each "world," we find that the Good/Good world is the winner, with a score of 4. The mixed egoist/altruist worlds come in second, with totals of 5, and the world of rational egoists is worst off with a 6. It is agreed that the Good/Good world of mutual restraint is the best society. *But then it follows that the best society is one in which the individual is second best off.* For, after all, each limits his egoism and scores a 2 instead of a 1.

This is what filled Nietzsche with contempt for Christian morality and English utilitarians. Social morality, he said, is a kind of treaty cowards and weaklings make who love their own freedom less than they fear the freedom of others, and so they sign it away for safety and security. The person who will not accept being second best off and who guiltlessly asserts himself Nietzsche calls the "monster filled with joy"; the Christians and utilitarians who teach us to feel guilty over violating social morality are "those English herding animals"; the victims of the system, who break the moral rules and feel guilty, are "pale criminals." There is no significant ethical difference between Nietzsche's view and the doctrines in the selfishness manuals listed in the previous chapter. Those books are inferior to Nietzsche in logic, literary quality, vision, candor, wit, and scholarship, but otherwise they are similar: "Put loyalty to yourself ahead of loyalty to institutions," "win by intimidation," and "conquer guilt." They betray the people who read them because they are not supermen.

So Nietzsche is correct: the best society is one in which the

	B is an Altruist	B is an Egoist
A is an Altruist	2/2 = 4	4/1 = 5
A is an Egoist	1/4 = 5	3/3 = 6

FIGURE 10. Prisoner's Dilemma: For Summed Possible Worlds

Here the value of each society is determined by summing the values won by the individuals in it. In the society that gets the best score no individual gets a best score.

individuals in it are second best off. One would be worse off in a world in which everyone tried to be superman and best off in a world in which one did what one wanted while other people followed the rules. We *are* weak, we *do* crave security and group membership, and we see no profit in a predatory world in which people are likely to do unto us as we do unto them. The difference between Nietzsche and the rest of us is that he would find admitting this intolerably humiliating. The issue lies at the heart of our thinking about individuals and society: It is a matter of whether or not we qualify our individualism and admit society is an "organic" entity in the sense that "best society" does not imply "best for me." And it does not, if in the best society I am second best off.

It is easy to show that a cooperative/altruistic society, considered as a collective entity, is best off, while each cooperator in it is second best off. We can demonstrate it in terms of the superior cost effectiveness, for societies, of altruistic over predatory behavior. If Jones robs Smith, Jones gains and Smith loses. Usually, however, Jones gains less than Smith loses. This is true in the vast majority of cases in which one person cheats, robs, assaults, betrays, maligns, rapes, dishonors, kills, or wrongfully neglects another: The loss to the victim is greater than the gain to the perpetrator. The malicious liar gains a momentary satisfaction but his victim may lose his job or be financially ruined. The burglar gets $50 from a fence, the victim, even if insured, suffers inconvenience and, more importantly, outrage and very often fear. Hence the entire two-person transaction produces a net loss.

Are altruist/beneficiary transactions similar to criminal/victim transactions in this respect? That is to say, are they symmetrical in that each produces a net loss, since the altruist, like the criminal's victim, incurs costs? As an argument for symmetry, think of meddlesome helpers. Dwell upon the countless ugly, unwanted, but expensive neckties given for Christmas every year, and consider the Good Samaritans who are drowned, cursed, or sued. But we know this isn't convincing: While altruism always costs something, these cases are exceptions and the benefit to the recipient usually greatly outweighs the cost, as when people are rescued from fires, accidents, and boring company; invalids and stranded motorists helped; directions given, and adults and children warned of various dangers and inconveniences. So the situations are non-symmetrical in that helping behavior yields a net gain, criminal behavior a net loss, to a society.

In real life it is common for individuals to gain from transactions in which their society is a net loser; in such cases social morality is often in genuine conflict with a person's rational self-interest. That fairness is on society's side can be seen when we acknowledge that no one can be better off *outside* a society of this kind, for those who cheat on the system require a sea of non-cheaters in which to swim and do their tricks. Accordingly, a rational individual's motives for restraint and for doing one's fair share must be some combination of sense of fairness, self-interest, strong group loyalties, and sheer habits of social morality acquired when young. This is the general answer to the question, "Why not cheat?" and is what is meant by the failure of selfishness as a foundation for the good society.

Of course, with a really bloody-minded version of Hobbes we can ground a safe society on pure selfishness: Have enough spies and

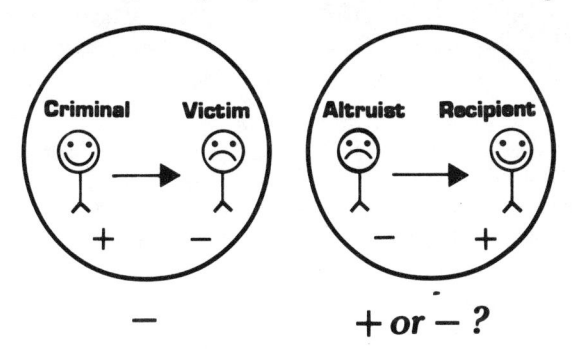

FIGURE 11. Criminal:Victim :: Altruist:Recipient

Are these symmetrical? Does the loss to the altruist outweigh the benefit to the recipient, just as the loss to the victim outweighs the benefit to the criminal?

police so that it is practically never in your interest to violate the rules. I want to use store policies to examine this idea. In a number of countries, non-communist as well as communist, it is usual to pay the cashier and give your receipt to a clerk before you receive an item. Moscow stores in particular exude a defensive, fortress-like mentality that seems to assume the customers will loot the store if given the slightest chance: You determine the price of what you want, line up to pay the cashier and get a receipt, give the receipt to a clerk who fetches your item from a shelf or case beyond your reach. There is no opportunity to shoplift; if you leaped across a counter to snatch and run it is more likely in Moscow than in New York that you would be stopped by other customers. On the other hand, it is amazing, when one thinks of it, to what extent Americans are trusted and set loose in stores. Some steal anyway, but most stores find the loss an acceptable write off. When it is not, they switch to the alternative, which is pay-in-advance and check everything.

The point is that everyone prefers the system of limited trust, if it will work. What makes it work? Perhaps most of us have tried self-analysis standing before a small two dollar item that is out of sight of clerks and other customers: "*Why* don't I slip it in my pocket?" The simplest answer seems to be the egoistic calculus: "The value is slight, the odds of discovery slight, but the punishment terrible—disgrace and a criminal record." Even if it were true (which it is not) that on that basis a perfectly rational egoist would never shoplift, most of us are neither perfectly rational nor perfectly egoistic. To see nothing but the egoistic calculus is to ignore habit, training, sense of honor, religion, and simple honesty. It is to write off, without argument or evidence, our principles and our childhood socialization. If self-interest were the *only* motive civilization could rely on, there would be more shoplifting and the universal adoption of pay-in-advance.

Civilized society depends on a social morality which requires small to moderate mutual sacrifices of self-interest, and on extremely rare occasions, considerable sacrifices. But a rational society does not tempt people *too* much, it does not make morality too expensive. It doesn't demand great sacrifices, except, again, in special and unusual circumstances such as war. We often leave our coats in unguarded coatrooms and expect to see them when we return, but we do not leave our life's savings or expensive cameras hanging there. If the store shelves held watches or bins of loose diamonds instead of toothpaste and ball point pens, more of us would steal.

Americans preach, more than most people, the doctrine of universal selfishness, and they trust each other to an amazing degree to pay their bills and find their coats and umbrellas on the hooks where they left them. The Russians preach the opposite, but the people are not trusted and they do not trust each other: Coatrooms are all attended, goods are paid for in advance, and everything is watched. Of course, the explanation of this is not simple. Russian coatrooms (and everything else in Russia) are watched by hired watchers partly in order to provide full employment. Russian citizens are trusted less partly because they *have* less, and it is the same in most poorer countries. Russians are in some respects more cooperative and altruistic than their American counterparts. Urban Russians probably can be counted on more to help victims of crime or accidents, and less to keep their hands off store goods, windshield wipers, coats, and other things that are either expensive or in short supply.

We cannot monitor every moment of our lives with laws, police, and watchers, hence every society must rely to some degree on social morality for mutual trust and cooperation. But a society cannot make it too difficult to be ethical, or too tempting to be unethical. This is partly a function of how difficult it is to afford (or find) the things on the store shelves, comparable items being in general "less worth stealing" in one country than in another. Ideology plays a role too. American businesses tolerate a small theft rate, but the Soviets tolerate none because their theory says people will not commit crime if they are raised according to Marxist-Leninist principles. It hurts them ideologically as well as economically that, under socialism, there is considerable behind-the-scenes theft in factories, or that store managers steal when a shipment of hard-to-find items arrives. Is it possible that it disturbs us ideologically *not* to have a certain amount of crime, which is why we tempt each other so much?—that it is as much a way of demonstrating to ourselves our egoistic individualism as it is a by-product of liberal democracy that we write off high rates of theft and even violence?

"But wouldn't anyone steal if the gain were sufficiently great and the risk sufficiently low, and doesn't this prove we are egoists after all?" Of course we would; and no, it doesn't. Perfectionists (and the young) think we must either be saints, or monsters restrained by fear. Sometimes we flip-flop from one view to the other: "If only we were brought up right and competition were eliminated, there would be no crime, we would need no police, and we would all love one another." And the same people may say, "We are all selfish atoms, and when we don't steal it is because the gain is outweighed by the risk of jail (and if we have a reputation, disgrace)." This is childish and unscientific; when we think like this we are perfect utopians whom the slightest brush with reality turns into perfect cynics.

The fallacy in this way of thinking goes back to Plato's *Republic*, where the young Glaucon tried to prove that morality is a sham by means of the fable of the Ring of Gyges: The "moral" shepherd Gyges found a ring that made him invisible at will, whereupon he went to the city, seduced the Queen, murdered the King, and seized the throne. From this Glaucon argued that we obey the rules of social morality only when we think we cannot get away with violating them: Either morality rules us even in Gyges' circumstances, or it is a sham.[4] What Glaucon could not tolerate is the idea that decent people can be tempted too strongly and then morality breaks down. Surely genuine morality would be impervious to temptation! Glaucon's intolerance of moral imperfection is not unlike Nietzsche's contempt for the weakness that makes us need morality and settle for being second best off. If every virtue is either incorruptible or a sham, every virtue is a sham. The interrogator who says he "has ways to make you talk," and does, commits the same fallacy when he concludes that courage is a sham. We must admit that if everyone is tempted like Gyges, a moral community is impossible. So the aim of a rational civilized society is to make it fairly easy for its citizens to follow the rules.

NINE

The Metaphysics of Self and Society

> Man cannot become attached to higher aims and submit to a rule if he sees nothing above him to which he belongs. To free him from all social pressure is to abandon him to himself and demoralize him. These are really the two characteristics of our moral situation. While the State becomes inflated and hypertrophied in order to obtain a firm enough grip upon individuals, but without succeeding, the latter, without mutual relationships, tumble over one another like so many liquid molecules, encountering no central energy to retain, fix and organize them.
>
> To remedy this evil, the restitution to local groups of something of their old autonomy is periodically suggested. This is called decentralization. But the only really useful decentralization is one which would simultaneously produce a greater concentration of social energies.
>
> —Emile Durkheim

Anglo-American social thought, from Hobbes and Locke to contemporary social scientists, considers just two foundations for the mutual restraint, cooperation, and commitment a society requires of its citizens if it is to be safe and satisfying: rational self-interest and impersonal social morality. I may be a good citizen because I think that is the best way to "look out for number one," or because I think it is my duty. The history of Western social thought, with the exception of German idealist philosophers and the Marxists, has primarily consisted in working out variations on these two themes.

The result has been a kind of "official theory" of human nature that attributes behavior to either selfishness or altruism and admits no third alternative: something in our brains or souls flips one way, or flops the other way, like a switch. Believers in universal selfishness, including most American social scientists, think the switch is permanently glued in the selfish position; but they still find these two motives the only conceivable ones. Hence group loyalty and sense-of-community, the third ground of social life, is either ignored or else some pallid form of it is assimilated to self-interest.

However, the fundamental force that holds societies together has rarely if ever been either rational selfishness or the cold demands of duty. There has always been a "third way." We need to acquire a deeper understanding of this third way, which I have by turns been calling group egoism, group loyalty, and community. The egoist acts because doing so benefits himself, the group egoist acts because doing so benefits or protects what he has come to regard as *his*, for example, his family, his neighborhood, his company, his city, his country, or his species. When we shift from egoism to group egoism, the self expands beyond selfishness: There occurs an extension of the self that disposes us to care and sacrifice for something because it is ours. Defenders of duty and morality despise egoists for regarding only themselves, but they cannot despise group egoists on that ground.

The egoist Ayn Rand spoke of "grey, debilitating duty" and she thundered that morality is your enemy unless it serves your happiness. But people who come to regard their city as *their own* will be disposed to love and care for it. They will feel pride when it flourishes, shame when it declines or is disgraced, and indignation or anger when it is threatened. There is nothing cold and grey about this and they would not regard obligations derived from civic or national loyalty as "their enemy," however unselfish these obligations may be.

The group egoist has made the move from "I do it for *me*" to "I do it for *my so-and-so*." When so-and-so is not just a personal possession, like a farm, but is a social unit such as my family, community, company, or labor union, I have a group loyalty. My norms are now social, which further removes them from selfishness: I can say not only that I work and care for the good of my community, I can say, together with other people, that I work and care for the good of *our* community. Thus the shift from "me first" to "mine first" is of the last moment: It is what makes a tribe or society possible because it creates a group of people who can say "ours first." And this in turn creates a shared, non-instrumental good, a *common good*. When the object of my group loyalty is not only social but is a political unit, we can say that I possess the basis of good citizenship toward my community, my country, or possibly the world community.

Group egoism (group loyalty) is a third category of the normative: There is the realm of impartial morality, of rules, obligations, and thou-shalt-nots; there is rational selfishness which, never completely confident of itself, hopes and only half believes that being a nice guy pays best. Distinct from these, and sharing features with each, is group loyalty, the paradigm of which is tribal morality.

In American social thought group loyalties are either warned against or ignored, for reasons that concern our ultra-individualist heritage and, as well, the tragedies of twentieth century history. For are not loyalties *biases*, cases of putting your own kind first? Social scientists remind us, when they mention loyalties at all, of the death and wretchedness that tribalism in the name of racism and nationalism have brought upon the world.

But they are ambivalent because there is also a tradition of honoring the distinction between "community" and "society." People cannot have sense-of-community, presumably a good thing, without simultaneously accepting special obligations to the community *and* the idea of a boundary to it, in other words, accepting the idea of insiders and outsiders, of "us" and "them." Anglo-American social thinkers have never put the pieces together, nor could they do so, for they want a number of incompatible things: the values of community and local loyalty, an impartial global morality, and nearly limitless individual rights. Forced to choose between an alienating and chaotic radical individualism, and the tribalism and collectivism of an organic theory of society, most of them opt for the former.

Yet it is obvious that group loyalties, more than rational selfishness or moral rules, are what keep the social organism alive. When people work for the good of a community, city, school, church, company, or country, their willingness to invest time, effort, and money come largely from their perception of the thing as *theirs*. They are not pushed by duty or pulled by self-love. They are, instead, pulled out of themselves, caught up in the vision of the good of something larger than themselves, which is theirs, and of which they hope to be proud.

Pride and shame are impossible unless one has either self-love or loyalty. Someone who cares nothing about himself cannot be proud or ashamed of himself. Someone who is proud or ashamed of a neighborhood must connect it with himself, view it as *his own* neighborhood. I cannot be proud of an iceberg, nor ashamed of it, unless I have somehow come to think of it as *my* iceberg, perhaps because some clever fellow sold it to me. So, too, a person who is capable of neither pride nor shame regarding his community views it as he does an iceberg: Something that is just there, to be coped with, and not his own in that non-legal sense of possession which is necessary for group loyalty.

We cannot, however, forget the need alluded to earlier to attempt a deeper understanding of the self and society. In the preceding chapters I talked as though there were little or no need to ask what was meant by "selfishness" or "the self," and it may seem that philosophizing about these matters has little importance for crime, schools, and good citizenship. But it isn't so; how one understands "the self" has all the importance in the world for how one sets about trying to achieve the good society.

It is doubtful that animals are capable of selfishness; this is not because they are noble or altruistic but because the very idea of the self is too sophisticated a notion for them. Probably only human beings can be selfish because only we have the degree of rationality required for it. What I mean is the following. A lower animal that reacts immediately to avoid what is painful or frightening and get what is pleasant thinks of itself, if we imagine it thinking, without the dimension of time. A mouse, to its own consciousness, is a thin time-slice, even though we know it may live for months. As we say, it lives for the instant, and it will do what gratifies it even if doing so causes its death a moment later. I shall call creatures that act in this way, and human beings when they emulate them, "pleasure/pain mechanisms." They do not act from self-interest or selfishness because the "self" is something that lives for weeks, or a month, or for years. They act instead for the sake of that thin time-slice, which is only a part of a self. To be conscious of oneself, in other words to know what one really is, is to be aware of a creature that endures through time, not one that exists only for a moment.

All kinds of animals do survive, of course, because evolution looked after tomorrow and next week: They do not—can not—think to the future, but their genetic program makes them find pleasure and pain in behavior which, more often than not, serves the self as a being that has a future. The caterpillar that eats and spins a cocoon acts in the interest of a being that includes the future moth—if we wished we could call this "behavioral selfishness" as a way of making a contrast with conscious selfishness. The caterpillar does not consciously act *from* self-interest; if it is conscious at all it is as a momentary time-slice and not as a being that endures through time.

There no doubt are degrees of this. A zebra or a bear, for all we know, has a tiny future it can worry about; but it is instinct, not thoughts of death by lions, that makes the zebra flee at a certain scent, and instinct, not thoughts of blizzards, that makes the bear seek a suitable place of hibernation. These animals, perhaps all of them except humans, and insofar as their behavior depends on felt reinforcements at all, are basically pleasure/pain mechanisms. It is doubtful any non-human can think of its own death, or its old age, or evaluate its life up to now.

Your idea of a self is complex. It is the idea that future states of a person, even after religious conversion or becoming senile, are still states of *you*, and that what hurts or pleases that person ten years from now hurts or pleases you. And self-interest, at its rational optimum, is the idea that those future pains and pleasures are as much yours as are present ones and, other things being equal, should count equally in your decisions of what to do. Of course, other things are never equal and it is always possible you will be dead in ten years, which is a rational ground for giving *some* edge to the present over the future. Nonetheless, we can understand ourselves in a way bears and caterpillars cannot, not as momentary time-slices but as time-worms: time-slices stacked in a long train extending from birth to death and comprising a single creature.

What the other animals cannot do at all we do imperfectly. "Imprudence" is a name we give to our imperfect rationality: We do not count future pains and pleasures as much as present or near ones, even though the future pains will hurt just as much as the present ones, and will hurt the same person. This is something everyone knows: If the likely bad effects of smoking won't show up for twenty years we behave almost as though the person likely to get sick in twenty years is someone else. Less commonly understood but equally plain is the reason why delayed criminal penalties are correlated with diminished deterrence: Criminals, just like cigarette smokers, imperfectly identify with their future selves, and heed less the punishment that does not come swiftly. It takes a degree of rationality no one possesses perfectly to see that the "you" of several years hence is just as much you as the "you" of this moment.

Sometimes people defend the idea that we always act from self-interest because they confuse the self with a pleasure/pain mechanism. Imagine a heroin addict who is reduced to committing night burglaries to support his habit and has lost his job, his wife and children whom he loves, and is watching his health deteriorate. Imagine also that he is intelligent, and now sits with his sleeve rolled up and the needle poised an inch above his vein. It is totally implausible to claim that the intelligent addict, when he goes ahead and takes his fix, believes what he is doing is best for him, on the whole and in the long run. "But he's addicted, and acts to get pleasure and avoid the pain of withdrawal, and thus acts selfishly." But of course he doesn't. The addict is destroying himself and knows it, and so he certainly isn't acting out of selfishness. He is acting as a pleasure/pain mechanism, as a bug acts, and at the same time acting contrary to self-interest. He is serving the good of a momentary time-slice, not the good of an enduring self.

This is what people who act imprudently from "weak will" are doing: In acting on the pleasures or discomforts of the moment they become pleasure/pain machines; they close their eyes to the rationality that understands future selves as identical with themselves. While weakness in the face of temptation can defeat self-interest, more interesting are people who lack, or have a very weak, concept of the self. A young person who jeopardizes his whole future as casually as he eats a hamburger is not a creature ruled by self-love, but in this kind of case it is not because of great temptation but because there does not exist, or does not yet exist or exist strongly enough, consciousness of a *person*, of an enduring being whose well-being he values.

So far I have suggested that humans, and perhaps only humans, can understand the self as a being who endures through time, changing greatly but remaining the person you care about in the special way you care about yourself. We also need to understand ourselves as distinct from other people. The first point involved acknowledging states of oneself that will exist in the *future*; now we must ask about self-identity and distinctness from others in the *present*. Both of these conceptions of the boundaries of the self vitally effect how we see ourselves in relation to society and how we are likely to behave. It is plain, for example, that a criminal who functions only as a pleasure/pain mechanism cannot usefully be reasoned with about his future.

I begin the discussion of this second aspect of the self with an analogy. Suppose you were offered a yacht, absolutely free, and told to choose from six side-by-side in the marina. It turns out that the eccentric millionaire offering this gift has provided six that are exactly alike, down to their colors and the details of their equipment. You might resort to whimsy: "Three is a nice number, so I pick yacht number three, counting from the left," but it is clear you can't place a higher *value* on one over the other if they are exactly alike. I mean any kind of value, not just dollar value. You cannot value one yacht over another unless you think there is some difference between them that makes a difference.

This tells us something about values: They appear at once to be subjective, a matter of judgment, and at the same time dependent on the real qualities of things. A good yacht must differ somehow from a bad one, and this is why the television commercial that said a certain brand of bread is "full of goodness" sounds slightly crazy. Do they pour in some wheat, yeast, the usual chemicals, and an ounce of goodness? The goodness isn't on a list of ingredients, as though someone might leave it out by mistake; this is what I meant by a "subjective" aspect. The goodness is instead a matter of a judgment we make *on the basis of its ingredients* (and their effects on us). The judgments we make about other people are similarly constrained: If a judge sentences Harry for ten years and Max for five, and they, their histories, and their crimes are perfectly similar, just like the yachts, we rightly accuse the judge of inconsistency.

The situation is strangely different when we come to how you value yourself (and here science fiction examples will help). Suppose someone could make six of "you," with the aid of a copying machine from the twenty-fifth century: You walk in one end of the machine and six of "you" walk out the other, identical in memories, thoughts, personalities, and bodily features; the six are then led off to six identical lab rooms. Now the problem, right off, is while there might be six of "you" *from an observer's point of view,* there certainly aren't, from *your* point of view: there are you and five copies. That is, no outside observer could justify special treatment for one of "you" over the others because, like the six yachts, you are all exactly alike. But from your own inner perspective you are completely distinct from the five replicas sitting in their five rooms (and thinking the thoughts you are thinking): You have two hands, not twelve, and if you pinch your hand you feel it but the replicas do not. If all six "clones" get toothaches and the scientist in charge says he will cure only one, it matters to you which he cures because you *feel* what happens to yourself and not what happens to them; but it cannot matter to an observer.

These "inner" and "outer" perspectives illustrate, respectively, nonsocial and social conceptions of the self. You can view yourself either way. The first conception allows a perfectly selfish individualism, the second is a perfectly social, collectivistic self. Your *nonsocial self* can put you (and, as we shall see, what is yours, such as your country) ahead of another person who may be exactly like you. It says, "I come first just because I am me," which sounds like a banality of nonsense, but is of the first importance for social thought: The possibility of this way of thinking is as essential for group loyalty as it is for egoism.

When you adopt the social perspective you appraise yourself as you do other people. You cannot favor yourself over another person just because "you are you," but must point to a difference between you. To your *social self* it can be relevant, in making a value judgment, that something causes pleasure, but not relevant that you yourself feel it. This public, social point of view is the basis of shared, social morality within a society, uniting the members under common rules.

Because, unlike robots, we are conscious, and unlike bugs we are rational, human beings are capable of operating from both points of view—from the egoist's all-important center of consciousness, and from the social conception of oneself as a being with qualities other people have too. The Golden Rule expresses the basis of social morality because part of what Christ meant was that we should think as social selves: He implied we should treat ourselves and other people by common principles. Normal persons feel the pull of each perspective and act from both at different times. Moreover, the same dual motivation reappears on another level, as we shall see in the next chapter, where I distinguish the patriot who puts America first because it is *his* country from the so-called patriot who believes his own country *deserves* to be put first.

The point of view of egoism can be philosophically puzzling. When I say, "I should keep the money because it will benefit *me*," I do not think of justifying features. It is enough that *I* will benefit. But what is this "I"? We have already seen that it is a thing that endures through time, despite changes, and cannot be understood by bears. Nevertheless, from the standpoint of egoism it doesn't matter what *kind* of thing the self is, it is simply "I," "me": I am a descriptionless point, a bare, featureless particular, a dimensionless kernel moving through time, and which lies behind all the features and properties I have. When I think as an egoist this qualityless kernel is the only thing that matters to me. This is why, as we saw in the last chapter, a collection of egoists has no secure common basis for the adjudication of disputes or the allocation of benefits: There is no common thing they love in the way each loves himself. What basis there is depends on the perceived usefulness of the society and its institutions to each individual. A society with this basis is necessarily an individualist one, its virtue is maximum liberty, its defects fragility and alienation.

Group loyalty is direct regard for the good of something distinct from oneself and it creates a moral community comprised of those who share this common good. Like selfishness it depends on prizing the self independently of its qualities. Think of family loyalty: It is obvious that I put my own family first because it is *mine* and not because I think that in some objective way it is better than other families. If I thought my family had royal blood or the best genes in the neighborhood, I might think it actually deserved special treatment; I would think my family was the best *kind* of family. But few of us think this way. We do not work and sacrifice for our families because they are rich, smart, beautiful, lovable, or utile, but because they are *ours*, with the full realization that, "objectively considered," there are other families with greater needs. I favor my family because of the relation it has to *me*; but this does not mean I think that *I* am

The Metaphysics of Self and Society / 121

Social Morality concerns the "internal affairs" of my moral communities, regulating interpersonal relations.

Group Egoism concerns the "external affairs" of my moral communities, by setting boundaries to my obligations.

The Self, the object of egoism.

FIGURE 12. Group Egoism, Morality, and Self

Self and Society: My loyalties define the domains in which I acknowledge obligations, at the boundaries of my species, my city, etc., thereby creating the boundaries of moral communities. This is something only my non-social self can do. On the other hand, my social self sees itself as just one among many in its community, and bound by its rules.

especially rich, smart, beautiful, or useful. I need not think I have special qualities in order to be an egoist, and I need not think my family or nation has special qualities in order for me to be a group egoist.

This is why some people condemn tribalism, patriotism, even community and family loyalty, as mere biases: "Why do you have stronger obligations to fight for so-and-so just because it is *your* so-and-so? It isn't any better just because it is yours." They are right, group loyalty is a bias. But in the next chapter we shall see how social morality is itself founded on group loyalties.

When entomologists discuss social insects they save the term "eusocial" for species at the highest level of sociality, and recognize lesser degrees of sociality beneath that. I wish similarly to distinguish between fully developed and incomplete (or deteriorated) human societies. Whether a society is fully developed depends not only on whether it has a satisfactory social morality that is successfully passed on to the young, but also on whether its members have common objects of love and loyalty and a conception of a common good. The paradigm of a fully developed society is a traditional, undisturbed tribe, not because technology and modernity are necessarily antisocial, but because both their group loyalty and their intra-group rules usually are strong and plain to see. A completely individualistic society is a truncated society because it does not supplement rational egoism with group egoism. In this sense the whole radical individualist conception of society is presocial, from Thomas Hobbes through modern libertarians such as Ayn Rand and Robert Nozick.

Group loyalty poses dilemmas for modern man that traditional tribes did not have to face. Our families, neighborhoods, and to a lesser extent our cities, are pretty much alike, and not socially and geographically inaccesible to one another the way jungle tribes are. I cannot help but see that my family or neighborhood is just one among many and that whatever is good about mine is equally good about thousands of others. So we are threatened with having to wear these narrow loyalties on our sleeves, in vulnerable nakedness, for next door to my family is another one, "just as good" from an impartial point of view, next to my community another just as deserving.

The reason it is hard to be loyal to a "clone" is that when you are proud of something you want to show other people the features that you are proud of; if these features in no way distinguish it from a thousand others, pride and loyalty will appear foolish. America, Italy, and large cities such as New York and Moscow differ greatly, making it easy to find unique features by which to identify them and of which one can be proud. Traditional tribes usually have no problem of this sort, for they have their own languages, spirits, and rituals.

Now imagine that not you but your best friend Freda is duplicated: she walks into the twenty-fifth century machine and six of "her" emerge from the other end. You would want to know *which* of these six is your friend. First you might try to track her, that is, not let the original Freda out of your sight as she goes through the machine and afterwards. When you took your eye off her and lost the track, you would hunt for individuating scars or mannerisms, and when that failed, eventually you would cease to care who was which and your loyalty to your friend would die. What this shows is that love and loyalty, like self-love, is for a *particular* individual and not for just anything of the right kind. For example, if a mother fears the death of the child she loves, it will not do to tell her not to worry because we will get her another one just as good; it is *that* child she loves.

Switch the case to neighborhood loyalty and imagine that someone is out to show a visitor the neighborhood he is proud of. He would be humiliated if he became confused and couldn't tell his neighborhood streets and houses from adjoining ones. Such confusion is easy enough in many American suburbs. If you could "clone" a person—actually make six of him—his concept of self-identity and self-regard would be thrown into confusion; if you clone his community, his group egoism is thrown into confusion. Hence sense of possession and loyalty toward one's community depend on how it is individuated and marked off from other communities.

While an object of group loyalty need not have features that make it *better* than other communities, it needs features that individuate it and set it apart from others. It is very difficult, if not impossible, to be proud of something that is exactly like what everyone else has. In addition, if my sense of self-identity in part derives from my social affiliations, from the clans and tribes I call my own—in other words, if my living quarters, community, job, and city partly define me, as I think they do, then seeing them duplicated promiscuously is damaging to my concept of self as well as to my loyalties. Self-identity depends partly on my territorial, institutional, and other *social* identities. Therefore clarity and coherence about my idea of a self depend on my ability to demarcate and reidentify my groups, territories, and social institutions.

Circling much of Moscow at the ends of the subway lines, like a great ring of Saturn, are hundreds of twelve- and sixteen-story white apartment buildings nearly exactly alike. It is an impossible shape for a neighborhood, people on opposite sides being separated by the mass of central Moscow. Is one's community a building, a street? If I pick up a pebble from the beach I can individuate it as "the pebble in *my* hand"—and from a strictly philosophical point of view that *would* do the trick. But I would feel foolish telling other people it was "*my* pebble" unless there were something distinctive about it, something that made it different from the millions of others on the beach.

What all this suggests is a fairly direct connection between the nature of the self and urban planning. The housing projects that sprang up in American cities beginning in the '50s were as monotonous as the Russian ones. To prize a dwelling or dwelling complex because it is *mine* (and hence want to be proud of it, and be less likely to vandalize it or let it go to ruin) is not to think it is better than its neighbors. But it does require features that individuate it publicly, features on which one can, so to speak, hang one's pride. Merely saying "my community is the one *I* live in" will not do, anymore than "my pebble is the one I hold in *my* hand." Group loyalties, however much they depend on a link with the conscious self, also depend on public criteria of identity.

We can summarize the difference between egoism and group egoism this way: The egoist puts himself ahead of others because, obviously, he *feels* what happens to himself and not what happens to others; so egoism confronts no problem of individuation: He knows that the tooth that hurts is *his* tooth. But when we turn from egoism to group egoism, what we prize cannot be individuated in this way. My family and neighborhood are mine but they are not me: I cannot distinguish my neighborhood from its "clone" as I can distinguish my toothache from my identical twin's toothache. My neighborhood is in the public realm of shared possessions; hence if I am loyal and proud of my neighborhood there must be something about its configuration, colors, customs, or architecture that makes it different from what is not mine.

This is one reason why public art and decoration is so important; for original art, unlike an assembly line product, is unique. Group egoism dies if I cannot tell my workplace or neighborhood from others for the same reason that egoism would die if I could not distinguish myself from other people. The individuating function of self-consciousness in the latter instance must be taken over by such things as public art in the former. And the function of the unique in creating and strengthening group loyalty is greatly enhanced if it is also grand. That is why great gorgeous skyscrapers, a giant modern sports stadium, a St. Louis arch are effective in creating civic pride and morale, and thus in catalyzing cultural and educational bequests. People who do not think these things are worth the money often do not understand the complex basis of their appeal.

It is one of the merits of pride and loyalty that what creates them need not be scarce things or necessities, the possession of which by my community or city diminishes yours or subtracts from its fair share. Sense of community does not depend on mine being the best or better than someone else's. It depends on two different things, first, a basis for distinguishing it from others, and second, *causes* of a sense of possession, of feeling that the community is *mine*.

It follows from these fairly abstract considerations that diversity is an essential part of any sound scheme of urban development, beginning with the smallest units of a society such as individual apartments, buildings, and parks. And insofar as a thing's history is more singular the older it is, history is the ally of community and therefore maintenance of the old an important cause of proprietary feelings toward one's community.

This goes against the grain of the dominant thinking in both the United States and the Soviet Union. We are now slightly more sensitive than the Soviets to the shortcomings of bulldozer mentality. We both crave monolithic solutions, in which we flex our national muscles and decide that what the whole nation or a whole city needs is so-and-so. Quantities of so-and-so's are then produced that are all alike—housing units, entire suburbs, trash receptacles, park benches, shopping centers. We clone our environments, depriving ourselves of the effects of gradual accretions and modifications made to what is old. Even a futurist and enemy of history such as Alvin Toffler sees this, thinking toward the end of *Future Shock* that we must fabricate traditions and rituals to serve in place of the past he gleefully sees being annihilated.[1] The irony is that a socialist such as Michael Harrington, who talks at length about alienation, argued that spanking new cities should be set down in the prairie. New cities in a prairie are a perfect formula for alienation.

Now we should step back and look at how these three motives—morality, rational selfishness, and group loyalty—might operate in citizens who are asked, say, to tax themselves for schools. It is difficult to know why people accept or reject school tax levies, so we can only speculate about the relative effectiveness of these motives. School levies recently have done poorly, forcing a few temporary system-wide closings and sharp cutbacks in school programs. Some people vote against school taxes to protest court-imposed integration plans, others because they are disgusted with what the schools offer with the funding they have, still others because they have children in Catholic or other private schools and are tired of paying twice. For the moment lay aside objections of this kind and suppose that an affluent suburban couple is asked to vote for a county-wide tax increase that will primarily benefit inner-city schools. Suppose further that this couple is rational; they will not believe *just anything* (this is one, obviously imperfect, way to predict how they will react to appeals).

Appeals to self-interest will simply be rejected as sophistical. "Vote for the tax and it will benefit you," the pro-tax people say, and our suburban couple, being rational, answers, "Nonsense." For the inner-city slum is fifteen miles away, they never go there, and they have good police protection in the suburb. The argument is simply no good, as indeed are most public appeals to self-interest as reasons for paying higher taxes, allowing halfway houses and group homes into the neighborhood, allowing expressways to be built through your neighborhood, and so on. It usually is just not true that these things are in your interest, including long-term interest, and the irony is that public officials and pro-tax groups often think any other kind of appeal is "unrealistic." What rational self-interest dictates is that you should support adequate or even generous school financing in your district until the day the last of your own children graduates, and not one day longer. Rational selfishness does not even require that you actually *pay* the taxes, if you can get away with not paying, because the default of a single taxpayer does not appreciably affect the quality of the schools.

Appeals to ethics do not fare much better, even though arguments for schools taxes based on fairness often are good ones. The basic argument is that since our schooling was supported by the taxes of strangers when we were children, it is our turn now and only fair to support the schooling of the next generation, even if they are all strangers. This argument is not completely persuasive for people who have children in private schools, and therefore pay for two systems. But even if an argument is accepted, there is no assurance it will be followed by action. And if the suburban couple is told that it is their *duty* to help the schools in the black slum, or that they *owe* poor blacks because other white people mistreated black people in the past, the reaction most likely will be indignation. If people do not already feel a moral obligation to do something, or if they are not moved by it, the reaction to being told they are unethical usually is indignation.

The appeals most likely to succeed are to group loyalties, both civic loyalty and loyalty to humanity. They can be reminded that having a good school system is good for their city, and here I assume there already exists a strong sense of possession toward a central metropolis which, while not where they live, is where they work, visit, and do major shopping. If the school system is good, the city's citizens will be better, crime and welfare will decrease, and corporations will want to settle in it; in a word, the city will flourish more than otherwise and be a fitter object of pride.

The success of such appeals depends on the antecedent existence of a sense of civic loyalty. If our hypothetical couple has this sense to a strong degree they will sacrifice to make their city something of which they can be proud rather than ashamed. If instead they are alienated, they will not care and arguments will be fruitless. Loyalty cannot be the conclusion of an argument. Arguing with a person that he ought to be loyal to his city or his neighborhood is like arguing that he ought to love someone, even when we think, given his circumstances, that he *should* feel love or loyalty. He either does or he doesn't, and hence the issue is a causal one, one that has to do with the spiritual, institutional, and physical attributes of a community that cause loyalty in its citizens, or alternatively, cause citizens to be alienated.

TEN

The Ethics of Parts and Wholes

> It is a known fact in human nature that its affections are commonly weak in proportion to the distance or diffusiveness of the object. Upon the same principle that a man is more attached to his family than to his neighborhood, to his neighborhood than to the community at large, the people of each State would be apt to feel a stronger bias towards their local governments than towards the government of the Union; unless the force of that principle should be destroyed by a much better administration of the latter.
> —Alexander Hamilton

One way to state the dilemma of modern man is that he belongs to too many tribes at once and becomes confused, and at the same time is tempted to retreat into himself and belong to nothing. Our ancient ancestors faced the problem of competing loyalties to a much lesser degree. Yet, the answer does not lie in eliminating group loyalties and replacing them with a single, global, impersonal loyalty. This probably could not be done and if it were we would be the more miserable for it. It would in any case not eliminate tribal morality but merely be a case of victorious tribal imperialism, one tribe—the global tribe—eliminating the multitude of loyalties we now have. Nor, on the level of our nation, is a single national loyalty that overpowers all others a rational goal; for when we take a hard look at the present state of American society it is clear that our social problems are not due nearly as much to the competition of loyalties as to their absence. In other words, they are due to alienation, loss of belonging, to not having affiliations about which one deeply cares. People whose primary interest is international and who are concerned with the dangerous competition between nations will see this differently. Shortly I shall consider that much maligned species of loyalty called patriotism.

Competition between neighborhood loyalty and civic loyalty is a microcosm that is on all fours with competition between national and global loyalty. Suppose the city wants to put an expressway through my neighborhood. Is it better or more rational to support my city to the disadvantage of my neighborhood, or to support my neighborhood to the disadvantage of my city? Am I a traitor to my neighborhood if my loyalty is to some larger whole?

An obvious first move is to ask why they should conflict. Perhaps rational people will see that the conflict is unreal and that what is good for the city is good for the neighborhood, and vice versa. The mayor and the city development director argue that the new expressway will make everyone better off. True, some people will have to move and those who stay will see, instead of familiar houses and trees, a huge concrete expressway and they will hear the roar of trailer trucks all night long. But they will be able more easily to get to the airport, or wherever. The city as a whole will be more attractive to business and conventions, which will mean more jobs and prosperity for everyone. Even the people in the neighborhood, the city will say, will be better off "on the whole and in the long run."

The neighborhood organization offers counter-arguments. Everyone will be better off if the expressway does not go through their neighborhood but takes the more rational route through yours. Or they may argue that sacrificing first this, then another established neighborhood in the name of progress eventually diminishes the quality of life for everyone; and that what is good for the neighborhood is good for the city, "on the whole and in the long run." The city argues that what is good for the whole is good for the part and the neighborhood argues that what is good for the part is good for the whole. No other line is politically possible: Each argues that the rational interests of both parties are served by its position, because any other defense implies that someone must be sacrificed, which produces an irresolvable adversarial situation and resentment on the part of the loser.

Most of us realize it is just plain false that what is good for the whole is always good for the part. What is good for the world may not be good for America, what is good for America may not be good for General Motors or New York, and what is good for New York may not be good for Greenwich Village. So, too, going the other way: What is good for Greenwich Village may not be good for New York, what is good for New York or General Motors may not be good for America, and what is good for America may not be good for the world. But then again, it may. There are, of course, many things we can do to benefit our cities or local communities that are non-competitive and do not subtract from the good of our nation or neighborhoods—I have in mind such things as neighborhood clean-ups and local charity. But even here, if we look at objective needs we will discover other communities more deserving; after all, no matter how badly off your community might be, you can be sure that fifty dollars does more to reduce suffering in Calcutta or Chad than it does at home.

While it cannot be denied that the good of the whole often is incompatible with the good of a part, yet it still might be argued that our loyalties, *when they are rational and ethical,* will not conflict. For agreeing with what I have said so far does not settle the issue whether it is better, when there is conflict or competition, to support the larger unit such as mankind or America, or the smaller, such as one's city or neighborhood. This introduces us to the problems of the ethics of parts and wholes. In a clash between my city and my neighborhood, am I obliged to support *whichever side* is likely to produce the most good? And, we must ask, the most good *for whom?*

The circle model in Figure 13 generates vivid images of how loyalties, morality, and the self are related. If we are egoists, the way to understand the circle diagram is to think of the ripple pattern produced by a pebble dropped in water. Ripples are strongest near the central generating point, which we can think of as the self, and become weaker and more attenuated as they move out. Our first obligations are to ourselves, egoists conclude, then to what is most intimately ours, and then, with diminishing force, to wider groups with which we identify. Wide loyalties, represented by wide ripples, while in principle infinite, ultimately die out. Egoists would delight in pressing the analogy with the physics of ripples: There can be no more energy in a wide ripple than in a narrow one, and if we think of these circles as enclosing people there will be less "energy"—benefit, concern, or love—for me to expend on each person in a big circle than in a small one.

Egoists think that whatever value I attach to my societies must be derived from the intimacy of its connections—social, legal, geographical—with the value I attach to *myself.* Sociobiologists offer a fairly exact parallel to the ripple model when they explain altruism by "kin selection," a postulated evolutionary mechanism that will be considered in the next chapter: They explain altruism by the degree of genetic investment an organism has in those around it, this genetic investment diminishing with social and geographical distance. From the perspective of the dominant ethical traditions—Kantian, Christian, Marxist, Utilitarian—this is a pessimistic conception of human nature. The pessimism, at least from those traditional points of view, lies in the suggestion that we are naturally disposed to identify with

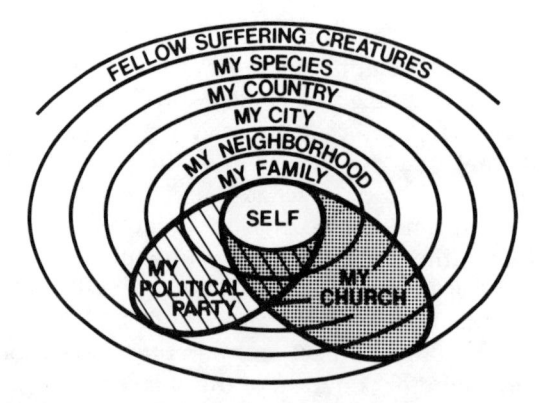

FIGURE 13. Nested and Overlapping Group Loyalties

The self is the "inward" logical limit on loyalty: When I shrink my commitments until I reach myself, I can pull in no further. Is there an "outer" limit, a widest loyalty, such as one's species or all living beings? There does not seem to be one that any arguments can prove, although there will be psychological limits that have biological and social causes.

smaller rather than larger tribes, and to have a weaker commitment to moral communities which are large and diverse. To put the matter starkly, are we by nature predisposed to value lives in inverse ratio to how far away they are? As a matter of sociology and the history of nationalism and tribalism there is considerable truth in the pessimistic view.

Consider another way to interpret the circle diagram. Modern liberals and utilitarians see the circles as enclosing ever larger areas with ever-larger needs. To them it is plain that our duty is to Humanity and that doing what benefits your neighborhood or country is wrong if it prevents a greater good for a larger whole. Hence, they say, the wider the loyalty, the greater its moral claim on us, and regional competition for resources or benefits is justified only when it is the more efficient way to maximize the good of everyone: The biggest circle is the only genuine one, the little ones inside have legitimacy only insofar as they serve the Good of the Whole. If you see that the new expressway will ruin your neighborhood, but also see that its benefit to the city is greater (however slightly) than the harm to your neighborhood, you must accept the expressway, for the simple reason that the total benefit is greater.

This position appears to present a dilemma for those who wish to take loyalties seriously. Should community leaders, mayors, or presidents always adopt the so-called impartial point of view regarding the allocation of effort and resources? They often will be disloyal to their constituencies if they do, and they will be judged unethical, from the viewpoint of the "general good," if they do not. The utilitarian asks, rhetorically, Does the mere fact that a university, community, or nation is *yours* add, even in the slightest degree, to what it deserves? Doesn't loyalty mean that you support policies because they benefit what is yours, even though from an impartial, ethical point of view these policies are not justified? On the other hand, if you are impartial, your community will not want you as their leader because you cannot be relied on to stand by them: You will be disloyal the minute you think the mayor has a better argument. So it looks as though you have to choose between doing what is right and being loyal; at least, this is how the utilitarian invites us to see things. Of course we all hope we can do what is best for everyone *and* remain loyal, but it takes someone with the mind of a Mary Poppins to think this is always possible.

There are a number of reasons why the utilitarian or "one world" attack on group loyalties is unconvincing. The first is that the utilitarians themselves simply assume that species loyalty is always the most demanding one. If it is claimed that it is the most demanding loyalty because it is the widest and the good and harm of everyone are at stake, the claim is incorrect. "Everyone" can be understood so as to exclude anyone, and while narrow understandings of "everyone" are common, wider conceptions of one's kind can be in terms of rational beings, beings capable of suffering, living beings—these are all alternative readings of "everyone." If family loyalty and patriotism are biases, in the sense of valuing a group more highly because it is one's own, so too is the claim that the greatest good is the happiness of the greatest number of human beings.

Utilitarians, who think making humanity the goal of morality is objective but having local loyalty is tribalism, confront a dilemma: If eliminating human suffering is more important than eliminating, say, animal suffering, either it is just a "bias" in favor of one's own species, or it is based on "justifying" features humans are supposed to have—commonly suggested are rationality, capacity for happiness, capacity for suffering, and a moral conscience.

However, any list of "objective" features presented to show that humans are more valuable than animals is bound to fail (even when we ignore the lack of moral proof of the features themselves), because of what we might call "the problem of imperfect specimens": It is inevitable that some senile or mentally retarded people will satisfy the list less well than chimpanzees or even the family dog. These "imperfect people" would lose their human rights. Perhaps we would have to conclude that they are more acceptable subjects for medical experiments than chimpanzees or dogs, if having human rights depends on having the objective features on the list.

Love of humanity has always been species loyalty, not an appraisal of worth based on "objective" criteria. In fact, the "ethics of love" is essentially tribal because the object of love is not an abstraction but a particular—one's lover, one's own family, community, nation, or species. Jesus asked us to love one another, period, without first checking whether someone who needs us satisfied philosophical criteria for full-blown personhood. When Mother Teresa visited war-ravaged Lebanon in 1982 she went first to a Beirut hospital for retarded children. She evacuated children who had no more potential for future happiness or for making scientific or artistic contributions to mankind than did the animals in the zoo. It was their being fellow human beings, not their rationality or the pleasure they would get or give, that counted with Mother Teresa, and it is for this kind of action that she was called a living saint.

Wide loyalties cannot be proven always to have greater moral authority than narrow ones. We are often urged to look beyond our community, city, or country in the name of impartiality, and treat what we had hitherto favored as our own as just one among many communities, cities, or countries. But this impartiality is never true impartiality, it is instead an invitation to give one's loyalty to a larger whole with which someone identifies; in other words, an invitation to join a larger tribe. If our first love is to some narrower group this forced shift may render our ethical concern and enthusiasm weak and pallid. Equal ethical concern for the whole of humanity is, for most of us, too diluted to be able to generate effective moral enthusiasm and too weak to outweigh narrow loyalties.

Sometimes people are unaware how tribal they are. An Ohio state legislator, after hearing me talk about these matters, announced he was a utilitarian; he did not seem to realize how attenuated his felt obligations and enthusiasm became beyond the boundaries of his district (and out of the range of his voters). Legislators are utilitarians regarding issues within their constituencies; they could not be utilitarians with regard to the whole world without their constituency being the world, and then Ohioans who want someone to represent *them* would find someone else. "Utility" is relative to a domain: To his Ohio constituents, the legislator who fairly serves their various interests is a perfect utilitarian, to people in Helsinki or Surabaya he is the perfect tribal moralist.

There is no hiding the evil to which unqualified tribal morality can lead, although it probably is not greater than the misery produced by the willingness to sacrifice anyone for the general good.

> While in the days of head-hunting Nagas viewed every outsider with the suspicion and latent hostility appropriate to relations with a potential enemy, they treated their kinfolk and co-villagers of both sexes in a relaxed spirit of camaraderie and good will, and appeared in their company as a gay, humorous and well-mannered people. . . . The discrepancy is probably characteristic of most societies permanently threatened by hostile attacks and conditioned to an institutionalized hostility vis-a-vis the members of out-groups.
>
> The Kalingas' attitude to homicide is similar to that of the Nagas. While the killing of a member of the in-group is looked upon with grave disapproval, . . .the killing of an outsider is regarded as morally neutral and in some cases even meritorious. . . . Here as among the Nagas we find that ideas of right and wrong conduct apply only to interaction with members of their own group, whereas the outsider is considered fair game. . . .[1]

Fürer-Haimendorf goes on to make the obvious point that this attitude to outsiders is not unique, the Spanish conquistadors having had a similar attitude toward new world Indians. Naga and Kalinga attitudes, we are told, hence do not betray an underdeveloped moral sense, but only "an intensive concentration of all sentiments of loyalty and moral obligation within comparatively narrow limits."[2] The problem with Nagas and Kalingas is not that they are loyal to their kind, but that they recognized no one else as belonging to their kind. They lacked multiple affiliations.

It is important to see that a person whose *only* loyalty is to humanity is a Naga writ large, another kind of one-tribe fanatic. These utilitarians may be even less tolerant than Nagas, given their intolerance of inside subgroups as well as outsiders. Nor is this position philosophically defensible: Utilitarians think a wider loyalty *must* carry greater weight just because it is wider; their slogan is "more is better." But the wider loyalty indentifies one's kind under a different description than the narrower loyalty, and the obligation one feels depends on this description: I have extremely weak loyalty to the whole of living nature, relative to loyalty to my species, and weaker species loyalty than family loyalty or national loyalty. More is not always better; it is not always better because it is not always more of the same thing: My daughter and your daughter may both be human beings, but they are not both members of my family. One should not simply *assume* that patriotism, community loyalty, and family loyalty count for less simply because they count for fewer. Human beings also are few, as part of the wider world of living beings.

What this implies is the defensibility of the position that sometimes what benefits my family obligates me more than does a greater benefit to the whole of humanity; and also that a still greater benefit (or threat) to humanity might nevertheless obligate me on the side of humanity. It implies the acceptance of a world in which rational, moral people can have loyalties that are in limited competition with those of other people, for example, members of different families, communities, or nations. If this is so, the rational community leader is not always obliged to be a traitor: He need not accept the expressway that obliterates his neighborhood just because he sees that it is likely to produce a small, offsetting greater good for some larger whole. If he is honest with himself, he admits that his own neighborhood counts more for him than do other people's neighborhoods. This is simply the equivalent, in microcosm, of the patriot who says that his own country counts more for him than do other people's countries and the human being who says that his own species counts more for him than other species.

Let us, then, consider patriotism. An idea so dear to people the world over, and held in such contempt by our intellectuals, deserves examination. One hundred and fifty years ago Tocqueville distinguished two kinds of patriotism:

> There is a patriotism which mainly springs from the disinterested, undefinable, and unpondered feeling that ties a man's heart to the place where he was born. This instinctive love is mingled with a taste for old habits, respect for ancestors, and memories of the past; those who feel it love their country as one loves one's father's house. They love the peace they enjoy there; they are attached to the quiet habits they have formed; they are attached to the memories it recalls; and they even find a certain attraction in living there in obedience. . . . Like all unpondered passions, this patriotism impels men to great ephemeral efforts, but not to continuous endeavor. Having saved the state in time of crisis, it often lets it decay in time of peace.[3]

This is the kind that is identical with sense of community, and is so fragile as well as passionate because it depends on a continued environment of mortal things—the buildings, towns, and people that cue those memories and without which our old habits make no sense.

> There is also another sort of patriotism more rational than that; less generous, perhaps less ardent, but more creative and more lasting, it is engendered by enlightenment, grows by the aid of laws and the exercise of rights, and in the end becomes, in a sense, mingled with personal interest. A man understands the influence which his country's well-being has on his own; he knows the law allows him to contribute to the production of this well-being, and he takes an interest in his country's prosperity, first as a thing useful to him and then as something he has created.

In this last phrase, perhaps the two kinds of patriotism merge, but Tocqueville surely thought that both should exist, supplementing, impassioning, and enlightening one another. If both die—the feeling for one's turf and people and the enlightened appreciation of political and economic institutions, it is then we have a suicidal society:

> Then men see their country only by a weak and doubtful light; their patriotism is not centered on the soil, which in their eyes is just inanimate earth, nor on the customs of their ancestors, which they have been taught to regard as a yoke, nor on religion, which they doubt, nor on the laws, which they do not make nor on the lawgiver, whom they fear and scorn. So they find their country nowhere, . . .and they retreat into a narrow and unenlightened egoism.[4]

Today in the United States, three main attitudes toward patriotism can be found, which I shall label *impartial patriotism*, *sports patriotism*, and *loyalty patriotism*. Both of Tocqueville's kinds are, I think, varieties of loyalty patriotism. Impartial patriots maintain that *only* impartial considerations count regarding which side to take in a conflict. If they defend their country's policy in a war or international confrontation they appeal only to truly international principles of political morality, for example, that their country is democratic, is on the side of "the people," or was intolerably provoked. They support *whichever* country has features such as these. They do not have (or claim not to have) group loyalty in the sense defined in the last chapter because the obligations they acknowledge do not depend at all on its being *their own* country. An impartial patriot says he supports his country because it has certain features; he has a list, again. And therefore he is committed to the position that if his country and its adversary exchanged these features, he should support the adversary.

If it really is true that he supports his country solely because he thinks it is in the right, the fact that it is his does not enter into his decision. Such "patriots" believe themselves to be objective, like disinterested observers, and simply lucky their own country is right, whereas I think most of us believe their reasons are rationalizations: We call impartial patriots "patriots" only because we think that, deep down, they are loyalty patriots. On the other hand, they might still be genuine loyalists, but *world* loyalists, and they confuse their global loyalty with national loyalty perhaps because they mistakenly think what is good for the world always serves the "true interests" of their country.

A loyalty patriot believes his obligation is partly determined by the fact that the good of *his* country is at stake. But he need not think it is *wholly* determined by this. He thinks the fact that America is his country can outweigh some (but not necessarily all) reasons of the sort a disinterested international observer would consider. The fact that a party to the dispute is his own country is a relevant consideration. To a loyalist, the thought, "A is my country," while it counts for something, may or may not outweigh global-interest arguments against reprisal or military intervention, whereas, to an impartial patriot, the thought, "A is my country," does not count for anything.

Can loyalty be based on the education, protection, and freedoms a country provides its citizens? On this view loyalty is gratitude to whatever country gave you these benefits. It is an awareness of debt, and hence in principle capable of being paid off, which seems quite different from loyalty. Moreover, while gratitude might justify ceremonial patriotism such as celebrations and flag-tending, it is questionable whether gratitude can ever justify putting your country first if ordinary moral reasons do not already justify it. For example, suppose that George and Harry are rivals in the heroin trade, and I owe George a debt of gratitude. If I help George kill Harry, it isn't any less murder because I owed gratitude to George.

The patriots' dilemma is that they seem forced to choose between the death of loyalty and mindless confrontations of pure tribalism. On the one hand, patriotism is just a bias if national interests must be completely subordinated to impersonal principles. Impartial patriots grasp this horn of the dilemma, but still call themselves patriots. On the other hand, suppose I believe it *does* count that America is my country and "impartial" principles do not automatically decide the case. What do I think *other countries' patriots* ought to do? If I think I should help America win in a competition with the USSR, must I not admit that the USSR's patriots should help their country win out over America? It isn't just that I admit that is what Russian patriots *think* they should do; I have to admit it is what they really should do, since it follows from the same argument that tells *me* what I really should do.

Sports patriots grasp this horn of the dilemma and attempt to cope with universalized patriotic obligations by modeling them after loyalties to sports teams. Suppose a loyal Ohio State football fan is asked by a philosopher, "But which team ought to win?" The fan doesn't want to say Ohio State *ought* to win because it is his team, nor that he should abandon his loyalty and support the team that deserves to win in the light of some criteria or other. The "ought" seems altogether too heavy and out of place here. If there is any "ought" at all, it is that each team ought to *try* to win, he says, and if he is pressed about which of them should succeed, "the best team should win."

A patriot who takes this line claims that each nation's citizens should further their respective national interests and, like football teams, try to do in their adversaries (assuming they have adversaries). His values are "trying" and, ultimately, such qualities as toughness and competence, so that the best may win. In defending this position the sports patriot seems to forget that he belongs to one of these nations. He is worse off than the impartial patriot, who at least rationalizes that his country is the best. Committed to universalizing, the sports patriot claims that when it comes to war country R ought to try to do in his country and his ought to try to do in R, with apparent indifference as to who should win. Sports patriotism makes patriots into mere fans whose partisanship is a mockery of the feelings patriots have toward their homeland.

This leaves us with loyalty patriotism. Can it be defended? Because patriotism is so often disdained, it may be useful to consider the case of family loyalty, for I think that what we can conclude about the one we can conclude about the other. We should see whether the *idea* of loyalty patriotism can be defended, and not a particular form of it. A felt obligation to assist one's family is a case of taking care of one's own. Yet, anyone who thinks small-group loyalties such as family loyalties are biases and we are always obliged to be "impartial," is invited to think of scenarios in which someone actually is impartial toward those close to him.

Imagine the following. A family is at the beach. As the father steps up on the pier he sees his daughter and her acquaintance fall out of their canoe, swim for a moment in different directions, and then both begin to drown. He immediately jumps in, and being sure he can save only one, lets his daughter drown and rescues the other girl. Asked why, he says that the acquaintance was well on her way to being a brilliant scientist, bound to contribute more to the general welfare than his daughter, and given that he could not save both, the choice he made produced more positive value. What do we think of this father? Would we want to shake his hand, or tell the story in the local paper as a moral lesson? Is he not instead a great fool and an object of pity and contempt? Indeed, it is the kind of incident we are embarrassed even to talk about, unlike cases of moral heroism or gross selfishness.

Perhaps someone will say, "Well, we are egoists and we respect egoism in others; we feel pity and contempt for the father because he sacrificed his own happiness in abandoning his daughter, and did it for the sake of some silly theory (utilitarianism)." This can be seen to be mistaken if we give the story a different twist. If the father had been in the canoe too and had sacrificed his own life, instead of his daughter's, in order to save the acquaintance, most of us might feel awe, but not contempt or pity. Therefore the bad emotion we feel in the first case isn't explained by the father's sacrifice of self-interest, for there is a *greater* sacrifice of self-interest in the second case and we do not feel that emotion in the second case. It is easy to say, "Yes, of course, we have special obligations to our children: the general good is better served if each takes care of his own." But how would thinking this way explain our feelings of contempt and embarrassment? Besides, letting his daughter drown serves the general good.

It is not just that people are as a matter of fact blindly loyal toward their families, communities, countries, or other societies, this being a fact about human nature we lament. On the contrary, loyalty behavior elicits approbation and opposite behavior disapproval. The contempt we feel for traitors is not unlike what we feel toward the father who lets his daughter drown.

What these various considerations suggest is that for most of us there is no single group loyalty that always wins in competition with other loyalties. Group loyalties vary greatly in relative strength from person to person, but people are generally considered to be fanatics if *nothing* ever counts for them except some single thing such as their families, political organization, or country. A fanatic is a one-tribe-person, the social networks which normally produce a number of nested and competing group loyalties somehow having broken down. For fanatics there is no ethics of parts and wholes, no dilemma of divided loyalties. However, for most of us there is no *single* thing which is the general good; there is the general good of my family, the general good of my community or nation, and so on.

Fanatic loyalists forget or ignore the fact that good and harm come in degrees, and they put their nation first not only when the issue is conquest or atomic annihilation, but also when the loss of national power, prosperity, or prestige is very slight and the corresponding benefit to the world is very great. If my strongest loyalty is to my family, it is clear that it comes first when its very existence is at stake. But this is hardly ever the case; more commonly I might be asked to sacrifice a Saturday family picnic to help a community organization. There is no inconsistency in thinking that one's highest loyalty is, say, family loyalty and at the same time being willing to make small family sacrifices for the sake of a large benefit for something else.

Recognizing that sacrifice and benefit come in degrees is of the upmost importance in deciding what it is rational of a society to ask from its citizens. In Chapter Eight I said people will usually act like egoists if social morality demands total sacrifice from them. A sane social morality exacts small to moderate sacrifices of self-interest and only in the most extreme circumstances demands more. The same thing is true on the level of group loyalties. Part of what it means to live in a pluralistic society is that different people have different strongest loyalties, some putting family highest, some their nation, others their political or ethnic group, or the world community. But if the sacrifices of what we hold most dear, demanded in the name of a larger good, are only small to moderate ones, cooperation generally can be expected. If someone's strongest loyalty is to his local community, this fact might not even be noticed if the sacrifices demanded for his city or nation are not large ones. An individualist who *never* lets social morality restrain self-interest is an egoist; a group egoist who *never* lets competing loyalties restrain or qualify his strongest loyalty is a fanatic.

We cannot make a go of contemporary American society unless each of its citizens has strong commitments to many tribes at once. The classical political philosophers spoke of factions as the death of the commonwealth. But "factions," understood as communities and not as interest groups, are the emotional foundation of our capacity to feel a larger national loyalty, without which we would be doomed. The political scientist John Agresto is one of many to say that the answer to factionalism as a threat to the republic is to multiply the number of factions: "If all factions are small, factionalism is powerless. . . ."[5] Equally importantly, if there are no small groups in which we are enmeshed we will never learn what loyalty is. There are a number of reasons why "small tribes are beautiful" that have to do with the psychology of community commitment and with crime prevention on the local level; but in large countries such as the U.S. and the USSR, it is these same reasons that generate the complexity of the ethics of parts and wholes. We must also be one people, with a common national good and a common core of social morality.

The only sane solution is that children be brought up to have a number of nested loyalties each of which can be overridden. Rational community leaders need not always be willing to sacrifice their communities for the greater good of their city or country. But sometimes they should. It depends on *how much* sacrifice is asked for, and on what is at stake for their city or country. "My family, right or wrong," "my country, right or wrong," and "the highest average happiness of all humanity, right or wrong," are no different logically and ethically from the egoist who says, "*me*, right or wrong." We are not obliged to be ashamed of our loyalties because they are parochial, tied to something we identify as our own, but we *are* obliged to become informed of the true differences and similarities between our own community, nation, and other parts and wholes. This knowledge can lead us to modify our loyalties, or enlarge them, or acquire new ones and new priorities among them.

ELEVEN

The Ethics of Evolution and the Evolution of Ethics

> We are not just rather like animals; we *are* animals.
>
> —Mary Midgley

The greatest influence on the idea of human nature since the beginning of Christianity has been Darwin's theory of human evolution. The idea that man is truly part of nature, in a literal, biological sense, prompts us to ask what kind of creature we can expect nature to produce. In the late nineteenth century the answer seemed obvious: What evolves will be selfish and ruthless, for the survivors have the offspring and only the few survive. The human nature that evolution would construct would be a package of traits and motives that best enabled individuals to survive and pass that package to their children; and what could this be except the most opportunistic and crafty nature possible?

Thomas Henry Huxley, the pioneer comparative anatomist and eloquent early defender of Darwinism, was trapped by this reasoning. He wrote a book called *Man as Part of Nature*, but he couldn't believe evolution produced our *whole* nature; evolution produced the ruthlessness, the bloody tooth and claw, as it does for all animals, but it couldn't explain the fact that humans can understand and follow Christian morality. Huxley couldn't see how ethics and spirituality could come from a jungle, and in his famous 1893 lecture, "Evolution and Ethics," he bifurcated human nature into flesh and spirit, good and evil, just as did the early Christian philosophers.[1] Our selfish animal nature is overlaid by a spiritual component that transcends evolution, a "special creation" for the soul if not for the body. Only in this way, Huxley thought, can we account for the gentler human sentiments of morality, altruism, and fairness, which blossom in the presence of society and intelligence.

British philosopher and sociologist Herbert Spencer was less interested in accounting for Christian morality. If evolution created humans and humans created society, it is natural, he reasoned, that human society like the forest and jungle should operate by the principle of the "survival of the fittest" (a phrase Spencer invented). His views found a ready audience. In America, the *laissez faire* capitalists and individualist entrepreneurs had been looking, since the start of the post Civil War boom, for an ideology that would fit and justify their behavior. Social Darwinism in the guise of Herbert Spencer's philosophy was just what they were waiting for; it was made for them. To tough Social Darwinians like William Graham Sumner, it justified the night watchman theory of government: "The proper function of government," Sumner said, "is to protect the property of men and the honor of women."[2] John Fiske, a philosopher-historian who hung about Harvard in the 1870s without ever being appointed to the faculty, thought Spencer was the "greatest mind since Newton." He usefully popularized the theory of evolution in countless lectures around the country, and in his *Cosmic Philosophy* combined evolution with a gaseous form of Christianity.

The American tycoons loved the explanation of society in terms of the survival of the fittest. It explained why they were rich and the poor were poor, and proved there was nothing to feel guilty about. For Spencer said, "If [people] are sufficiently complete to live, they *do* live, and it is well they should live. If they are not sufficiently complete to live, they die, and it is best they should die."[3] Andrew Carnegie became Spencer's friend and wrote *The Gospel of Wealth*, in which he discovered that morality was not so much a matter of constraints on him while he was getting rich as it was an opportunity for beneficence after he was rich. John D. Rockefeller, noting that God made Nature, Nature made the laws of social evolution, and these laws made him rich, concluded, "God gave me my money."[4] The American Social Darwinians, unlike Huxley, did not see a conflict between ethics and a purely competitive, loser-and-winner, theory of society. And the Protestant work ethic was safe, hard work being a primary characteristic of the fit.

Spencer's views about human nature and society did not go unchallenged, but the best of the turn-of-the-century challengers was a Russian emigré in England who said things Carnegie and Rockefeller had little interest in hearing. Peter Kropotkin was a Russian prince who as a boy in St. Petersburg was trained to be a page for the Tsar. He grew into an anarchist of whom the Soviets now are proud. Given duties in Siberia as an inspector and administrator, he spent much of his time observing the local animals. What Kropotkin saw in the evolutionary process was the opposite of what Spencer and his

American followers saw. Animals routinely cooperated with members of their own species, he said in his *Mutual Aid* (1902). Altruism and mutual assistance weren't behavior animals engaged in mysteriously and at their peril; such behavior was, on the contrary, *how* they survived. Other things being equal, a flock whose members were innately disposed to help one another had an advantage in Darwinian fitness over a flock that did not exhibit mutual aid. Human beings, the most social of the higher animals, evolved, even more than the animals of the tundra, to be cooperators rather than competitors. Kropotkin concluded that the kind of society that was "natural" and consonant with the "laws of evolution" was not the competitive struggle Spencer defended, but cooperative anarchism.

Recent work in sociobiology shows Kropotkin to be the winner, on the biological if not the political issue, in his argument with Spencer. One might think the conclusion would be that they are both partly right and partly wrong. But this isn't so, because of an asymmetry in their positions. Kropotkin and other defenders of innate altruism and cooperation are content to argue that we are genetically disposed to be *sometimes*—often enough—cooperative, whereas their opponents argue that our biological nature is 100 percent opportunistic and exploitative.

For a long time, however, Kropotkin's position was thought to be untenable because it apparently depended on the evolution of fitter groups—herds and troops of animals—and not just on the evolution of fitter *individual* animals. In other words, and putting it in biological terminology, Kropotkin's view seemed to depend on "group selection" and not just on individual selection. As we shall see, it was not until the mid-twentieth century that the grave theoretical difficulties with the possibility of any kind of group selection began to be resolved.

Actually, Darwin had seen it all, both the problem and a glimmer of a solution. He was too smart to be a Social Darwinian but also too smart not to be puzzled about how an animal's altruism and cooperativeness could give it increased survival potential. He knew that animals helped one another with warning cries, defense, care of the young, and so on. But doesn't all altruism involve taking risks, however small? If you stop to give aid or directions to a stranger, this subtracts time and energy, even if just a little, from your own aims and projects. Can we understand how what disposes us to be Good Samaritans did not get selected out, over the course of thousands of generations? Darwin had said that the greatest threat he perceived to his theory was the extreme altruism and self-sacrifice found among social insects. How in the world can you pass on an altruistic trait if that trait includes sterility (worker bees, for example) or if it gets you killed before you have children? Even the tiniest cost attached to altruism would seem to be enough to make altruism disappear, given the millions of years evolution has to work its effects.

The theoretical problem that especially seemed to ruin Kropotkin's conclusion about society was this: It seems that all natural selection is individual selection because it is *individuals* who pass on genes to their children, and if in the long run altruistic cooperators take more risks than opportunists, it looks as though altruistic tendencies must get eliminated in the course of time. The problem is that whatever we may wish to say about the advantages of a cooperative group as a whole, *within the group* cooperators seem at a selective disadvantage vis-à-vis egoists. Think of the egoist/altruist "worlds" in the Prisoner's Dilemma boxes of Chapter Eight. And if each individual in a group must, for these reasons, be selfish, the group will be selfish, even though it *also* seems obvious that a group of animals that provides mutual aid has a selective advantage over a group that doesn't. It is the Prisoner's Dilemma all over again. Group selection, most biologists concluded, doesn't work. We have already seen, however, in the computer contest winner "Tit-for-Tat," that it is not at all obvious that, in the long run, cooperators take more risks than opportunists. But the biologists had to develop their theories for natural environments, not computer programs, and the problem of how cooperation could be selected in evolution was daunting.

Consider a flock of birds whose members give warning cries when they see the hawk approaching. It seems obvious that a flock that gives warning cries will do better than one that does not, for each bird in the flock will be warned earlier if the first bird to spot the predator lets out a squawk. But how can the genetic disposition to give a warning cry spread through the flock? It starts with a mutation rate for squawk genes, let us assume, but the few mutant squawkers are immediately at a disadvantage relative to the non-squawkers in the flock. The hawk has some ability to locate sounds, so the squawker is more likely than non-squawkers to be eaten before it can reproduce: another illustration of the point that altruism implies taking risks. If our noble squawkers, in serving their fellow birds, attract hawks to themselves, their squawk-genes are going to be relatively poor bets for getting passed on and spreading through the flock. So, it seemed, nice birds finish last, in spite of the fact that if, by magic, the whole flock got the squawk-genes, it would have an advantage in fitness over a flock of non-squawkers.

It was only in the 1960s and 1970s that what Prince Kropotkin observed taking place among his Siberian animals and Darwin observed among the social insects began to get explained, by population biologists, in a theoretically satisfying way. The trick was to explain how evolution could produce altruism without appealing to traditional group selection, and population biologists such as W. D. Hamilton and Robert Trivers began to come up with theories.

Hamilton introduced the idea of *inclusive fitness*, although earlier others, including Darwin, had had a glimmer of it. It is quite simple: One way to help pass on your kind of genes is to increase the fitness of your relatives, since they share your genes in proportion to how closely or distantly they are related to you. (Cousins have on average one eighth of your genes, siblings average one half, whereas each parent has exactly one half of your genes.) Inclusive fitness in the alarm-giving bird case is simply the sum of the alarm-giver's fitness (diminished because he attracts hawks) and the effects his behavior has on the fitness of his relatives (increased because he warns them of hawks). The alarm-giving genes spread if the gain to the relatives (weighted for the proportion of his genes each relative carries) outweighs the loss to the alarm giver. Hamilton summarizes his view this way:

> For a hereditary tendency to perform an action of this kind to evolve the benefit to a sib must average at least twice the loss to the individual, the benefit to a half-sib must be at least four times the loss, to a cousin eight times and so on. To express the matter more vividly, in the world of our model organisms, whose behavior is determined strictly by genotype, we expect to find that no one is prepared to sacrifice his life for any single person but that everyone will sacrifice it when he can thereby save more than two brothers, or four half-brothers, or eight first cousins. . . .[5]

Robert Trivers's theory of reciprocal altruism is a complementary, not a competing, theory of the evolution of altruism.[6] It enables us to expand our explanations beyond a circle of relatives. Trivers hypothesizes that some of our early ancestors became genetically predisposed to help other altruists more readily than non-altruists—in other words, to be nicer to nice guys than to bad guys. If you and I are both genetically disposed to help helpers, and I help you, my act enhances my individual fitness because it identifies me to you as a suitable person to be helped when the occasion arises. If I pull you out of the river or save you from the cave lion, the small but certain risk my altruism requires is outweighed by the great though uncertain gain of future rescue.

Evidence of a general sort for Trivers's claim is what in Chapter Eight I called the cost-effectiveness of altruistic transactions: The two-party transaction yields a net gain, so if one has equal or near equal shots at playing both roles in the transaction, one gains in the long run. But the really impressive evidence in support of reciprocal altruism as a strategy that could evolve in small hominid clans is the success of Tit-for-Tat in Robert Axelrod's computer tournaments. For Tit-for-Tat is nearly identical with reciprocal altruism as Trivers describes it; in each, one cooperates with cooperators but not noncooperators. Tit-for-Tat is even a slightly stronger form of cooperation, for unlike reciprocal altruism it stipulates cooperation before you know whether or not the other person is a cooperator.

Kin selection explains how altruism could evolve even when it is genuinely self-sacrificial. Trivers's theory of reciprocal altruism, on the other hand, aims to show that altruistic acts merely appear to be self-sacrificial: Altruism benefits the altruist because it identifies him to other altruists as a potential recipient of altruistic acts. Reciprocal altruism increases relative individual fitness because it has built into it the Sword of Hobbes: The sovereign is replaced by the tendency each reciprocal altruist has to ignore drowning egoists. Trivers also hypothesized that we evolved tendencies to detect and punish egoists who try to pass as reciprocal altruists; this punishment aspect is another similarity with Tit-for-Tat.

Reciprocal altruism is a biologist's answer to the question, "Why not cheat, why not be a free rider within a scheme of social cooperation?," the answer being a biological version of the familiar view that social pressure makes us helpful and cooperative. It can be in our interest not to cheat either because there is a sovereign with a big enough sword, or because evolution gave most of us genes that dispose us to punish free riders and leave egoist opportunists in the quicksand. But it is *not* an answer to the question, "Do I, as an individual in modern society, have a *good reason* not to be a free rider?," for the reasons given in Chapter Eight.

Part of understanding the evolution of social behavior is seeing that *animals, including early humans, did not have to understand the consequences of their behavior in order for it to be selected*. This means that in the first stage of understanding how human sociality works we can forget about motives: Hominids do not have to be able to figure out that cooperative behavior pays, in order for a disposition to evolve; and because it could evolve without their knowing it was in their interest, we cannot infer anything about their motives. Neither do we have any choice in the matter: Emotions do not leave bones or shells behind, which makes impossible any direct evidence about the emotions of hominids.

This allows us to talk about what I called "behavioral selfishness," that is, predisposed behavior that *as a matter of fact* is in the individual's long-range interest, regardless of what the individual thinks about it. He himself may think it is altruistic, or neither altruistic nor selfish but just a matter of urges. The universal selfishness doctrine is highly dubious in the light of reciprocal altruism and kin-selection altruism, since those behavioral dispositions had to evolve long before anyone was smart enough to understand their consequences. Since human behavior, unlike bug behavior, is mediated by motives of some kind or other, we might hypothesize that reciprocal altruistic and kin-altruistic behavior were prompted by direct wants and urges not tied to calculation of any kind.

Although explaining how the genes for reciprocal altruism could survive or spread when there were only a few reciprocal altruists is a serious problem, it is tempting to look around us and say, "Yes, this is how people behave: We are much more inclined to be reciprocal altruists than promiscuous altruists or egoists." Are we not favorably inclined toward helpful people, cold and unresponsive toward unhelpful people, and disinclined to turn the other cheek? And if actual hostility to non-cooperators is also selected for, might we not have the beginning of the pervasive idea that criminals *deserve* to be punished? Utilitarians and modern liberals like to point out that retributive punishment is revenge and revenge is a primitive, biologically based urge. I suspect they are correct, although I am not sure why they think this is a criticism of retribution. This is an issue we must examine in a later chapter.

I have described two arguments by biologists for the view that altruistic behavior is predisposed by our genes. Yet, biologists such as Edward O. Wilson and Richard Dawkins tell us the genes are "selfish."[7] And some of these, such as Wilson, argue *both* that we can be altruistic and that our genes are always selfish. What are we to make of this? Sociobiologists have enjoyed taunting us with the idea—undoubtedly true—that the "aim" or "goal" of genes is nothing more than self-replication; and then going on to say that the animals who carry the genes, together with their whole intellectual and cultural lives, have no purpose in nature other than to serve as temporary, protective sacks for genes. Wilson tells us, "Spirituality is just one more Darwinian enabling device." Nevertheless we know (and Wilson knows) that our aims go beyond this. We seek happiness and fulfillment and not just the perpetuation of our DNA. The idea of a "purpose" in nature is in any case a metaphor; so, too, is the idea that genes have purposes, unlike the conscious purposes human beings have. The thought of competing with our own DNA is a confusing one: We need to become clear about exactly who or what is being selfish and who or what is being altruistic.

Suppose I am a member of a hominid band 300,000 years ago and genetically disposed to help others within a limited geographical or social space; the people I help are more likely to be relatives than those outside this "space," although I, small-brained brute that I am, know nothing about that. This "kin altruism" puts me, and the individual genes in me, at risk and at a disadvantage relative to non-helpers; it prompts me, and the genes I carry, to act in a way truly contrary to self-interest. Kin-altruism benefits neither me nor the particular genes inside me. So when Edward O. Wilson and others say our genes are selfish, they cannot mean *individual* genes, for they sacrifice themselves whenever the person they are trapped in sacrifices himself: If I am destroyed, the DNA in my body is destroyed too. These biologists mean instead a gene *type*—an assemblage of genes of a given kind scattered widely but particularly densely among my relatives. Richard Dawkins makes the distinction as follows: "What is the selfish gene? It is not just one single physical bit of DNA. Just as in the primeval soup, it is ALL REPLICAS of a particular bit of DNA, distributed through the world."[8]

So when biologists say the genes are selfish, they mean by "a gene" a gene type or kind, a colony-individual, what we may call a super individual. By a super individual I mean a collection of things of the same kind, thought of as a single organism, each member of which aims impartially at the good of every member of the collection. In this way the gene type perpetuates itself even though each individual gene is ready to sacrifice itself. Entomologists like to think of ant colonies as super individuals: The colony is the organism and the individual ants are its parts, they simply being more widely separated spatially than is usual for the parts of an organism.

Perfect collectivism—the polar opposite of the individualism of Hobbes, Locke, and John Stuart Mill—is an organic society: The State is the true organism; it is a super individual and the individual citizens are its parts or organs. For Hegel the Prussian State was something like this. If you are a member of a super individual you are like a liver or a pair of lungs: It makes sense to talk about your good only in terms of the contribution you make to the good of the organism. The notion of a super individual is relative to one's perspective. We can readily switch from thinking of a person as a part of a super individual (a citizen of a smotheringly collectivistic state, or a member of a fanatic army or religious order), to thinking of a person as himself a super individual who is served by *his* parts—his various organs or cells.

It is in this sense that a gene can be selfish: It can be a super individual, served by its members through their serving each other,

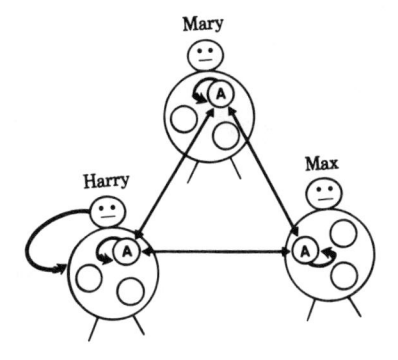

FIGURE 14. Selfish Genes vs. Selfish People

Here is illustrated the difference between a selfish person and a selfish super individual. The A-gene is a super individual, its parts scattered in different people. It is selfish because its parts each follow the Golden Rule with regard to their kind, thus benefitting the whole. The arrows indicate who helps whom. The A-gene in Harry is indifferent whether it survives or its other instances in Harry's relatives survive. But *Harry* certainly cares, at least when he is not being fed motives by his A-gene. *His* selfishness aims at himself, not at Mary and Max who are different people. Harry is a particular, the A-gene is scattered about. So the A-gene prompts Harry with motives which, from Harry's point of view, are altruistic, and from the super individual A-gene's point of view, selfish.

and it can potentially compete with the persons who are host to them. On this model my *individual* genes are impartial altruists, perfectly indifferent to whether it is they who are replicated, or instead other members of their kind in my relatives. Their altruism disposes me, their host, toward altruism, and this is the basis of kin-selection altruism. Who or what benefits from this? Clearly, the *gene type* or super individual, through the sacrifice of the individual genes (along with the individual person who bears them). In this way we can resolve the apparent paradox of "selfish" genes prompting sacrificial altruism by the persons who contain them.

The fitness of that scattered individual which is the gene type is identical with what Hamilton called inclusive fitness: this, we remember, is not the fitness of an individual but of an assemblage of genes of the same kind. Kin selection is a solution to the problem of group selection; that is, it *is* a kind of group selection, explainable through the idea of the gene type as a selfish super individual that is served by the altruism of its constituent members. A hominid whose actions are explained by kin selection practices genuine self-sacrifice; a hominid whose action is explained by reciprocal altruism practices subtle selfishness. Neither is a promiscuous altruist, that is, someone who will be altruistic toward anyone.

Philosophers have been as suspicious as social scientists about the light biological considerations can shed on values and society. Edward O. Wilson, in an opening paragraph of *Sociobiology* that reads like a challenge to a duel, staked the biologists' claim to a role in explaining values.

> The biologist, who is concerned with questions of physiology and evolutionary history, realizes that self-knowledge is constrained and shaped by the emotional control centers in the hypothalamus and limbic system of the brain. These centers flood our consciousness with all the emotions—hate, love, guilt, fear, and others—that are consulted by ethical philosophers who wish to intuit the standards of good and evil. What, we are then compelled to ask, made the hypothalamus and limbic system? They evolved by natural selection. That simple biological statement must be pursued to explain ethics and ethical philosophers, if not epistemology and epistemologists, at all depths.[9]

The ethical philosopher Peter Singer is more sympathetic than most to the idea of a core of ethics somehow based on our biological nature. But when Edward O. Wilson suggests that biology might "explain" him, and ethics, at all depths, Singer is the model moral philosopher, assuming that scientists either are going to commit the "naturalistic fallacy" or say things about ethics of little philosophical importance:

> No science is ever going to discover ethical premises inherent in our biological nature, because ethical premises are not the kind of thing discovered by scientific investigation. We do not find our ethical premises in our biological nature, or under cabbages either. We choose them.[10]

Singer is saying that we cannot deduce, from the fact that we evolved to love children and avoid incest, that children are valuable and incest bad. Moral philosophers have lectured scientists so long and so tediously about the "naturalistic fallacy"—the idea that one cannot deduce values from facts—and have had so little else to say about science and ethics, that they are seldom read by social scientists and biologists. Anglo-American philosophers have been trained since Russell, Moore, and Wittgenstein at the beginning of this century to believe that their only legitimate activity is the analysis of concepts and language. This is a pity, for the socially important and intellectually exciting problems are inextricably both philosophical and scientific. If we place great value on the lives of children and believe incest wicked *because* certain emotional responses evolved (rather than, say, because of some quirk of our local culture), that is an important thing to know in constructing a rational social philosophy.

There are difficulties with Singer's idea that we "choose" our ethical premises. I do not think anyone has ever chosen an ethical belief or, for that matter, any kind of belief. I can choose to move my body—to stand up, sit down, or talk—but I no more choose to believe rape is wrong than I choose to believe Chicago is in Illinois or Komodo dragons eat meat; I am *caused* to believe these things by my perceptions, my feelings, and my other beliefs. Insofar as people "believe what they want," it is by choosing not to take steps to check things out. On the positive side, we can be caused to believe (or doubt) something by the evidence we gather. For this reason we can say that scientific investigation is *inviting causation*: It is inviting the causation of a belief by what we hope will be evidence for the truth of the belief.

The isolation of most moral philosophers from the intellectual mainstream can be seen in this very characteristic passage in which Singer criticizes E. O. Wilson's objections to the political philosopher John Rawls:

> When Wilson objects to Rawls's theory of justice because it is "in no way explanatory or predictive with reference to human beings," he reveals a deep misunderstanding of what ethics and ethical philosophers are about. Neither Rawls nor other contemporary ethical philosophers are trying to explain or predict human actions. If they were, they would be scientists, not philosophers—and we would still need ethical philosophers to puzzle over what we ought to do.[11]

This old-fashioned view of moral philosophy says that philosophers must not explain anything or discuss causes, lest they be scientists. To make empirical claims is not only amateurish dabbling in science but also sullies the purity of philosophy. Instead, philosophers "puzzle over what we ought to do," which is to say, they painstakingly examine words and concepts, like tea leaves in the bottom of a cup, and then tell us what is right and wrong. Singer continues:

> [Wilson] says that "ethical philosophers who wish to intuit the standards of good and evil" are really just consulting their "emotional control centers." If ethical judgments were nothing but the outflow of our emotional control centers, it would be as inappropriate to criticize ethical judgments as it is to criticize gastronomic preferences. Endorsing capital punishment would be as much an expression of our feeling as taking our tea with lemon, rather than milk.[12]

Those who, like Wilson and myself, ground ethics in our "emotional control centers," that is, in evolved human nature, are not speaking of the morality of lowering the Ohio income tax, or even the morality of capital punishment; these matters depend on lots of factual knowledge because they are high up in the superstructure of ethics and not part of a cross-cultural, basic core. The emotions common to our species tell us that we do not want to freeze, starve, or be burned to a crisp; that we want to be accepted and belong to something, and we do not want to be assaulted, rejected, or banished. These shared wants and fears cause us to have corresponding shared and very basic "thou shalts" and "thou shalt nots." Species-wide emotions about tea with lemon and the ethics of corporate mergers have not yet evolved.

TWELVE

Human Nature and the Social Contract

> The social contract theory of ethics held that our rules of right and wrong sprang from some distant Foundation Day on which previously independent rational human beings came together to hammer out a basis for setting up the first human society. Two hundred years ago this seemed a plausible alternative to the then orthodox idea that morality represented the decrees of a divine lawgiver. It attracted some of the sharpest and most skeptical thinkers in Western social philosophy. If, however, we now know that we have lived in groups longer than we have been rational human beings, we can also be sure that we restrained our behavior toward our fellows before we were rational human beings.
>
> —Peter Singer

Once upon a time long ago people wandered the jungle as solitary creatures and they were very poor. Having no society or common good to bind them together, they fought over caves and carcasses, which made social interaction nasty and brutish. Without the association of their fellow humans they lacked the benefits of common provisioning and defense, they were preyed upon by big cats, and their lives were short. Finding this a bore these rational, selfish savages said, "enough of this, let's make a civilization with rules of social morality," and actually did it.

Thus goes the social contract theory of the origin of society. Even if it made sense (which it doesn't) to say humans invented cooperative society, we couldn't *remain* selfish atoms; for as we have seen, rational selfishness tells us to cheat selectively on the system and accept the social contract with our fingers crossed behind our backs. And yet if it were our *nature* to be selfish atoms we couldn't change either. To enter society is to enter a moral community, it is to submit to a social morality and acknowledge a non-instrumental common good. We, or our ancestors, cannot enter society as though it were like entering Chicago or Hungary. We can enter *a* society, for example, the Masons, only if we are already social by having been socialized from infancy into some other society.

If we were, in our presocietal jungle, *by nature* selfish creatures, do we acquire another nature, perhaps become another species, when we present our exit visas and leave the state of nature? Among social contract thinkers, only Thomas Hobbes, the first and smartest of them, clearly sees the impossibility of this. If our nature is selfish, inventing society isn't going to change it. Hobbes's humans are as egoistic in society as in the state of nature.

Chapters Seven and Eight criticized the view that motives of rational selfishness can suffice to produce adequate citizens. In Chapters Nine and Ten I argued it was essential that human beings belong to groups and that individualism be tempered with collectivism, if we are to thrive and be a people, a moral community. Now we need to continue the evolutionary theme begun in the last chapter and ask if the individualist assumptions that lie behind the social contract theory of society have scientific plausibility.

The social contract account of organized society says that law and governmental power are justified when they are what people in a "state of nature" would mutually accept: They would trade insecurity and unlimited freedom for security and fair, mutual limitations on their freedom. Although I could be wrong, I don't think any philosopher has ever gone so far as to claim there was an actual, datable, social contract, as there was a real signing of the Magna Carta, and which took place on the last day of an actual state of nature. Social contract philosophers, from Hobbes through Locke and Rousseau to John Rawls, appear to think this unimportant and they usually hint that the social contract is "hypothetical"—that it is the sort of agreement rational individuals of roughly equal power *would* make were they to find themselves in a state of nature.

If we were societyless egoists wandering the jungle, or as the Harvard philosopher John Rawls suggests, floating in hyperspace choosing principles of justice to govern the world we will be born into (and not knowing whether we will be born black or white, male or female, stupid or clever)—*if* any of this were so, then it is natural to suppose *we would choose a social organization that was tailored to cope with egoists*. Hobbes would have us appoint a sovereign and hand him the sword of political power.[1] Being an egoist the sovereign will do what he wants, and being rational he will want laws that maintain order and reduce the level of mutual throat-cutting, because without order he cannot collect enough taxes to live like a sovereign. His egoistic subjects want exactly the same thing, since, also being rational, they see that supporting one sovereign who has the sword is better than everyone having a sword in a "war of all against all." Hobbes never suggested that the sovereign or the citizens would ever be anything but the perfect egoists with which he began.

John Rawls, however, would have us give up egoism. We are asked to imagine ourselves to be rational egoists who are unborn spirits, floating behind a "veil of ignorance" regarding our future abilities and social class, and worrying about tomorrow, at which time we will be born into the real world. This imaginary world of ignorance, which he calls the "original position," is Rawls's version of the state of nature.[2] In it, he says, rational egoists will choose principles to live by, which by definition are fair, because it cannot be in anyone's interest to bias the principles in favor of landlords or tenants, men or women, and so on. What principles, then, will we choose, while imagining ourselves to be egoistic ghosts in hyperspace, ignorant of our future incarnations? On proper reflection, he says, we will first choose the most extensive liberty that could be shared by all. And second, we will let some people become rich and powerful if, through a combination of the invisible hand of the marketplace and the visible hand of the tax collector, redistribution of wealth made everyone better off, especially the "least advantaged." The political position these principles represent is not revolutionary, it is not very different from that of the Left wing of the Democratic party.

The liberal Rawls and the libertarian Robert Nozick, also a Harvard philosopher, often are pitted against each other in philosophy classes. For Rawls, nothing but economic efficiency can justify anyone having better or worse than anyone else, for Rawls assumes a doctrine of social determinism from which it follows that no one *deserves* his success: "Even the willingness to make an effort, to try, and so to be deserving in the ordinary sense is itself dependent upon happy family and social circumstances."[3] Thus, to be talented, to be smiled on by fortune, is no longer innocent: One must, out of fairness, pay reparations. The fruits of my labors belong as much to you as to me and, if psychology didn't get in the way, should be distributed equally to everyone in the world. For Rawls, justice permits unequal wealth not because the rich and talented merit or are entitled to more, but because of the economic efficiency of differential reward: Absolute equality of reward would kill the motivation of the talented. High producers of wealth and jobs are milk cows, to be milked (by taxation) up to that point where, if they were milked more they would produce less. Efficiency and the fear of resentment, not merit, justify letting some people get rich.

It is important to see that this example of modern liberalism has nothing whatever to do with community or group commitments; it is just a matter of the equal distributive rights of individual persons, as determined by abstract principles of justice and utility. True enough, the state makes demands on the individual; but it simply wants your money, to satisfy its principles of fair distribution, it doesn't demand your loyalty or affection. Rawls's conception of the state and the individual's relation to it is thoroughly individualistic: The state is a guarantor of rights and an income redistribution machine, balancing the envy of the poor against the resentment of the successful, the result being called justice.

Robert Nozick argued that the state has no right to take my profits even if you need them more than I. But he stands with Rawls in denying that citizens have obligations to society beyond payment for services and the restraints of justice. He says,

> . . . the legitimate powers of a protective association are merely the *sum* of the individual rights that its members or clients transfer to the association. No new rights and powers arise; each right of the association is decomposable without residue into those individual rights held by distinct individuals acting alone in a state of nature.[4]

For each of these philosophers, civil society is not an object of love and loyalty but a machine to which you owe nothing but taxes. You pay your money, your garbage is collected, and the account is quits, there is no residue of debit or credit. Each conceives of the relation of the individual to organized society as coldly and commercially as one's relation to a store, except that Rawls thinks it should be a big store and Nozick thinks it should be a small store.

Rawls does not think real people are exclusive egoists, because he thinks it is possible to live by his two principles of justice. Why, however, do real people get their principles of justice chosen for them by imaginary egoists? This is typical, individualist, social contract thinking. Why is what egoists would choose behind the "veil of ignorance" *relevant* to what is just and fair for human beings if human beings are not egoists? If horses needed principles to live by would they ask cows or crocodiles, even rational ones, to pick them? The explanation of this peculiar method lies in the assumptions of the social contractarian tradition.

It cannot be denied that earlier liberals tried to make community a reality, in some sense of that generous term. William Schambra has argued, for example, that the New Deal liberals attempted this. They wanted, he said, to combine the Federalists' large commercial state with the communalism the Anti-Federalists felt required local participation and small community loyalties. The New Deal liberals, Schambra says, were utopians who tried to have it both ways: They wanted to "create the sense of community thought possible by the Anti-Federalists only in the small republic, on a national scale."[5] They were to have "a true sense of national community," facilitated by equalizing wealth and power as much as possible. "The contemporary left," Schambra says, "embraces only the Anti-Federalist principles of community and equality . . .," and he seems to accept an intimate linkage between those two ideas.

It is part of the mythology of liberal individualism that wealth and power is the problem and getting enough of it is the solution. It isn't only that thinking equalizing money and power will produce community is a mistake, which it is. Those who praise community as a good that comes with equality of wealth and political power often mean no more than equality, "community" being emptied of meaning and turned into a pleasant sounding title to drape upon the egalitarian society. Egalitarianism is not community; indeed, people who insist on equality commonly are enemies of community, which after all includes the idea of insiders and outsiders. The recent American Left loved justice and equality, understood as the rights of individuals against the social will, and their fraternization with community usually did not go beyond food co-ops.

We can talk about the kinds of business arrangements rational egoists might choose, when they realize with horror they must live together; but they are not the kinds of social arrangements *human beings* throughout their history have found themselves in nor are they what people would choose in a hypothetical situation. The evidence indicates social contract thinkers are mistaken about the nature of the human beings they philosophize about. We very probably were social animals and group loyalists even before we evolved into human beings. Social arrangements rational egoists would choose have little to do with the motivations and institutions in actual human societies. The social contractarians changed the subject from human beings, who are tribal creatures, to rational egoists, who are some other kind of creature: They philosophized about the wrong animal.

What most likely really happened, historically speaking, is that people always lived in troops and clans, and what moved them always was a combination of self-interest and basic non-selfish wants aimed at the good of kin and clan. This is an evolutionary matter: The tendency to have group egoistic, tribal attitudes probably evolved before our prehuman ancestors were advanced enough even to be called hominids. There never was a presocial stage, at least not for millions of years; there almost certainly never was a race of early humans or hominids whose behavior was exclusively selfish; and there never were humans, or creatures on the way to becoming humans, who would choose the kind of society that the philosophers' rational egoists (or Martians for that matter) would choose. No existing human society is as individualistic as social contract theory, from Hobbes to Rawls, predicts. All real societies are, in differing degrees, organic ones, which means we are both egoists and group egoists. Extreme individualists, however, assume that tribal morality and group loyalty are a learned thing, overlaid by convention on human nature.

The idea that people at some time *thought up* the idea of social living can be seen to be a conceit, with no scientific basis, when we consider our very early ancestry and make some comparisons with other animals.

> The two traits, large prey size and social hunting, are unquestionably linked. Lions, which are the only social members of the cat family, double the catch when hunting in prides. . . . Primitive men are ecological analogs of lions, wolves, and hyenas. Alone among the primates, with the marginal exception of the chimpanzees, they have adopted pack hunting in the pursuit of big game. And they resemble four-footed carnivores more than other primates by virtue of habitually slaughtering surplus prey, storing food, feeding solid food to their young, dividing labor, practicing cannibalism, and interacting aggressively with competing species. Bones and stone tools dug from ancient campsites in Africa, Europe, and Asia indicate that this way of life persisted for a million years or longer and was abandoned in most societies only during the last few thousands of years. Thus the selection pressures of hunter-gatherer existence have persisted for over 99 percent of human genetic evolution.[6]

But then does innate sociality require us to deny the importance of culture? Hardly, for culture is how we express our nature; cultures are the natural products of our innate needs, fears, sources of satisfaction, big brains, and diverse environments.

For most of the twentieth century, American social scientists clung to the view that human society is something we invented, and which we retain only by convention. The sociologist Don Martindale reflects the common view when he says, "Man is one of the most social of all the creatures, but unique in the nature of sociality. He is social by learning and not by instinct."[7] The idea that human society is an invention, to be contrasted with the "natural" condition of man, never seems to have been supported by any empirical evidence, although it is clearly an empirical hypothesis. The past decade shows signs of a change, the received doctrine coming under increasing challenges. Contrast Martindale's 1963 view that man is "social by learning and not by instinct" with the 1978 statement of psychologists Robert Hogan and Nicholas Emler:

> One of the most remarkable features of current social psychology is its systematic denial of man's social nature. This might seem a contradiction, for what could social psychology be but the study of man's social nature. And yet the central thesis of the discipline is that social psychology is an individual psychology, that social behavior is to be understood in terms of personal psychological qualities.

On the contrary, Hogan and Emler claim,

> Society is not only a condition of life for every person and something he or she is invariably born into, it is an irreducible characteristic of the species.[8]

Few deny that until very recently a second assumption of the psychologists was the doctrine of universal selfishness. In the words of the psychologist Martin Hoffman, "The doctrinaire view in psychology has been that altruism can ultimately be explained in terms of egoistic, self-serving motives. Although widespread, this assumption remains untested—perhaps a reflection of Western philosophical thought."[9] And Daniel Batson says: "Current [psychological] theories tend to be egoistic; they are built on the assumption that everything we do is ultimately directed toward the end state goal of benefitting ourselves." But he goes on to say, "In the past few years, a number of researchers have hypothesized that this motivation [empathy] might be truly altruistic, that is, directed toward the end state goal of reducing the other's distress."[10]

The idea of human society as independent of the natural, biological world is also a legacy of early Christianity. It was not part of their world view that man is part of nature: God made nature specifically to serve man's needs, and eventually He would destroy it all again—animals, oceans, stars—because we had sinned. The anthropocentrism aside, the forces in this drama were human free will and God's commands. The conceptual scheme of the early Christians ruled out the idea that *nature* might give man sociality, for near animists that they were, they never asked "*how* does it happen," but "*who* did it." One of the main thrusts of the developing scientific world view thirteen hundred years later was to explain, by unraveling one riddle after another, the respects in which human behavior, anatomy, mind, and values are continuous with and enmeshed in the rest of nature.

Sophisticated religious thought complements rather than competes with biological origins: The laws of nature, whatever scientists discover them to be and including the laws of human evolution, cannot be other than God's laws. (This is not to say sophisticated religious thought is winning: Witness the success of those who wish to substitute Genesis for scientific biology in frightening the publishing companies into removing the theory of evolution from high school biology textbooks. Biblical biology might be fun if it included an explanation of how 50,000 species of South American beetles made their way, two by two, to Noah's ark, and then back again to South America.) The increasing awareness that man is as "naturally" a social animal as ants, dolphins, and wolves is part of the ages-long process of bringing man home to nature. It is in part sinful pride, in part simple ignorance about what makes us tick, that leads people to assume that we, but not "animals," are clever enough and plastic enough to invent social life.

To say we are "naturally" social means evolution made us into creatures emotionally equipped for and dependent on common features of social living, including socialization of the young, mutual aid, ritual, social roles, useful work, personal responsibility, and other elements of what we may call our Pleistocene Inheritance. If this is so, what is the significance of the social contract myth for understanding society—the story of a state of nature in which selfish, solitary creatures decide life is more secure if they invent society? We must say, I think, that because the social contractarians speculated about a made-up creature, social contract theory is not likely to provide an especially illuminating account of creatures genetically programmed to be social. For what makes sense of society for a race of social, tribal creatures who are, simultaneously, egoists, group egoists, and moralists is not likely to make sense for a race of egoistic, individualist atoms.

For these reasons it is doubtful whether the whole social contract tradition is relevant to an accurate understanding of human society. Mary Midgley points to innate sociality as the crucial criticism:

> Every existing animal species has its *own* nature, its own hierarchy of instincts—in a sense, its own virtues. In social animals, such as ourselves and the wolves, . . . it is plain that we are much better fitted to live socially than to live alone or in anarchy. . . . Rousseau's or Hobbes's state of nature would be fine for intelligent crocodiles, if there were any. For people it is a baseless fantasy.[11]

The objection that no one takes social contract stories literally, as actual history, misses the point of my criticism: In spinning their myths, social contractarians presuppose theories about human nature and the relation of individuals to society. These theories have social and political policy implications that directly compete with other conceptions. Midgley nicely makes the point regarding Hobbes and Rousseau.

> The State of Nature and the Social Contract are not just literary devices, nor are they merely metaphors about people's present psychology. They imply something about human origins, namely that we *are as if* the Contract story had been true, and therefore cannot (for instance) have evolved from the reverse direction. To that extent they form an empirical hypothesis about the past, which has been falsified. Similarly Rousseau, when in the *Discourse on Inequality* he spoke of primitive man as solitary, as "meeting other men perhaps once or twice in a lifetime, without knowing each other and without speaking," was not just adding illustrative embroidery to his analysis of political obligation. Certainly what he says is primarily meant as a piece of timeless psychology, as a claim about what people are like now in their deepest motivation. But it does also have a literal, historical meaning, because such accounts of how people are are not compatible with just any story about their past.[12]

As an example of this incompatibility, consider the multiple, competing loyalties I have described and defended in earlier chapters. Today they are called "mediating structures" and are understood collectivistically by some writers and as interest groups by others; but to eighteenth-century social contractarians they were "factions," a mortal threat to the commonwealth.

> But when cabals and partial associations are formed at the expense of the great association, the will of each such association, though *general* with regard to its members, is *private* with regard to the State. . . . It is therefore of the utmost importance for obtaining the expression of the general will, that no partial society should be formed in the State. . . .[13]

Thus for Rousseau the state cannot share your loyalty with another, any more than can your spouse your bed or your God share your devotion. Rousseau, and indeed the great majority of eighteenth- and nineteenth-century social thinkers including both Marx and Mill, simply would not think in terms of multiple, nested, overlapping, and competing loyalties all of limited authority. The very idea of a social contract nourishes a "one tribe" model, especially if we think of a social contract like a marriage contract or like a business contract that excludes competitors. What I mean is that while social contractarians might accept many tribes, each on its own island and formed and bound by its own contract, each must be pure, its contract disallowing sub-societies or "factions" nested within it and challenging its moral authority. On the other hand biologically innate sociality, which contains no idea of simple or unitary lines of authority, grows more complex over time and naturally accommodates nested and overlapping group loyalties.

Tribal morality, wherever we find it in families, fraternal organizations, corporations, street gangs, and nations, is predisposed by our genetic program. During our long, hunter-gatherer prehistory there was biological selection for the mutual concession and cooperation that are essential for group life. Anthropologists agree that our hominid and early human ancestors banded together for cooperative hunting, food gathering, and out of respect for animal competitors and predators.

This banding together wasn't the result of a social contract, made by egoistic hominids deliberating under a Pleistocene equivalent of Rousseau's communal oak tree. It all began long before we were smart enough to do any such thing. It was not a matter of an agreement but of natural selection for deep wants and aversions, about the nature of which I shall speculate in the next chapter. As in the case of any adaptive process, those who had the emotional equipment for group life lived in groups, those who did not conform or accept group goals lived outside the group and either starved or got eaten by saber-toothed cats. Put a little more cautiously, they reproduced somewhat less than their more social competitors.

We might speculate that the similarities found in primitive tribes around the world today reveal a social organization very similar to what natural selection predisposed in us during the past several hundred thousand years. In other words we can postulate a common or average condition of human life, one that changed very little over a very long time prior to our ability to tinker with it, and which represents the kinds of social practices and institutions that existed in the environments late hominids and early humans confronted. Needs and fears that suited us to social institutions that enabled us to survive would have had time to be biologically selected and become part of human nature.

There is nothing remarkable or even very controversial in postulating the evolution of wants, fears, and emotions that are triggered in specific situations, including social ones. Things so simple as an animal's fear of certain sounds and scents, response to courtship ritual, or rage when you approach its young or invade its territory, are examples of *emotional*, as distinct from physical, adaptations to an environment. It is likely that our predispositions to respond emotionally changed more slowly over the past several hundred millennia than our intelligence. Perhaps, while our brains were growing at a fantastic rate (by evolutionary standards) new emotional predispositions evolved. I do not know what these might be, but I assume that most of the old emotions, needs, and fears remained, and it is this that I am supposing unites modern city dwellers, members of contemporary primitive tribes, and our ancestors of the late Pleistocene and early Holocene, and which I have been calling our Pleistocene Inheritance. It assumes there are no *socially* significant genetic differences among present-day humans, whatever their cultures, and minimal differences between us and our ancient ancestors.

This scenario gives us a new conception of the "state of nature," one that contrasts sharply with the state of nature as Hobbes and his successors conceived it. What I have in mind is a historical and empirical model conceived of as a state of culture under long-term primitive conditions: What I postulate are close analogies between present-day primitive tribes in the jungles of the Philippines, New Guinea, or the Amazon basin and their ancestors in similar environments 100 thousand years ago and more. Thus, on my model, you *can* get a visa for the "state of nature": You can board an airplane and visit stone age societies in New Guinea or the Amazon basin.

Since evolution never ceases, this is a constantly changing as well as historical and revisionist idea of the state of nature. There would be differences, probably small ones, between the genetic predispositions for social life among our recent Pleistocene ancestors, the Cro-Magnons, and a contemporary tribe in the Amazon basin, and perhaps no socially relevant genetic differences at all between the Amazon tribe and New Yorkers. An empirical conception of a "natural state" of cultures and societies, of which late Pleistocene hunter-gatherer bands are examples and recent Holocene primitive tribes approximations, is more helpful for understanding present-day society than the speculations of Hobbes, Locke, and Rousseau.

The phrase "natural state" is in order here because we are talking about a social setting of very long duration in which most of the emotional and brain evolution that made us peculiarly human took place, and in which for hundreds of millennia our technical mastery of nature was minimal and relatively unchanging. We have become used to a world that is significantly different every fifty years; our ancient ancestors lived in one in which society probably changed less in 50,000 years than it has in the past fifty years. The "state of nature" conceived as our evolutionary past is important if the social emotions and responses we feel now had evolved to "fit" what we can call the social geometry and dynamics of Late Pleistocene times. For then the social institutions that function successfully in Manhattan or Belgrade are likely to be "tribal surrogates" or analogues, which together comprise a social geometry roughly congruent—though hardly identical—with the interpersonal social patterns around those ancient caves and campfires.

The idea of getting clues to Manhattan social institutions and practices that hurt or succor us emotionally, from institutions and practices in clans back in Pleistocene times when our emotional responses got "fixed," comes across suggestively in this reflection of Fürer-Haimendorf about South Asian tribes.

> Throughout the greater part of his history man has led the nomadic life of hunters and foodgatherers, roaming in small bands over a world sparsely populated and untamed by human civilizing effort. Today . . . they form so infinitesimally small a fraction of present-day mankind that we might well be tempted to disregard them in a study of moral attitudes and human values. Yet, such a decision would be unwarranted. . . . They represent patterns of society comparable in many respects to those which must have prevailed throughout the hundreds of millennia which elapsed between the emergence of man as a rational being and the development of the more complex communities of settled populations engaged in agriculture or other forms of systematic food production. No modern anthropologist will claim that tiny groups of present-day foodgatherers . . . are exact replicas of the men of the old stone-age, but there remains the fact that the economic basis of their social and cultural life is remarkably similar to that of paleolithic foodgatherers or hunters. Neither had they nor had paleolithic man seriously begun to transform nature, and a close adjustment of their whole style of life to environmental conditions and resources imposed on both a pattern of behavior confined of necessity to narrow limits.[14]

There can be no hiding the fact that there are problems with analogies between modern tribes in the jungle and ice age tribes living in plains or tundra regions. A greater understanding of variety and similarity in cultures, whether North American plains and forest Indians, Eskimos, Kalahari desert dwellers, East African tribes, Australian aborigines, and Amazon or African jungle tribes, would contribute more toward understanding human sociality than the traditional, philosophers' conception of the "state of nature." It would be useful too if we knew more about the increasing biological and cultural differences between contemporary primitives and people older than the recent Pleistocene, such as Neanderthals, homo Erectus, or the earlier hominids.

This way of looking at things says that the basis of society and social morality is not the hypothetical "social contract" egoistic individuals *would* make but complex emotional "ready responses" and pro-social dispositions evolution *has* made. When we try to reconstruct the social life of ancient man under our new, admittedly loose and changing model of a "state of nature," what we find is evidence for a mixture of strong group loyalties with altruistic and individualistic impulses, an overwhelming need for social belonging, culture, ritual and ceremony, procedures of child rearing and social indoctrination, and sexual regulation and custom including pair bonding and incest taboos. We find social animals. And since we share their genetic heritage, we carry the stamp of their world in our deepest feelings and needs. How could it be otherwise, for evolution has not had time to change what became fixed during our sojourn in the "state of nature."

THIRTEEN

Our Secret Pleistocene Inheritance

> The trouble with [man] is, of course, that he comes half-finished. Man is innately programmed in such a way that he needs a culture to complete him. Culture is not an alternative or replacement for instinct, but its outgrowth and supplement. Man is like one of those versatile cake mixes that can be variously prepared to end up as different kinds of cake—but never, it must be noted, as a boiled egg or smoked salmon.
>
> —Mary Midgley

> In other words, man's whole system of innate activities and reactions is phylogenetically so constructed, so "calculated" by evolution, as to need to be complemented by cultural traditions. For instance, all the tremendous neurosensory apparatus of human speech is phylogenetically evolved, but so constructed that its function presupposes the existence of a culturally developed language which the infant has to learn.
>
> —Conrad Lorenz

Long ago, when unconventional people fell on hard times we would wag our fingers and say they had tried to live contrary to what nature (or God) intended. Today, technology, affluence, and the values revolution have dramatically changed how we live, both in the main streams and experimental subcultures. And we have fallen on hard times, at least relative to what we have come to expect given our political freedom, mastery of nature, and incredible (by ancient standards) economic prosperity. There indeed are respects in which we are living contrary to nature, but we are only beginning to understand what this means.

It is, of course, an ancient idea. The Chinese Taoists made life in accord with nature their ideal ("be like water" and follow the natural ways and bends of things, Lao Tzu said) and the Stoics made it the cornerstone of their ethical life. As we have seen, the idea of life in accord with nature fell into disrepute in modern times when it was used to argue that women belonged in the kitchen, blacks in the cotton fields, and in general to support nastier parts of the status quo. Now, examples given of life in accord with nature are not the lives of Taoists and Stoics, which were noble, but bigotries and absurdities that mock the idea.

Over thousands of generations the advantages and requirements of hunting-gathering social life leave their mark on our *emotional* makeup, not just on our behavior. We are not bugs who mechanically catch their prey and spin their cocoons as their DNA directs them; we are more complex creatures whose innate behavior works through wants, fears, and external sources of satisfaction and anxiety. Perhaps bugs simply *do*—eat, spin, burrow, copulate—but people *want* and *fear,* and on that basis *do*. Because we, unlike bugs, are creatures with mental and emotional lives, our innate behavior is mediated by the felt satisfaction or anxiety it causes us. These satisfactions and anxieties are the reinforcements by which psychologists explain behavior. The psychologists may take a positive reinforcement, like a mother's smile, or a negative one, such as a hard stare, as simply given, for perhaps it is not thought their business to discover *why* something reinforces.

But *we* must ask why if we seek clues to human nature and the structure this nature gives to human sociality. For example, if in almost any culture delinquents are intimidated by loud, disapproving uproar by those around them, and their pro-social behavior is positively reinforced by rituals, we add these phenomena to our list to be investigated more closely. They are potential components of our "Pleistocene inheritance." I call it that, but some of the social situations that please us or fill us with anxiety and misery come in part from still more ancient influences on our brains. In *The Dragons of Eden* Carl Sagan tells us:

> The deep and ancient parts [of the brain] are functioning still. . . . If the preceding view is correct, we should expect the R- [reptilian] complex in the human brain to be in some sense performing dinosaur functions still; and the limbic cortex to be thinking the thoughts of pumas and ground sloths. . . . [Paul] MacLean has shown that the r-complex plays an important role in aggressive behavior, territoriality, ritual and the establishment of social hierarchies.[1]

In hunting-gathering society people knew well those with whom they lived, worked, and played. Social interactions were personal, tied to familiar faces, places, and ways of doing things. Beyond the circle of routine, the familiar, and the whole net of clan life, waited hunger, exposure, and the leopards. Lacking courts, jails, and probation officers, our ancestors necessarily depended on group reactions as the mechanisms of social control.

> The nomad in forest or bush, whose material possessions are often so scanty that the members of a family can carry with them all that they own, relies on his kinsmen or friends for company, security and comfort. He knows no other entertainment than their conversation and perhaps an occasional dance, requires their help in sickness and emergencies, and finds round the camp fires of his group the kind of comfort and shelter which in later stages of civilization man expects when entering his more solid home. Relations with his fellow-men are therefore of paramount importance for the primitive hunter or jungle nomad and it is not unlikely that the universal human craving for social approval was developed during the hundred thousands of years when man, struggling for domination over a largely hostile and threatening nature, had no other comfort and support than the friendship and sympathy of the few other human beings who constituted his group.[2]

I suggested we can find a "state of nature," of sorts, in primitive tribes where needs and comforts, and in-group and out-group relations, are reduced to essentials—as close as we can hope to find to the society of our late Pleistocene ancestors. Among the Daflas, primitive cultivators in India's North East hill country, a single long-house is the social unit, ruled by one senior man. The world beyond the confines of an individual long-house is, almost, Hobbes's state of nature, and within each, a petty sovereign. Long-houses are grouped in villages, but there is no authority beyond the long-house, no one to enforce sanctions. Justice, for wrongs done by one household against another—cheating in trade, abduction, unpaid bride prices—is retaliation by the aggrieved together with his friends and whomever he can enlist. A feud, with exchanges of raids, may continue for years, but attempts may be made to negotiate with the aid of a gingdung, a go-between who has diplomatic immunity. Conferences are held, cases argued, peace pacts concluded between long-houses as between nation states, within a network of inter-long-house custom as fragile as international law among sovereign nations.

> [Q]uestions of right and wrong are continuously discussed in the course of a dispute. In the mind of the Dafla there is a great difference between "justified retaliation" and "unprovoked robbery".... The peculiar situation in Dafla society is due mainly to the unusual smallness of the in-

> group. As the inhabitants of one long-house constitute the only real in-group most economic and social contacts are between autonomous and independent bodies. . . . One has only to listen to a Dafla arguing his case in the course of peace-negotiations and enumerating the injuries inflicted on himself or his close kin, to realize that in describing the high-handedness of his adversaries he is appealing to a sense of justice and to moral values he presumes his listener will share with him. By accusing his enemies of treachery, breach of promise, outright lies, unprovoked aggression, robbery, theft or similar acts, he manifests his conviction that his audience will be moved to indignation. . . .[3]

Is it that society as we know it requires a larger critical mass? With a larger society comes a moral community: Third parties take an interest in disputes, and thus are born crime and punishment and officials, as distinct from feuds, victims, and retaliation.

Throughout our long prehistory there was less that hunter-gatherer bands could get away with, compared with modern man, without risking extinction. Life was so difficult and full cooperation in proven routines so essential that injury and death were the usual price of nonconformity. Certainly there were other major causes of death such as disease, accident, and perhaps infanticide, and certain types of innovation would have been highly adaptive; however, in the long run selective pressure greatly favored emotional dependence on conforming, cooperative routines. In our modern society we readily understand how distressing group exclusion is to children—the image of children made to feel left out is familiar and understood. We also understand, perhaps with decreasing lucidity, the need of handicapped and retarded people to feel accepted and recognized as useful in a local community, and the need of old people for familiar faces and surroundings that affect their perception of security. Less well understood, in good part because of our love affair with autonomy and inner-directedness, is the need well-functioning adults at the height of their powers have.

Group egoism, in the form of genetically predisposed loyalties to extended families, clans, and their territories, is an obvious candidate for one of the more important emotions that would evolve. We see what probably are its ancient forms in the herding instincts and territoriality of other animals, and its conceptualized, human form as the primary social glue of present-day tribes and societies. It is reasonable to suppose that Pleistocene environments would favor its evolution.

Franz Boas describes the conservatism and minimal individualism of primitive life.

> The dislike of anything deviating from the custom of the land is even more strongly marked than in our civilization. If it is not the custom to sleep in a house with feet turned towards the fire, a violation of this custom is dreaded and avoided. . . . We are justified in concluding from our own experience, that as among ourselves, so among primitive tribes, the resistance to a deviation from firmly established customs is due to an emotional reaction, not to conscious reasoning.[4]

In primitive society, Boas continues,

> the child in whom the habitual behavior of his surroundings has not yet developed will acquire much of it by unconscious imitation. In many cases, however, it will act in a way different from the customary manner, and will be corrected by its elders. Any one familiar with primitive life will know that the children are constantly exhorted to follow the example of their elders, and every collection of carefully recorded traditions contains numerous references to advice given by parents to children, impressing them with the duty to observe the customs of the tribe. . . . The essential result of this inquiry is the conclusion that the origin of customs of primitive man must not be looked for in rational processes.[5]

When in 1975 Edward O. Wilson suggested that humans might possess "conformer genes," an uproar ensued that probably is best explained as a reaction by people contemptuous of conformity to certain qualities they attribute to the American middle class. Wilson's critics perhaps thought he meant there was some specific thing—such as Protestant middle-class capitalism—to which genes make us conform. They seemed to worry that our very DNA might be bourgeois. Harvard biologist Richard Lewontin attacked Wilson's views as a form of genetic determinism that provides a rationalization for the political status quo:

> [T]heories of the physical body and the body politic come together in biological determinism, an ideology that both justifies current social arrangements and claims them to be the inevitable consequences of the facts of life.[6]

Someone who didn't know where Lewontin lived might wonder which "current social arrangements" he had in mind: Those in China, Sweden, South Africa, or the USSR? If biological determinism justifies any of these it justifies them all (and past ones too—the Dutch Republic and the Rome of Emperor Heliogabalus). Since the status quo is different in different times and places it becomes difficult to see who is supposed to believe that biological determinism justifies anything. Along with many scientists of the Left and others deeply suspicious of evolutionary hypotheses about society, Lewontin thought that sociobiological theories, and indeed any hypotheses about human nature and society, implied we were unfree to make social reforms or mount revolutions. He writes that according to such views, "Politics becomes a branch of molecular biology, and our social and political institutions are as immutable as the chemicals of which we are made."[7]

Again one wonders who is supposed to believe this; if all the world had the same social and political institutions it would be slightly less silly. As it is, the straw doctrine Lewontin invents and attacks does seem to imply that Americans and Chinese and Swedes are made of different chemicals because they have different social institutions (and Albanians made of very queer chemicals).

It is a fallacy to think genetic causes make any kind of social behavior inevitable. Genetic causes are tendencies, dispositions, which produce their effects only in certain environments: Change the environment and the genes will be inoperative or will produce a different effect. For example, it is possible that many people (but not all) have a genetic makeup that will give them lung cancer *if* they smoke cigarettes, and which is much less likely to give them lung cancer if they do not smoke cigarettes. Or there might be a genetic cause that will make those who have the gene (or genes) homosexuals *if* they are treated in certain ways as children, and otherwise not.

At the same time the evidence of anthropologists such as Boas is that people generally conform to the culture of their group. This would be a banality not worth mentioning were it not for those who wish to cause children to grow up with a particular ideology, but who at the same time raise an outcry against "determinism" when biologists discuss social causation. Midgley describes the confused animosity to human nature to which this leads.

> Every attack on [E. O. Wilson] I have seen protests strongly at his saying that "human beings are absurdly easy to indoctrinate; they *seek* it," and "men would rather believe than know". Now this seems simply to be an explicit statement of the force of social conditioning, which is the very fact he is accused of neglecting. People are indeed very easily indoctrinated by their societies. That is what makes their nature so much harder to study than that of other species. But anyone who holds that we really *have no nature* is surely forced to believe that we are, not just absurdly, but *infinitely* easy to indoctrinate, since we can have no inborn tendencies that either deflect or resist the process. . . . The notion that we "have a nature," far from threatening the concept of freedom, is absolutely

essential to it. If we were genuinely plastic and indeterminate at birth, there could be no reason why society should not stamp us into any shape that might suit it. . . .[8]

We have already seen that to talk about human nature is not to suggest there are genes that make one vote Republican or approve of nuclear power plants; and that to assert the origin of conformism in our biological history is not to suggest that a person brought up among socialists (or capitalists) *must* be a socialist (or a capitalist). That people largely *do* conform to the society around them is an undeniable fact; if it were not so, no tribe would last beyond a generation with its culture intact, which is a way of saying there could be no culture, and therefore no human life as we know it. Wilson was talking about the fact *that* we conform and much less about *what* it is to which we conform.

It would be preposterous to think that any theory about human nature and society might prove humans are perfect conformists, or for that matter inveterate nonconformists, when anyone who reads the paper or watches TV sees around him a world full of both rebellion and conformity. The degree to which people conform, and the degree to which they rebel, is whatever careful observation and the study of history show it to be. That most people conform as much as they do is, I suppose, an acute disappointment to those who passionately desire radical change but who, like communists in America or anti-communist dissidents in the USSR, find most people to be conformists. But if humans did not conform on very basic levels, we could not have cultures, and would not be social animals, and hence would not be humans.

Today we can afford a sub-population of rebels, hippies, or bohemians because we produce surplus goods, cure diseases, and have vanquished the leopards and cave lions. Our ancestors no more could afford this than can present-day stone-age tribes. Today's bohemians quickly develop their own supportive, conforming communities—their niches—that are affordable within advanced cultures but not elsewhere.

The selective pressure for social conformity is both cultural and genetic. Cultural selection works quickly and is Lamarckian, that is, it passes on to the next generation practices people have *learned* and which have won out in competition with others. Biological selection is slow and works through *genetical* influences on the fears, wants, and emotions of those who survive and have children. This genetic legacy is our Pleistocene inheritance, and makes us crave a supporting and largely conforming community, at the same time providing enough non-conformity for social evolution to take place and to eliminate boredom. Consequently our innate tendency to conform is not just an evolutionary fossil—an emotional equivalent of the appendix, ripe for social or psychotheraputic excision. Our emotional need for acceptance in smallish social units is still part of us to the degree that frustrating it makes us unhappy and insecure, and unlike the appendix there is no surgical procedure that can remove it.

The important difference between present-day social life and our ancestral clan life results from technology. The broad features of social life in the past evolved as adaptations to a natural environment one had relatively little power to manipulate: The sources of uncultivated food, the consequences of incest, predators, human competitors, disease, available shelter, and the necessity of cooperation for defense and hunting—all these were simply given, and over the millennia made their contributions to the human nature we now possess. In the late Pleistocene the environmental constraints which originally produced people's genetic predispositions for clan life *still confronted them each day to reinforce (or gradually change) the social systems.*

In the case of modern man, however, our culture has become our environment and selection has become "soft" because we have, among other things, banished the predatory cats and the immediate biological consequences of deviation from sexual regulations. As a result, our Pleistocene genes have become our *secret* Pleistocene inheritance: We experiment with social schemes and when we go too far, what makes us miserable is not so much the natural environment, which we have largely mastered, but the emotional needs and aversions we carry out of our tribal past. We might not have the slightest idea why society begins to go sour and people become dissatisfied, alienated, and socially destructive, while living in the midst of material prosperity and political freedom. If solutions are proposed that confine themselves to providing individuals with more money and political power, they are unlikely to touch the source of the problems.

Consider an analogy that concerns disturbing our fit with the physical environment. People, like all living things, evolved in relation to a range of environments, and those who had the most or healthiest offspring passed on characteristics suited to living in those environments. Our hominid ancestors lived in tropical and subtropical environments and when they were becoming human spread over the world; they found livable niches almost everywhere except in the air, under water, and where there was no water at all. We adapted, over hundreds of thousands of years, to the chemicals in our food, air, and the rest of our environment, meaning that those who weren't poisoned or given cancer and other diseases had better chances to pass on their genes and are, for that reason, like the people we see around us now. Actually, it is not hundreds of thousands, but many millions of years, for important adaptations are no respecters of species boundaries: We were being bred for tolerance of our chemical environments from the start, long before we were hominids or even mammals.

Now, at the end of the twentieth century, we have the power to radically change our physical environment, including the chemicals and foreign protein with which we surround ourselves, exposing us to carcinogens and poisons to which we have not had millions of years to adapt. We can understand part of the present-day increase in cancer in evolutionary terms when we hypothesize that what is carcinogenic is relative to the makeup of the creature exposed to it: If asbestos had always been as common as green leaves, the fibers constantly swirling in the wind, land creatures would have evolved lungs, if they evolved lungs at all, which were less likely to be made cancerous by asbestos. If we kept our present American urban environment stable for hundreds of thousands of years, the survivors would live in a benign environment of familiar exhaust fumes and other hydrocarbons, industrial chemicals, tobacco smoke, and food preservatives.

Other animals meet new evolutionary pressure only when it comes from external sources—glaciers, receding seas, new predators, human beings—but we are the only animal for whom sudden, "hard" selective pressure can be of our own doing. We most commonly think of the aftermath of atomic war, but we are already creating new selective pressures in these less cataclysmic ways I have described. To take a slightly whimsical example, think of the natural selection for young adults who can drive a car fast on Saturday night, often intoxicated, and of the improved competence under those conditions that 10,000 years of present-style highway slaughter would bring.

Now, I wish to extend the point about carcinogens to the subtler and more controversial realm of social and antisocial feelings, to alienation and its opposite, and to the emotions in general. Our power to experiment with our social environment can hurt us emotionally and spiritually just as our power to experiment with our chemical environment can hurt us physically. Corresponding to new chemicals, some of which are poisonous, carcinogenic, or harmful mutagens, are new ways to live together, raise our children, and pass our time, some of which make us wretched, insecure, hostile, uncaring, and alienated. If we need to hunt down bad chemicals one by one, we need to hunt down, one by one, misery-producing social settings. The analogy is close: If chemical tolerances got established by a long process of adaptation, our emotional thresholds and tolerances are adaptations to a somewhat shorter period of human and hominid social life. And if, in a brief one-hundred-year technical and economic surge, we can surround ourselves with new, disease-causing chemicals, we also can immerse ourselves in new social environments which frustrate the social emotions we need and fill us with insecurity, indifference, or hostility. Our Pleistocene inheritance can sting us in ways that seem invisible, for our emotional miseries cannot be put under a microscope like cancerous cells or brought into a lab for experiments.

There seems little doubt that in America our tribal natures are wrenched and frustrated by social processes which have altered the family, courtship, and sexual customs, changed our symbols, altered or eliminated our rituals, and in general made community and institutional loyalties more difficult to form and sustain. The automobile, large impersonal shopping centers, frequent corporate transfers from city to city, suburbs that are without stores, sidewalks, or even a mailbox, the segregation of the young from adults, the old from everyone in "golden age villages," the intentional downplaying of ceremony and communal demands on the young, and the demolition of old neighborhoods and buildings on which the memories and very self-identity of the elderly depend—all these things and more are destructive of intimate social networks without which human social animals become miserable. What emerges is the hypothesis that human lives are structured by the requirements for survival in social groups with social institutions that fall within certain limits. The key to this structure is the emotions we feel in different situations.

Sexual customs that are universal—incest taboo and pair bonding—are taught by culture and at the same time are as innate as human language and bird songs.

> In every society in the world sexual relations between siblings or parents and offspring are forbidden, abhorred, and extremely rare. . . . There is evidence . . . that this response exists not only becuase parents and society in general forbid or disapprove of such behavior but also because the individuals that might be involved themselves avoid it. Few persons could describe the developmental or learning experiences that produce this avoidance in themselves but none can deny its universality throughout the world. The exceptions are always peculiar, such as brother-sister marriages allowed only in royal lines in ancient Egypt and Hawaii, or father-daughter sexual relations in certain African tribes which are restricted to ceremonial situations associated with the father's departure on a hunt. . . . We do know that among sexual organisms all but a few peculiar species consistently outbreed. In other words, we humans share the tendency to outbreed with nearly all sexual species.[9]

Incest taboo is an example of a practice we learn more about when we consider other species. Nearly every animal that reproduces sexually has a mechanism for minimizing incest, for the reason that sex with siblings, parents, and even first cousins greatly increases the chance that the offspring will get a deadly recessive gene from both parents—a gene that is harmless if inherited from just one parent but harmful or deadly in a double dose. There are three main ways animals avoid incest. They can abandon their young: The turtle lays its eggs on the beach and swims away and the baby turtles disperse when they hatch; the moth lays its eggs on a leaf and flies away—the sexless caterpillars often stay together but when they turn into moths they disperse. Abandonment doesn't work for animals that must care for their young, such as birds and mammals. Common practice here is that the young are kicked out of the nest or lair when they reach sexual maturity, or sometimes, the parents leave them.

Neither of these mechanisms will do for the great apes and humans, who often keep their young around beyond sexual maturity. Jane Goodall, in her extended studies of chimpanzees in Tanzania, describes a female chimp named Flo who walked about accompanied by her sexually mature son. When she was in heat Flo copulated with all the males around, with the exception of her son. How does this work? Physical distancing is ruled out when family units stay together, so a plausible hypothesis, easily applicable to humans too, suggests an emotional mechanism: a lack of sexual interest, or even distaste, for those who occupy a close social and geographical space and are likely to be close relatives. In studies of unrelated young people raised communally in Israeli Kibbutzim, Joseph Shepher discovered no cases at all of intra-peer group marriages, and no heterosexual activity between native adolescents in the one Kibbutz he studied in detail. Shepher believes collective peer group education and a close physical relationship during the first six years results in sexual avoidance and exogamy.[10]

Pair bonding is a somewhat looser matter; but the evolution of sexual, romantic love between mates is, by itself, a formidable obstacle to completely casual and promiscuous sex and an indication that one side of human nature, at least, wants couples to stay together. Some people can handle recreational sex and some cannot. Some are willing to pay an emotional price, some just think they are. That there almost always is a price to pay seems beyond doubt, although it is not easy to understand why this is so or even what the exact nature of that price is. Perhaps it is part of our Pleistocene inheritance we do not yet fully understand; but as Iris Murdoch said, "there is nothing like early promiscuous sex for dispelling life's bright mysterious expectations."[11] In raising children rational parents must act on the best bet, which is that their child will be best off if he or she does *not* decontextualize sex and is fairly serious and cautious about sexual relationships.

Questions about the wise and the unwise, the legal, the moral, and the policies of a healthy society, come together in the issue of homosexuality. Presently, a man (or a woman) has a perfect legal right to be a homosexual and, if so inclined, spend his evenings in homosexual pick-up bars. Nor are there grounds for moral criticism. Just *being* a homosexual does not imply harmful or dishonorable behavior; if he obeys the law the police have no right to bother him; if he does his work and does not proselytize, society has no right to torment or even criticize him and his employer no right to fire him or delay his promotions. If he gets a terrible disease that is highly correlated with homosexual promiscuity, he deserves compassionate medical care as much as do cigarette smokers who get lung cancer or people who crashed because they drove too fast. He has a legal and moral right to *toleration*.

But for all that, toleration does not mean approval and is consistent with society's doing everything in its power to minimize the number of homosexuals and their influence on the young. The position I think reasonable is that our attitude toward homosexuals should be like our attitude toward midgets: No one ought, just because they are midgets, to question their morality or competence, be biased in employment, or harass, ridicule, or humiliate them. But there are some jobs for which a midget is naturally unsuited, such as a basketball player or the American ambassador to a sensitive third-world country. But imagine that a certain environment—a diet or smoking when very young—increased the likelihood of becoming a midget. Parents, and society in general, would do everything possible to prevent children from becoming midgets; but when some did anyway, they should fully accept them. This is a perfectly consistent position.

No parents view the possibility of their child growing up homosexual with anything but fear and dismay, for they know (or should know, the propaganda of homosexuals and relativists notwithstanding) that homosexuals are more likely to be unhappy, lonely, to miss the warmth, emotional support, security, and pride of a family, and (particularly in the case of men) have immature and unstable sex lives. Like childhood without a father, homosexuality is a cross to bear, not an "equally valid alternative life style" whose only disadvantage is the prejudice of others. Even if no one ever had the slightest disapproval of homosexuals, and you had the power to make a soon-to-be-born child homosexual or heterosexual, it would be mad to toss a coin.

It has been argued that parents' dismay at homosexuality is just the selfish desire for grandchildren to dote over. This is a difficult argument to understand. It is not as though they are forbidding children to be homosexual who want to be homosexual, much as they might from selfish reasons forbid a marriage. It is not as though being homosexual was something the child wanted, like a fast motorcycle, and the parents said No; the teenager just finds himself homosexual. He doesn't have a choice in the matter, there is nothing to forbid that hasn't already happened, and certainly parent selfishness does not come into the matter, for if the child is *not* homosexual he will not want to be. We are dealing with causes and scarcely at all with choices. It is more like fear our children will be sterile or midgets, if we thought certain environments contribute to causing these conditions.

At some major universities homosexuals, in the name of "gay rights," have demanded university-sponsored dances. The universities should do that if they wish to tell their young student body that being homosexual is as desirable a way of life as being heterosexual, getting married, and raising children. A university is free to broadcast that attitude if that is what it believes. But we know it isn't true. The proper attitude toward homosexuality is to politely ignore it, the way one ignores someone's clubbed foot. Homosexuals no doubt will be indignant and say homosexuality is a sexual preference, a life style, not a disability like a clubbed foot, and they may quote the decree of the American Psychiatric Association that homosexuality is not a pathological condition, a decree only slightly more plausible than the Roman emperor Constantine's announcement that homosexuality is the cause of earthquakes. I wonder how many of these psychiatrists would toss a coin to decide the "sexual preference" of their own sons and daughters, if a coin toss could determine the matter.

Of course, a university that rejects homosexual dances seems to be assuming that homosexuality is infectious, or at least, that some young people will be pushed over the edge by this kind of societal approval and opportunity who otherwise would not. I said earlier that forbidding a child to be homosexual is absurd. It isn't a matter of choice like deciding to go to bed with someone. But what causes it is hardly 100 percent genetic, nor can we assume the die is cast in childhood. If homosexuality is viewed with full approval, if this results in more young people experimenting, or experimenting more deeply and openly, and that in turn increases the number of committed, life-long homosexuals, then the college is giving some of its students a whole homosexual life as part of its education, and which a different policy would not have caused. Is it not possible that a number of somewhat conservative, conventional, or timid people have homosexual urges they keep to themselves all their lives, because of societal disapproval, live happy or reasonably happy married lives instead, and are the better off for it?

While different sexual practices, within limits, are found all over the world, some kind of sexual regulation or other is found everywhere. What was bizarre about American society during the past two decades was not *how* it proposed to regulate sex, but that we moved in the direction of not regulating it at all.[12] Midgley generalizes the point:

> We are free to change things within a certain range. Understanding that range is the first step on our way. By contrast, if it were true that people's emotional needs were entirely acquired, things would be black indeed for the reformer. Oppressors would only need to condition people earlier and more thoroughly to enjoy slavery; after that it would be impossible to object to it. . . . *What* customs we learn depends on chance, but *that* we learn some customs does not. There is variation in manners, in clothes and ornaments, in what is praised and blamed, in sexual customs and moral standards generally, in homes and property, in songs, dances, jokes, and stories, in how we mourn our dead, in the way our entry into adult life is marked, in forms of marriage, trading, quarreling, work, and friendship. But *that* all these things are present, and present in some definite accepted form, is something that does not vary. . . .[13]

It is obvious enough that if society is to function it must have the cooperation and the restraint of the individuals in it. I suggest the converse is equally important: If individuals are to function they need social membership and social morality, not just for protection but as an absolutely essential part of the structured life humans require if they are to live well. And insofar as socialization is part of social morality, socialization too is something individuals need for their own emotional well-being and not merely something society needs from them.

FOURTEEN
Human Nature and Society

> As the ethologists have continued to remind us—one of the distinguishing features of the species Homo sapiens is that we are social animals. Sooner or later—and in between—we need each other.
> —Urie Bronfenbrenner

> It is not only that . . . a life without piety, including piety to the past, courts grief and does damage to the life of the living individual. The respectful treatment of traditions is also enjoined on us by awareness that to refuse a tradition is not a guarantee that it will be well replaced.
> —Edward Shils

I have suggested there are ways to conduct a society which, without harming us materially or even diminishing freedom, make almost everyone miserable; and there are forms of social living which incline us to be content and cooperative even in the midst of poverty and physical insecurity. Each of these forms and practices is another knot in a human social net whose design is not entirely of our making, a sociality that supports us as much as it confines. In this chapter I wish to continue the discussion of "tribal surrogates" that sustain urban life, and of other practices that alienate us.

These hypotheses will not please people who are outraged at the very idea of human nature. Those who simply do not, *will* not, believe in human nature, are strange bedfellows indeed: Existentialists who believe that free will is everything; homosexual liberationists who like to think it an accident of culture, indeed, a mere heterosexist bias, that most people are sexually interested in members of the opposite sex; radical feminists who likewise believe that practically every human emotion comes from culture; some deeply religious people who simply never acquired the idea of man's continuity with the rest of nature;

the politically suspicious who think all motives are political and human nature a stage prop of racists, reactionaries, and warriors; and moral and social revolutionaries, mainly of the Left, who cannot abide the idea that they may have company at the helm of history in the form of gene-based limits on their ability to mold a new human personality. All these people will perceive the idea of a "Secret Pleistocene Inheritance" as a threat; to some of them, it is.

It is time to pause and consider this matter of nature and nurture. The main thing to see is that all human behavior has both innate and learned components, and calling it one or the other reflects our interests as much as anything; it does not imply an exclusive "either/or." We learn many things we are innately primed to learn, such as language and (I wish to hypothesize) socialization and ritualized social behavior. Learning them depends in turn on simpler behavior, such as babbling and imitating that involve learning only in the most minimal ways.

Even a robin building a nest learns partly by trial and error which materials to use and exactly where to put them, but its performance is nonetheless innate and it never ends up building an oriole's nest. Conrad Lorenz has given a marvelous account of how bird songs are acquired by a combination of innate capacities and learning.[1] Sometimes a poor bird, raised by the experimenter without ever hearing the song of its species, would give out with some garbled fragment of its song. Birds of other species would fetch nearly their whole song from their racial memories, and yet others would make more or less unsuccessful attempts to pick up the songs of alien species they were allowed to hear. The genetic priming was necessary but usually not sufficient; the learning was not sufficient; when we had *both* the birds learned the songs of their species. There cannot be simpler and clearer example of the need a creature has for both the innate and the learned, for nature and culture. I wish I were able to show, as simply and elegantly as Lorenz has for bird songs, the role of both in the successful raising of children, and that some children grow up like those birds who never heard their song, or who were played the wrong one.

We are genetically primed to learn, and to teach some things and not others. So the innate and the learned aren't mutually exclusive: There is even a lucrative book trade in teaching people how to perform sexual intercourse. In the case of sex (but not suckling or breathing) we are *predisposed to learn*. Learning is also required because of different roles and taboos regarding sex in different cultures. But for all that, sex is innate. So it is a mistake to say, "No, it is not innate, for look how one must learn"; a child learns how to eat and how to walk, but we are also creatures who evolved to do these things (and to teach our children how to do them). It is equally a mistake to say, "No, it is not learned, for it is universal, necessary for survival, and look at how good the evolutionary explanation is." We *evolved* to be creatures who *learn* (and are taught) to live together in cooperative groups with shared, common goods. How important a genetic component is depends on how miserable and unpredictable we become when some aspect of a society's way of life is changed and there is no materially obvious way in which things have gone wrong.

It is perfectly possible to educate members of a society in ways directly contrary to strong genetic predispositions: We might try teaching mothers never to handle their infants, or near universal homosexuality as a method of population control, or completely free incest as a logical extension of the sexual revolution; we might train children never to smile, scorn having any special affection for a regular sex partner, decree that adults never live more than six months in the same locality, make illegal all ritual and ceremony; we could segregate the old from the rest of us and segregate youths from adult life and work, never indicate to either that they are needed in any way, and never teach the young the rules, values, and traditions of their culture. If we could accomplish these things our society would die like that of the Ik or some of the uprooted American Indian tribes. We have already tried some of them and were fortunate enough to fail before it was too late. The Russians, whose ideology commits them to an almost totally plastic human nature, experimented with completely collectivistic child rearing—in its heyday mothers would be lucky to catch occasional glimpses of their children behind glass, and the Russians were forced by the misery they produced to back off.

The basic non-economic reason why "small is beautiful" is that people can remember, recognize, and be remembered in small social units more easily than in large ones; there simply are fewer faces and places. Long ago, likelihood of survival was increased for those who were emotionally at ease in such societies rather than in anonymous or widely dispersed ones. This creates biologically based size constraints on the social units in which we most easily feel at home. Reciprocal altruism, for example, depends on meeting helpers and non-helpers again and remembering them, and therefore could evolve only in middle-sized groups, not too large or small for this process to work. In our ancient brains we *feel* what is too large and too small. Perhaps we have a partial explanation (in addition to the obvious one concerning crime and safety) of the recent surge of Americans from cities to small towns, as the large cities have become more homogeneous and anonymous and the ethnic sub-units have declined.

People swarm to the burgeoning capitals of the developing nations to make their fortunes, as they did to American cities until recently; people leaving American cities do not have this economic pressure. Social units that are vastly larger than ancient clans run up against our need for familiar and comfortable turf. It is not that we cannot also love large things, such as New York, America, or humanity, but that our strongest need is for group affiliations that parallel most closely those of our past. The traditional urban solution is the neighborhood, usually individuated along ethnic lines. These neighborhoods, however ethnic, were essentially *places* and there is a risk in wantonly substituting spatially scattered communities based on function or common interests for communities based on geography: Clubs need places, clubhouses.

It is in form more than size that our prehistoric emotions recognize reflections of equally prehistoric pathways, places of shelter, ranges, and cringe at what is unfamiliar, exposed, or devoid of distinguishing marks. Middle- and low-income city dwellers are more likely to think as *theirs* a neighborhood which is a warren of familiar streets, shops, taverns, and places where they are known personally. They are less likely to develop a sense of possession for uniform housing projects, or for shopping centers whose stores have clerks whose eyes manage never to meet theirs. We should ask ourselves which of these environments is closer to how Gonds, Nagas, and Arapesh live today, and we should consider the similarities between displacing the residents of an old neighborhood in order to build a housing project and resettling a tribe.

A study compared West German children from 18 new model communities with children in older cities.

> Amid soaring rectangular shapes of apartment houses with shaded walks, big lawns and fenced-in play areas, the children for whom much of this has been designed apparently feel isolated, regimented and bored. . . . The children gauged their freedom not by the extent of open areas around them but by the liberty they had to be among people and things that excited them and fired their imagination.[2]

Urie Bronfenbrenner, in reporting this, concludes, "Much of what happens to children and families is determined by the ecology of the neighborhood in which the family lives."

By the late sixties 14,000 shopping centers had been built in the

United States. If the shopping center is huge and far away, one of the major activities of our lives, gathering provisions, takes place in an environment of strangers. Sociologists have pointed out that in this respect women have been worse off than men. Men typically work with co-workers with whom they develop tribal affiliations and a miniature moral community, whereas women who keep house and go shopping have less opportunity to do this. The collective hunting of prehistoric men continues today, equally collectively, in offices and factories. But twentieth-century housework, grocery gathering, and child tending probably are more isolating than they were in prehistoric times. Emile Durkheim comments on the minimal collective life of women in nineteenth-century France, in language not intended to give offense but less circumspect than would be used today:

> Man is actively involved in [social life], while woman does little more than look on from a distance. Consequently man is much more highly socialized than woman. His tastes, aspirations and humor have in large part a collective origin, while his companion's are more directly influenced by her organism. [Marriage] cannot simultaneously be agreeable to two persons, one of whom is almost entirely the product of society, while the other has remained to a far greater extent the product of nature. It is by no means certain that this opposition must necessarily be maintained.[3]

The loyalties we develop for our shops, offices, or companies, are not easily directed toward shopping centers. Perhaps the isolation of the housewife is a short-lived, temporary phenomenon. Things may appear to be going full circle as more and more women return to work; but not really, since this time they don't work in fields and villages with their children but downtown in offices, further isolating the children and segregating them from the world of adult work.

Very expensive gasoline or increased fear of auto emissions might stimulate the revival of small neighborhood stores, and encourage the creation of local parks and better sidewalks so that people can use baby carriages (a rare sight today). These things are not as trivial as they sound because, cumulatively, they help create a frequently traversed territory near home that contains familiar faces. As it is, neighborhood sidewalks are decrepit; newer suburbs have neither sidewalks nor local stores, requiring people to drive to mail a letter or buy a loaf of bread, which, of course, is considered evidence of their superior class status. This radical break with traditional village logistical systems for the sake of prestige has absurd consequences for retirees in Florida, who buy homes in tracts without sidewalks and three miles from the nearest store. They soon become too infirm to drive; but local stores, sidewalks, or even a bus line, would cheapen the neighborhood, so they are forced to sell and move to nursing homes sooner than they would in a neighborhood that had the traditional range of support facilities.

A community one easily identifies with and cares about is a familiar one with familiar people, and therefore needs to contain small stores. Small stores are not as anonymous as large ones because they have owners who work there, give the store a character of its own, and come to know their customers. Such businesses serve to concretely individuate a neighborhood; they enable us to say "because it's mine" and "because it's special" at the same time. Nor ought sense of possession in a neighborhood be effortless to come by. Perhaps, long ago, there were good biological reasons for not making clans too easy to join, good reasons for clannishness.

You are more likely to have strong community loyalty, other things being equal, if your community has intricacy, complex byways, clear boundaries, a name, ideosyncratic stores and businesses, all of which you know and which a stranger passing through does not know and would have to learn. You can say, "This is mine, and it does not instantly become yours just by driving in for a visit." Complexity and the sheer difficulty of learning how to get about and find things are part of the poor person's exclusivity, playing the role high property values play for the rich. Prefabrication and uniformity from neighborhood to neighborhood rob a community of its mysteries, foreclose any sense of special ownership, kill pride, and ruin the question, "What is it really like to live there?" The uniformity of a cloned neighborhood bores us; its lack of what is unique and ideosyncratic threatens our sense of self-identity; and its lack of anything that is grand, "neat," striking, or symbolic, frustrates our need to identify with something larger than ourselves and which compensates for our sense of anonymity and insignificance.

Some readers may feel impatient with talk about needs to belong to what is grand and to compensate for insignificance: The *lumpen Proletariat* and failed clerks of the world need their Hitlers and Nürnberg rallies. But is it not possible that this need is simply our innate collectivism, bred into us by a million years or more of group life, and its natural object—this "something larger than ourselves"—is the small clan and its modern surrogates in community, workplace, and neighborhood, rather than Hegel's or Hitler's conception of the state? There is nothing inherently sinister in the idea of a universal need to belong to something "larger" or "grander" than ourselves. The argument that it is sinister is the propaganda of radical individualism. The minute we acknowledge shared non-selfish values we have something larger than ourselves that we wish to possess or identify with.

Our need to belong and be caught up in shared concerns that transcend the self more easily turns sinister if we are alienated from our mainstream societies: Street gangs and other hostile sub-groups exist when mainstream collective affiliations are frustrated. The very language in which collective belonging is described often is denigrating—"compensating for insignificance," being "other directed" rather than autonomous. Expressing it in biological rather than psychological terms avoids the innuendo: We evolved a need to belong to social groups because doing so protected us from predators and helped in the hunt.

The seriousness of joining a social group is expressed in rites of initiation and in ritual and ceremony in general. Initiation affirms the value of belonging: It is a serious ceremony in which a price and a vow are exacted, and old members notified that the new entrant belongs and can be relied on. Ritual and ceremony are part of our form of life. When forced exile or an overwhelming alien society destroy them, a culture can wither and die, like that of the Ik, the Cherokee of Carolina, or African slaves in America. If cultural identity and with it a sense of individual worth is tied to an innate need for ceremony, tradition, symbols of belonging, socialization, and shared activities, then the problem those tribes faced we face too. For, ironically, from a surfeit of power and the opportunities power creates we have been dismantling the infrastructure of our own culture.

Even the abandonment of simple ceremonies is something we do at our peril. Suppose getting married requires paying ten dollars to the state for a blood test and nothing more: Your cancelled check is your proof of marriage and neither church nor state is interested in the name of the person you marry. Various people—bohemians, the alienated, beady-eyed utilitarians—will say, "Why not?" But it is through ritual and ceremony that the social will speaks; when they are stilled, it is stilled, and then we will care less, if we care anything at all, about the institutions on which a viable society depends.

Most animals are creatures of habit, insecure when things are unfamiliar, and there is little reason to think this is learned in humans but innate in all the other creatures of the world. In all animals that have any emotions at all, we should expect natural selection for an emotional makeup that reinforces behavior that did not get us eaten, injured, or starved. The conservative nature of tribal life fixes on the familiar. When we recognize this as an emotional heritage we carry today, one thing we should expect is that a sense of neighborhood belonging depends on the stabililty and continuity of the physical environment.

Thus the bulldozer is an enemy of community and it is better, when our aim is community building, to repair the old than demolish and rebuild. The importance of the familiar seems to increase with a person's age: An aged person's sense of belonging, even his sense of self-identity, commonly comes to depend more and more on memories of what occurred in the physical environment—it is the places where things happened that become more vivid as current happenings become less so. Like an old cat that for years has sniffed every square foot of the urban acre it wanders in, it is common enough for an elderly person to become very distressed when the old neighborhood is wiped away by bulldozers. Harry Truman of Mt. St. Helens fame, who lies buried in the volcano because he wouldn't leave home, is not all that unusual.

Corporations strengthen community loyalties when they transfer executives less frequently, the corporate transfer being another enemy of community. The mobility of Americans has been exaggerated, however, and holds more for some groups than others: American cities and towns are full of people who have lived there all their lives and whose parents and even grandparents are no more than fifteen miles away. One way staying put is relevant to sense-of-community concerns the relations between professional and community service people and their clients. There are reasons why police, clergy, judges, and even schoolteachers and firefighters are posted away from their home neighborhoods and are moved about: It combats favoritism, cronyism, and in the case of police, opportunities for corruption. But the negative consequences may outweigh the advantages. When these service personnel work for years in one place, preferably in their home neighborhoods, it reinforces their commitment, personalizes their relations with their clients—another tribal analogue—and produces an atmosphere of stability as well as familiar faces to which young people growing up in the neighborhood feel answerable.

When we think of good and bad neighborhoods to live in we usually pay insufficient attention to the bonds between community and aesthetics; and when we do attend to the aesthetic we thoroughly relativize it to personal taste and to associations with wealth and power. Aesthetics in the sense I mean is the whole realm of how things look: If one way things look pleases and another displeases, that is a matter of the artistic, of aesthetics. It is also a perfectly objective feature of a community: Slums *look* bad, and that is one important reason why people do not enjoy living in them. Wealthy neighborhoods look good. They do not look good just because the neat lawns, trees, and large, well-maintained houses are signs of wealth, it being the association with the idea of wealth that pleases.

To think this way is to get things backwards: Our fixation on wealth and power makes it hard to believe that other things have effects in their own right. The wealthy can *choose* the way their neighborhoods look and if trash and rusted autos in the front yard and the elimination of trees and orderly greenery pleased them, then *that* would be the look of wealth. The shame or disgust people feel toward a neighborhood that is shabby, dirty, monotonous, and devoid of green spaces is not just disgust at poverty and powerlessness, but disgust at the shabbiness and monotony. The visual appearance of a neighborhood is in itself a significant determinant of whether people like or dislike it, it is not just a symbol of "more practical matters" such as wealth.

Outdoor aesthetics, however, merges with the practical in the sense that what looks nice very probably has its causal basis in what makes (or long ago made) it easier for us to survive: What is dirty or littered can cause disease, injury, or ruin clothing, what is overgrown can get in one's way and hide snakes, and what is monotonous and uniform lacks navigational landmarks and also threatens one's sense of self-identity.

Psychologically, what is disorderly, dirty, and undecorated with careful artistic expression suggests proprietors who are sloppy, dispirited, or even dangerous. This is why the dispute over "graffiti art" in and on the New York subway cars is not just an artistic dispute. Those who, like the mayor of New York, fight against graffiti are fighting for the city's self-respect. While on a symposium with some of New York's noted graffiti artists and the intellectuals who praise them, I had explained to me the mystique of graffiti art. The art intellectuals, who lived in neat suburbs 500 miles from the New York subway, talked about graffiti as the only way the disadvantaged can express themselves. The artists said it was fun, that it only was pure when done at night in the subway yards where the transit police would chase them, and nowadays it was a good way to start an art career. The graffiti artists who have become successful now paint in studios. If a customer demands authenticity some will prop a stretched canvas against a wall in a littered vacant lot, spray-paint a piece of decorative art, and sell it in an East Village or SoHo gallery to an Upper East Side collector.

It is unimportant to argue whether graffiti is art, or even good art; I am inclined to think almost anything can be art if enough people wish to call it so. The point is, whatever else it may be, it is tolerated vandalism. It is the failure of society to defend itself against the desecration of its public possessions, it is a message to the marginally loyal that at the center is a failure of conviction or resolve. The toleration of and apologies for filth in Times Square and graffiti on the subways is a little gesture toward societal suicide; it is a battle won by radical individualism in its war with civilized society.

The grand and the impressive are species of the aesthetic, and our need for what is grand is not just weakness but craving for identity-creating affiliations. It is a collective, social need, not an egoistic one. The mechanisms by which tribal affiliation is reinforced in the modern state have included conquering armies, strutting bands, pomp and rigamarole, frequent contrived crises, and impressive monuments and structures. But the physical focal points of social belonging need not be warlike or in any way sinister; they commonly include skyscrapers, a handsome downtown, or a sports arena and team.

Utilitarians and Marxists will say we are being swindled, that the city fathers and ruling circles are simply selling more people's opium. But the fact is that community possessions of which we can be proud usually satisfy us more lastingly than do larger diameter sewer lines— the cold porridge utilitarians say is good for us. It is best, of course, if the symbolic and grand is also useful. The Moscow subway is in all these respects a creation of genius. Muscovites are immensely proud of it and their pride transfers to their city and, their rulers hope, to their government. The subway stations are beautiful and the service first-rate—if an escalator breaks down it is repaired immediately, the whole system receiving first-class maintenance in dramatic contrast with the rest of the city. Visually it is serious and formal, with busts of Lenin or other communist saints and martyrs in every station, and aurally ritualized, the same recorded voice on every train in every station saying, "Caution, the door is closing. The next station is. . . ." Each train has the same number of cars exactly filling each platform. Like a nightly dance in the jungle these orderly repetitions project a sense of grandeur, permanence, and security.

The Moscow subway is not vandalized or desecrated. To this we may respond, "Ha! They will be pounced on at once and carted off to Siberia." Not quite: Fellow passengers will pounce, they almost certainly will shout, scold, shame you, and perhaps hold you until a militiaman comes. It would take immense nerve, or tremendous hostility, to deface or vandalize an American subway car or station if it looked like Moscow's and the people were likely to react like Muscovites. And these is still more to it. Is it not possible, as the economist Wilford L'Esperance suggested, that people naturally respect what is excellent? That is, quite apart from the community pride excellence engenders, that people easily tell a thing of structural and functional excellence from the shoddy and the mediocre and are less inclined to smash or deface it? And by excellent I mean the excellently done: substantial, hence probably expensive, and of excellent materials and workmanship, I do not mean artistically excellent or "important" in the opinion of art critics.

What would be the New York response to subway stations and service that were up to the standards of the Moscow subway? Those who are ruled by hostility would have to be restrained, and we would be at some disadvantage because we are not trained as children to intervene, to mob the predator. Perhaps those who yearn for things around them worthy of pride would help. Several years ago a professional plasterer repaired a ceiling in a rental house I own in a lower-middle-class area of the city and dumped his debris in the back yard rather than haul it away. When I complained, he was indignant because he felt, in the unconscious channels of his brain, that he did what was fitting and right for the neighborhood. The street *was* a bit seedy and he would never have done it in the suburbs.

Public art is everything from statuary and architectural embellishment to the design of a park and its benches. What is important about public art is not that some critic thinks it is "important," but that, like all original art, it is unique and something nobody else has. Hence artists (including architects), because they aim to make what the world never saw before, are the people who best can individuate communities, parks, and buildings. If, as I have argued, it is difficult to have sense of pride and possession toward a "clone," we need the artist to help make what is ours publicly distinguishable from what is not.

This is a social role contemporary painters and sculptors unfortunately reject. Architects and landscape architects, because their work is lived in and walked on, have little choice but to merge their self-expression with the way of life of their society. Painters and sculptors do not and that is the problem. Fine artists are alienated professionally: Their work often ignores or mocks the social world around them; it has lost connection with the concerns of the society in which they move and which supports them. Medieval painters served God and society; nineteenth-century painters sought to capture reality. Each was motivated by something outside themselves, but most contemporary painters and sculptors shrink reality to the geometrical point that is their ego and if they notice society at all it is to be its judge, not its servant. What interests them all too often, is not the world, or even the problem of understanding the world, but the autonomy of their creative acts.

Soviet public art is commemorative and inspirational. Moscow is full of granite and bronze heros, museums display some vast canvases of dark-suited party officials. American art is free, but it is hardly inspirational and often is out of joint with the physical, social, and intellectual ambience of the park, lobby, or campus for which it was commissioned. Art mirrors and exaggerates the spirit of the times. There is no clearer expression of hyper-individualism than the inward, self-centered, and sometimes downright dangerous art fads of the '60s and '70s.

Humans are almost certainly territorial animals and our sense of proprietorship toward a neighborhood or nation creates solidarity with those with whom we share the territory. Most of our strongest group loyalties are tied not only to language and religion but to geography—to neighborhoods, hunting and foraging territories, villages and nations. There is evidence that people whose sense of security is fragile cling to home territories. Elderly people resist being uprooted; delinquent youths fear strange environments and tend to seek work in their immediate neighborhoods.[4] For numerous species of animals a territory is where it feels safe, knows its way about and isn't lost, and finds the emotional resources to defend itself with ferocity. What moves Conrad Lorenz's territorial fish to defend their spot of sandy aquarium bottom and moved Poles to fight invading Germans and Russians in the autumn of 1939 are similar evolutionary products.

Robert Audrey was thought overbold to assert that human territoriality supports the institution of private property, thus explaining why Soviet collective farms are so less efficient than the private plots of Soviet farmers.[5] Nevertheless, on a smaller scale, the householder feels possessive of his yard, carefully marks its borders, chases out trespassing children, and usually takes good care of it. Is the suburbanite's garden or the fenced city yard that different from the "turf" of a street gang? And is it not plausible that these are cultural overlays on territorial impulses as innate as the boundary-marking of an Alaskan wolf? Because for social animals a territory can "belong" to more than one individual, it is historically a primary basis on which "mine" becomes "ours," as when I feel possessive of my neighborhood and not just my yard and thus join a clan.

Human beings the world over are strongly moved by ritual and ceremony. In America there is no cause of social cohesion and pro-social behavior so important and at the same time so ridiculed as ritual and ceremony. The parades, rallies, weddings, funerals, and religious services of modern society move us as deeply and effectively as a New Guinea tribe is by its dances and ceremonies. For each of us they serve—and are exploited—to pull us out of our selfish concerns and make us willing to do almost anything in the name of tribe or nation. When a person speaks casually and informally he speaks for himself; when he speaks in a ritual or ceremony the tribe, its values, and its traditions speak through him. How it came about so universally to be this way I do not know. It is a sign of a strong, healthy culture that its rituals are unaffected by modern technology and civilization. The smiling Balinese Hindus, unaffected and unembarrassed by the Indonesian Muslims and the ever larger swarms of European and Japanese tourists, every day make tens of thousands of ceremonial, public offerings to their numerous gods.

It is to be expected that individualist thinkers in modern democracies view ritual as their natural enemy. The anthropologist Hervé Varenne, echoing Tocqueville's observations 150 years earlier, remarked that modern democrats everywhere show a strong antipathy for anything that smacks of ritualism.[6] They hate secular ritual for tapping emotions that compete with and overpower their principles and ideals. The power ritual and ceremony have to move us lies outside the individual, its engine is group egoism, not egoism. Ceremonies are levers attached to emotions more ancient than our species; when pulled they call up group loyalties that shoulder aside self-love and in a tribal crisis such as war make us interrupt careers, take great personal risks, and forget personal crises, neuroses, or thoughts of suicide. Thus, in the contest for control of a person, ritual and ceremony do battle with egoism and individualism.

Excessive individualism logically and inexorably leads to the elimination of ritual, which diminishes the social bonds. When reformers banish ritual from schools, juvenile justice procedures, and community life—on the grounds they are useless and more suitable for dictators and New Guinea tribes—they banish an essential element of human social life. Juvenile authorities who completely shed their formality risk shedding their authority and influence and becoming, in the eyes of the delinquent, just more individuals preaching as have dozens before. Varenne says:

> The rejection of ritual in the modern world . . . is based on a false premise: that social life is possible without ritual. In fact, what distinguishes men and women from animals and machines is their ability to symbolize and to act through collective rituals. Such rituals express in artistic, dramatic form the values that are most important to the persons who perform the rituals. . . .[7]

When I participate in a ceremony I imply that I take seriously the enterprise of which it is part. If, as innate sociality implies, valuing oneself depends on valuing something besides oneself, a life devoid of ceremony and ritual is likely to be a life the individual does not take seriously. The connection with values is easily overlooked because we closet them away out of public view and think we can have common values without their public expression. "To be important and to be learned, values must be acted out or expressed—not only in words, but also in gestures, posture, etiquette, demeanor, and, indeed, ritual."[8]

The most telltale mark of anomie and alienation is the abandonment of ceremony, for everyone senses that to continue the ceremonies would publicly attribute worth and commitment one doesn't feel. We can locate alienated individuals and families by noting the abandonment of ritual and ceremony. The deep connection between ceremony and earnest commitment can be seen in people who simply *cannot* bring themselves, say, to salute a flag or sing an anthem. It is why oaths of allegiance are worth bothering with. People say, can't one just lie? But an oath is not just a promise, it is a *ceremony*. It is a public *act* of allegiance, not just a promise of allegiance. When we want to mock an institution we mock its ceremonies, when we cease to respect it or take it seriously we withdraw from its ceremonies, and when we see it has none to begin with we conclude that no one thinks it is worth much. Conversely, getting people to participate in school or civic ceremonies is a cause of their accepting the school or community as *theirs* and as an object of respect. When a community asks people to participate in a ritual, it acknowledges them as members and expects a commitment in return.

The expectation of commitment is psychologically sound if the target population is appropriate. Why these connections exist is difficult to understand, but perhaps the explanation is something like the following. The grain of truth in those sententious, oleaginous, self-help books which say "smile!", when you feel like drowning yourself, is that feelings are causally tied to their natural physical expressions: The one is very difficult without the other, but if you can bring off the behavior it drags the feeling along. That is why it is so fanciful, in literature, to imagine people who cry when they are happy and laugh when they are sad. If, as the evidence strongly indicates, participating in an institution's ceremonies and prizing the institution are similarly tied together, each difficult to bring off without the other, then it is less likely that ritual and ceremony are cultural inventions, and more likely, for reasons we do not fully understand, that they are expressions of human nature.

This is admittedly speculative: Ritual and ceremony are *natural* behavioral expressions of commitment and sense-of-belonging, as a smile is a natural expression of pleasure. Perhaps they can be traced back to the courtship rituals and territory-marking rituals of many species of animals, back to times before we were human; but that is a speculation that cannot be pursued here. Whatever the basis is for this linkage, requiring young people to participate in ceremonies in school, church, ROTC, their families, or their communities, will be an effective cause of loyalty to the social units that own the ceremonies. This only sounds problematic when put in theoretical terms; everybody accepts it in practical cases: We feared the effects of Hitler's giant youth rallies and we routinely utilize the power of pep rallies and marriage ceremonies.

The anthropologist Ralph Ross stated the essential social functions of ritual and ceremony:

> [Rituals] permit us to share the deep emotional commitments which are the cement of society. Secular rituals share with religious ceremony the elements of celebration, dedication, and consecration. . . . The familiarity of the ritual, the others who perform it at the same time, the feeling that we are connected with something larger than ourselves, that we are accepted, that we have a place where we belong—these . . . are in some ways the most important things about them.[9]

A psychologist came to a similar conclusion in listing the functions of ritual:

1. Providing mental anchorage and orientation.
2. Boundary making and role differentiation, as between the sacred and profane, in-group and out-group.
3. Conflict reduction, tension release, and the allaying of anxiety, as in sports, expiatory acts, etc.
4. Bonding and linking the individual to society, providing a sense of solidarity and membership through shared participation.[10]

We might add lending earnestness to one's life and protection against a sense of meaninglessness. Ritual and ceremony are preeminent proof of group belonging because they are not just evidence but actual *instances* of participation and belonging. The herding behavior of Thompson's gazelle, the evening meal in suburbia, and a High Mass all are rituals and, simultaneously, instances of group participation. Varenne suggests we can know what we really believe in "*only* through evident symbolic and ritual acts. Such acts, when they are effective, are usually not termed ritual, and may appear to be simple routines, or habits, or even spontaneous. But they are public, they involve others, and they appear in essentially predictable fashions."[11] Varenne is not the first thinker to see that routine is ritual; psychiatrists for a long time have called pathological routines "rituals." The anthropologist I. M. Lewis sums up the ways in which ritual is a part of the very essence of our sociality:

> So we see that ritual ... perpetuates that sense of continuity and changelessness to which so many traditional societies attach such importance. In the same spirit ritual can also be employed to encapsulate and dramatize duty, obedience, and obligation. In general, the ethnographic evidence suggests that those who perform collective public or "communal" rituals do so because they share other highly valued interests. The composition of a ritual congregation is thus a rough and ready guide to the range of collaboration and commitment in a community. People here are standing up and may be counted. They wish to be seen. If old so-and-so is not at X's funeral or Y's wedding without good excuse, the absence is significant: it represents a gesture of disrespect, an indication that the missing guest is outside the bounds of current "togetherness." This, of course, is why people choose the most widely publicized rituals to stage dramatic "walk-outs". . . . Many anthropologists ... see the principal function of communal ritual to be the "expression" or reaffirmation of sentiments of collective loyalty. People assemble ritually, it is argued, *in order to show* and further reinforce their existing sense of identity and cohesion.[12]

Psychotherapists and drug therapists have begun to understand and use ritual. At San Francisco's Haight-Ashbury Free Medical Clinic, workers observed the rituals associated with heroin use and then developed a competing, ceremonial detoxification process they called "rites of passage."[13] More recent work at George Washington University Medical Center concluded that alcoholic families whose family rituals had waned or been altered were more likely to pass on alcoholism to their children than alcoholic families whose rituals remained intact.

Family ritual is little appreciated, seldom studied, and very likely of immense importance to our well-being. If the family is a miniature tribe and moral community, and tribes need ritual, we can expect family rituals and ceremonies to be important features of happy, stable families with secure and socially well-integrated children. Almost anyone will, on reflection, be able to think of examples from one's own experience or the families of friends.

One of the marks of the liberated, permissive family we were asked to admire in the recent past is its casualness. We were to "hang loose" and go our own ways; rules and structure made one "uptight." Casualness and the emphasis on children's rights diminished family ritual. The result was children who passed through a family life that had been divested of ritual and who, looking back several years later, found it harder to view their growing up with satisfaction. Casualness and informality in the important social activities of one's life constitute a psychological blunder of the first magnitude. It strips them of dignity, meaning, and seriousness.

Many family rituals are fairly standard from family to family—going to church, birthday and holiday celebrations, and so on. The interesting ones are unique to a family. Some evolve and become family traditions, others can simply be invented, on the spot, by a parent who sees that family rituals bring to the children and the whole family a sense of magic and earnestness. The idea of a family ritual, minimally, is keeping something routinized to a fixed procedure, time, and place, and the requirement of participation by relevant family members. All examples are silly and boring to outsiders, as silly as Shriners' rituals, baptism, Christmas trees, or cheerleaders.

Every attempt should be made to understand what makes families flourish, for particularly in our black slums the nuclear family is an endangered species, while nonetheless there is strong evidence it is important to the normal development of children. The family is our most ancient society and the different species of love that bind families together are neither mysteries nor illusions but obvious evolutionary products. Consider infants, and the reason why they are not all strangled. Infants are shrieking, useless, mess-making, demanding creatures. Child abuse by a father who has just lost his job and spends a sweltering summer night in a one-room apartment with a colicky, screaming infant is something most of us can comprehand. Yet infants are cared for in the most trying circumstances because parental love evolved by natural selection. Otherwise no one in their right minds would care for infants.

Romantic, sexual love evolved as one of the reinforcers of pair bonding, which is another mechanism for the lengthy care young humans require. As the ethologist Irenaus Eibl-Eibesfeldt put it, "The roots of love are not in sexuality, although love makes use of it for the secondary strengthening of the bond."[14] It is a biological fact and not a cultural convention that a man and woman who copulate with each other on a regular basis tend to have strong feelings for one another including love, possessiveness, and if there are rivals, jealousy. To some people this is one more inconvenience that attends sex, like venereal disease, plaguing couples who try non-possessive sexual relations. But the purpose of sexual love is collaboration in the care of children, and the purpose of sex itself is to create genetic diversity. From a biological point of view sex is a tool with several uses, not an end in itself.

FIFTEEN

Race

> The most formidable evil threatening the future of the United States is the presence of the blacks on their soil. From whatever angle one sets out to inquire into the present embarrassments or future dangers facing the United States, one is almost always brought up against this basic fact.
> —Alexis de Tocqueville

> My optimism is based upon the belief that this society cannot continue and function effectively, in the latter part of the twentieth century, the beginning of the twenty-first century, with the cancer of an oppressed, rejected, depressed underclass in its cities. I have given up believing society is going to do something about the black underclass, because of moral concerns. I do believe this society is going to save itself, is going to do something about the black underclass because it's going to have one damn fiscal, urban crisis after another, until it does it.
> —Kenneth T. Clark

A society can commit suicide and still be there, going about its business, as dead as can be; for the people in it don't fall down dead and the courts and schools do not suddenly vanish. But a society that commits suicide is one nobody wants to live in and children raised in it are very likely to grow up ruined. Our worst slums, most of them black, are dead societies, the vital signs of societal life—ceremony, care for the look of things, supervision of the young, family pride and honor, and sense-of-community—having stopped. In our mostly black, urban slums are large numbers of young people who simply do not participate in the complex procedures by which young people, throughout the world, are made members of their tribes and moral communities: They are not socialized at all.

In the United States the lives of whites, blacks, and to a lesser extent Native Americans, depend on one another to a degree most people do not recognize. Just one aspect of this is the dependence of a person's self-concept both on the health of his nested societies and on whether they accept him. It is a testimony to the genius of Tocqueville that he saw these relationships with such clarity, and saw the difference between two kinds of social destruction.

> In one blow oppression has deprived the descendants of the Africans of almost all the privileges of humanity. The United States Negro has lost even the memory of his homeland; he no longer understands the language his fathers spoke; he has abjured their religion and forgotten their mores. Ceasing to belong to Africa, he has acquired no right to the blessing of Europe; he is left in suspense between two societies and isolated between two peoples, sold by one and repudiated by the other; in the whole world there is nothing but his master's hearth to provide him with some semblance of a homeland. . . . The Negro makes a thousand fruitless efforts to insinuate himself into a society that repulses him; he adapts himself to his oppressors' tastes, adopting their opinions and hoping by imitation to join their community. From birth he has been told that his race is naturally inferior to the white man and almost believing that, he holds himself in contempt. He sees a trace of slavery in his every feature, and if he could he would gladly repudiate himself entirely.[1]

The Indian, on the other hand, has a culture to remember:

> In contrast, the pretended nobility of his origin fills the whole imagination of the Indian. He lives and dies amid these proud dreams. Far from wishing to adapt his mores to ours, he regards barbarism as the distinctive emblem of his race, and in repulsing civilization he is perhaps less moved by hatred against it than by fear of resembling the Europeans.[2]

The one group was transported, and as slaves inevitably had the closest social and economic interactions with their masters, the other was simply conquered and pushed away. The Indians clung to their culture, but a third-generation African slave had almost nothing African to remember. The Indians, like the Ik, watched their culture—their tribes—gradually die before their eyes, while the Africans, with no past to cling to, were emotionally free to become part of whatever the white man would permit. In the 1830s Tocqueville saw the difference between the quick death of African culture and resultant orphan status of blacks, and the long, debilitating sickness of Indian culture:

> In its dealings with the North American Indians, the European tyranny weakened their feeling for their country, dispersed their families, obscured their traditions, and broke their chain of memories; it also changed their customs and increased their desires beyond reason, making them more disorderly and less civilized than they had been before. At the same time, the moral and physical condition of these peoples has constantly deteriorated, and in becoming more wretched, they have also become more barbarous. Nevertheless, . . . although they can destroy them, [the Europeans] have not been able to establish order or to subdue them. . . . All the Indian tribes who once inhabited the territory of New England . . . now live only in men's memories. . . . I have met the last of the Iroquois; they were begging.[3]

In each case there is the killing of a culture, with the attendant spiritual, moral, and even physical deteriorioation of the individuals in these cultures, but by very different means: In the one case, before your very eyes, with language intact, romanticized memories of a way of life, and sacred rituals reduced to tourist attractions. In the other, a culture destroyed without a trace, the memories, language, and ceremonies wiped out long before you were born. One can murder nearly all of a people without murdering their culture and one can murder a culture without murdering the people in it. In the former case, as with Jews, the survivors can flourish; but in the latter they languish.

The Indian lived for the past, the black slave for a future of equality with his masters. The past is irretrievable, but there is always a future. This is one reason why the American Indian problem is more intractable than the Negro problem: Indian culture is only half dead, making full integration and Indian reservations equally unacceptable. Whereas blacks, having been culturally orphaned, have no genuine culture of their own to oppose to full Americanization, only that which comes from their history of slavery and discrimination.

A century and one half later American society remains tormented and threatened by the problem of race. If, tonight in our sleep, every shred of race prejudice drops away from every American, white and black, it will still be so. The problem that plagues us today, particularly regarding the black underclass in urban slums, is what the sociologist William Julius Wilson has called "historical discrimination"—which means, simply, the consequences of the past.

Is it possible, thinking of the black urban underclass, that what makes the Indian problem intractable is now beginning to make the Negro problem equally so? Are black slums becoming like Indian reservations?—we decide that the black slum has its own culture, not to be disturbed, and we simply leave the blacks to stew there, like Indians in their reservations? Apart from the difference that black slums are right in our midst and not in faraway deserts, thinking this way commits a historical fallacy: There is no black American culture to disturb, on a par with Indian culture, but just a slum way of life that is wholly the product of slavery and discrimination. "Getting rid of the ghetto" is not like "getting rid of the reservations": One is not killing a culture, not even a sick one.

In 1950, 18 percent of black families were female-headed; in 1969, the proportion rose to 27 percent; in 1973 it was 35 percent, in 1983 more than 50 percent. The out-of-wedlock birth rate for blacks under 18 years old is eight times as high as the rate for whites under 18. In the Central Harlem health district in 1983, 79.9 percent of the babies were born out of wedlock. As Ann Hulbert describes it,

> 56 percent of all black babies are born out of wedlock, almost 40 percent of them to teenagers. Those single mothers and their children, whose numbers have been growing rapidly for two decades, are being left behind in poverty while black married couples are moving into the middle class.[4]

Crime in black slums worsened during the twenty years of the civil rights revolution during which the black middle class grew. The increases in crime and fatherless families cannot be wholly explained by a race discrimination that surely did not worsen during that period. Sociologist William Julius Wilson argued, amidst controversy, for what he called the declining significance of race in the black slums.

> . . . it would be difficult indeed to comprehend the plight of inner-city blacks by exclusively focusing on racial discrimination. For in a very real sense, the current problems of lower-class blacks are substantially related to fundamental structural changes in the economy. A history of discrimination and oppression created a huge black underclass, and the technological and economic revolutions have combined to insure it a permanent status. By the same token, it would also be difficult to explain the rapid economic improvement of the more privileged blacks by arguing that the traditional forms of racial segregation and discrimination still characterize the labor market in American industries.[5]

One needs, Wilson suggests,

> to beat down the mythology developed by the black intelligentsia: blacks regardless of their station in life have a uniform experience in a racist society. This is pure mythology; it effectively obscures the unique problems experienced by the black poor in this period of our advanced industrial society. . . . It is not privileged black college graduates who are experiencing a sharp rise in unemployment, a decline in labor force participation.

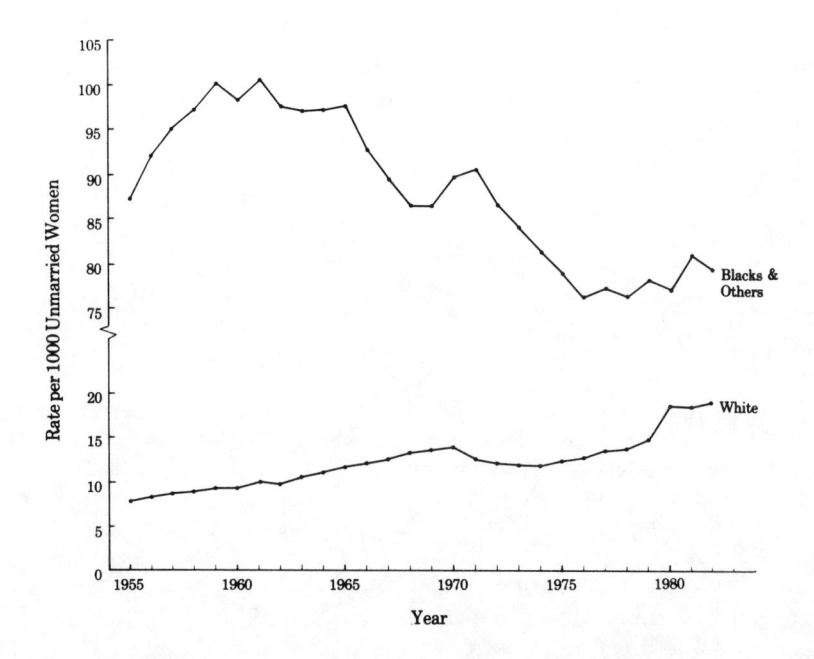

FIGURE 15. Out-of-Wedlock Birth Rates, by Race

The difference between rates of out-of-wedlock births for blacks and whites is very great. The white rate is rising rapidly, that for blacks has actually declined. The recent attention to the enormous proportion of blacks born out of wedlock is not because it has just been noticed, or is a new phenomenon, as is the case with whites. It is hard not to surmise that no one cared, until links with serious problems for these children were publicized, and the out-of-wedlock birth rate for whites also began to skyrocket.

Data from *U.S. Statistical Abstracts* and *Historical Statistics of the U.S.*

Criminologist James Q. Wilson and others have also argued for the decreased importance of racial discrimination: "Indeed, much of what passes for 'race prejudice' today may be little more than class prejudice, with race used as a rough indicator of approximate social class."[6] Of course, using the race of an individual as a "rough indicator" of social class, where being in that social class counts against you, is still race prejudice.

However, with the exception of William Julius Wilson and a few others, black intellectuals say black progress is an illusion, that racism is just as strong but takes different and subtler forms, and affirmative action and the black middle class have not gone beyond tokenism.[7] Do they really believe this or is it strategy? Do they think that if they admit to real progress whites who have helped will call it a day? Are they just not about to forgive after these 300 years, hence not about to admit any decent behavior by whites? Or is it fear of a transference of responsibility for ghastly black slum conditions from whites back to themselves, to the extent discrimination is less of a force? I think it is all of these.

But anyone who, like myself, grew up in Chicago in the '40s and early '50s *knows* they are wrong. One needs to jog memory, to the time when nearly everyone referred to blacks as niggers; when you never saw a black person in an office or behind the counter, but only Pullman porters, laborers, janitors, maids; when most whites thought blacks smelled bad inherently; when a black person could not buy a drink or a meal without going to a black neighborhood; and when the police paid only the slightest attention, if any at all, to black crime victims.

The idea that the cause of the black urban underclass is innate mental inferiority is still widely believed, in my opinion, but seldom mentioned in public. Many intellectuals and public officials with impeccable liberal credentials believe it, but do not think they are racists because they do not harbor hostile thoughts toward blacks and they sincerely condemn discrimination. They need to look up the word "racism" in the dictionary. Actually, a mental difference of fifteen IQ points (one white/black innate difference that has been proposed) probably is inadequate to explain the black crime and heroin statistics, the desertion and illegitimacy rates, and the sordidness of the worst of the black slums.

But the problem is not, in the first place, one that has to do with innate intelligence. What causes the continuation of the black underclass is not lack of intelligence, and only partly the technological revolution that William J. Wilson mentions. It is instead an almost complete absence of socialization into civil society, that is, into a moral community in which people share a work ethic, social morality, personal virtues, mutual trust, and personal accountability. Indeed, relatively slow-witted or even retarded whites, when socialized into a supportive community that treats them fairly, assures them they belong and gives them an opportunity to be useful, are scarcely less likely than people of normal intelligence to be decent, hard-working, law-abiding citizens. It is highly probable that a major cause—perhaps *the* major cause—of the lack of socialization of slum blacks is the destruction of the black nuclear family.

Socially suicidal practices that have been more tolerated in the black slums than elsewhere have to do with families and sex. A satisfying society depends on stable families which make their children know they are loved, cared for, and closely watched over—families that work at internalizing in their children rules, good character traits, and a willingness to accept discipline and the answer "No." Most people have always known, without any need for data from expensive surveys and experiments, that young children raised without both parents (or parent substitutes) are at risk. Many, such as Urie Bronfenbrenner, assumed that father absence is more harmful to young boys than girls; but nobody knows this for sure because the effect of father absence on girls has not been studied enough. Reporting on a study he made of middle-class American adolescents, Bronfenbrenner said,

> Perhaps because it was more pronounced, absence of the father was more critical than that of the mother, particularly in its effect on boys. Similar results have been reported in studies of the effects of father absence among soldiers' families during World War II, in homes of Norwegian sailors and whalers, and households with missing fathers both in the West Indies and the United States. In general, father absence contributes to low motivation for achievement, inability to defer immediate rewards for later benefits, low self-esteem, susceptibility to group influence (e.g., children with absent fathers are more likely to "go along with the gang"), and juvenile delinquency. All of these effects are much more marked for boys than for girls.
>
> [Father absence] not only affects the behavior of the child directly but also influences the mother in the direction of greater over-protectiveness. The effect of both of these tendencies is especially critical for boys. Children from father-absent homes, at least initially, are more submissive, dependent, effeminate, and susceptible to group influence, with the later course of development being determined by the character of the group in which the child finds himself. Thus in lower-class Negro families, where father absence is particularly common, the typically passive and dependent boy readily transfers his attachment to the gang, where, to earn and keep his place, he must demonstrate his toughness and aggressiveness.[8]

As reported by the National Association of Elementary School Principals, a 1980 survey of 19,000 elementary and high school students revealed that children living with only one parent are twice as likely as other students to get "D" and "F" grades and to become high school dropouts. The report goes on to say that in 1980 there were 12 million one-parent children in the schools. Low achievement was 40 percent for one-parent children and 24 percent for two-parent children. The high school expulsion rate was three times as high and the dropout rate twice as high for single-parent children.

There are problems long known to be correlated with broken homes, which almost always means fatherless homes: There are higher rates of crime, delinquency, and psychosexual maladies. Since fully half of young black children are growing up without fathers, it is not implausible to suggest that this fact alone accounts for much of the black crime, school dropouts, and emotional disorders, and that a resuscitation of the black family would do much to reverse the situation. It is not obvious that a concerted, multifaceted effort to create and preserve two-parent black families would fail, since no such attempt has been made. It is not just a matter of jobs (though creating more jobs plainly would help) since the progressive destruction of the black nuclear family since 1950 is not paralleled by a proportionate decrease in black employment.

One reason why there has been no great rush to rescue the black nuclear family is that many educators and social welfare people think it doesn't matter. They think that whether one has two parents or one, a communal family, lives in a promiscuous or sexually conservative environment, is homosexual or heterosexual, has middle-class values or different ones, or gets pregnant as an unmarried teenager—that all these modes of social life are just different, not better or worse than anything else. They are lifestyles with no objective merit or demerit, their value relative to each individual's "value system," and in a democracy to be accorded equal rights and respect. According to this way of thinking, school books and the media ought not to portray one style of life as though it were superior or the only correct way to live.

People have the legal right to lead lives such that, if everyone lived like that, our society would disintegrate; they are ways of life the society encourages at its peril. In an individualist democracy the boundary of the legal extends way beyond the boundaries of the wise, the moral, the socially desirable. If these boundaries coincide, we have complete paternalism, incompatible with an open society: Everything judged unwise, immoral, or socially undesirable is made a crime. The rulers have made the fundamental decision to give the people what is good for them, not what they want. Tempting to Americans is the other side of the same coin: Nothing is better or worse than anything else so long as it is legal. These are two ways in which law swallows up morality and wisdom, which is a kind of parricide since law is the child of social morality and has neither point nor justification without it.

In an individualist society we easily confuse the immoral and the unwise with matters of law and rights; as though, if we do not have good grounds for making some behavior illegal it is not open to criticism. Often, people whose political or social views are criticized as stupid, wrong, or harmful protest that they have a right to their views and that their critics are trying to censor or jail them. But the critic usually is out to refute them, or ridicule their position, not have them arrested or censored, public refutation in any case being more effective. Presently, an unmarried teenage girl has a perfect *legal* right to get pregnant again and again, and have the welfare department support her, her illegitimate children, and her children's illegitimate children. But she is foolish and harms everyone concerned, from infant to taxpayer. The schools and *every arm of organized society* should condemn that way of life and use every device at their disposal to steer young people away from it.

The pregnant teenager should be treated as an object of shame and disgrace by the welfare, school, and municipal officials with whom she comes in contact, which is compatible with their simultaneously being helpful. For quite apart from the probable effectiveness of near universal disapproval by the larger society around her, her way of life is, quite objectively, shameful and disgraceful: She is not self-disciplined nor does she plan for the future, she is not financially responsible because she makes the taxpayers support her, she is egregiously irresponsible as a parent because she is raising children without sufficient maturity, without a father for the children, and in greater poverty than if she waited until marriage and the completion of her education. She, and her boyfriends, provide a poor model for her children, and she has put herself in a position that makes developing her talents and finding a career extraordinarily difficult. If she were white, poor, and our neighbor's daughter, we would have little difficulty coming to this judgment.

If she and her boyfriend—teenaged, poor, high school dropouts, and knowing next to nothing—are to be shamed, what are we to say of the adults around her who signal in a hundred ways that her way of life is acceptable? They ought to know better. Professional educators and civil libertarians, sitting in their comfortable suburban studies listening to their daughters practice the violin, may say we have no right to make judgments about black teenagers in their slum. The relevant question is, Would you find this an acceptable way for *your* daughter to be raised—getting pregnant unmarried at fifteen, dropping out of high school without any job skills, foregoing the development of her innate talents, and living on welfare? What future do you envision for her adulthood from this starting point, beyond poverty and the risk of prostitution, violence, and drugs? Some people may view the slum teenager as a manipulated *thing*, a creation of capitalism or racism, and think that when socialism comes the problem will go away; but if socialism comes the first thing the authorities will do is shame people who live that way.

And what are the prospects for boys born to unmarried, uneducated, teenaged mothers living on welfare in a slum? How will they acquire the character, discipline, and knowledge that will equip them for a successful life? What happens inside them because they have no fathers? They are black and have to worry about discrimination and racial slurs; but that seems minor compared with the smorgasbord of horrors waiting for them in the streets outside—drugs, pimping, crime, homosexual prostitution, physical danger, short, pointless jobs, and the likelihood of a short, pointless life.

The very thought of taking forceful action to rescue these children from a life that ranges from the hopeless to the sordid completely terrifies educators and public officials precisely because most of these young people are black: May middle-aged white people, the descendants of slaveholders and lynchers, *morally criticize* the sexual behavior of young black women, the descendants of slaves? May the concentration camp guard wag his finger morally at the behavior of his victims behind the barbed wire? Are we not blaming the victim? So the entire social welfare and educational establishment is frozen into stone by the mere thought of the rebuke, "Who are *you* to criticize. . . ."

Yet, is not the toleration of this way of life by an adult establishment able to influence it the worst kind of child neglect, and for girls, a vicious kind of sexism? Young teenage girls, who should be doing homework and taking music lessons, are subject to the grossest sexual exploitation, and become no more than meat for the neighborhood men and teenaged boys. Instead of training for a productive and satisfying future they get pregnant and go on welfare, and no one comes down hard on the prevalent attitude that it is "in" and fun to have a baby, and proves they are women. It is not even a case of saying, "don't have a career, get married and have babies"; we in effect say instead, "get pregnant, don't bother with marriage, don't bother with a career, live on the dole, have children who will do the same thing."

There is no evidence that the character, work ethic, social and sexual morality, and general upbringing we think desirable for middle-class children is not equally desirable for the poor including the poor in the worst black slums. Or is there something called black culture such that the early promiscuity, unmarried pregnancy, and lack of strict socialization we deplore in whites can be all right for slum blacks because they have a different culture? How could that be so? Does such upbringing *benefit* pregnant black teenagers or young black men who are functionally illiterate and lack an adequate work ethic? Are these characteristics one views with pride in a black community? We should not forget that these questions must be pursued against the background that about 40 percent of young blacks are functionally illiterate and over 50 percent have no fathers.

In many cities there are curfews for children and teenagers, for example, they must be off the streets by 11 P.M. weeknights and midnight weekends. These curfews often are effective in keeping young people off the streets at times when they are more likely to be preyed upon or get in trouble. However, in Times Square, other areas of New York, and in parts of Washington, Chicago, and most large cities, one sees teenagers, some of them young girls not more than 14, walking about at all hours of the night. Some are prostitutes, some runaways, many of them, perhaps most, black or Hispanic. It is another case where the municipal authorities have been practicing social triage. Given the nature of these neighborhoods, there is an even better reason than in the suburbs to scoop up all these children, every night, and make their parents come downtown at 3 A.M. and get them.

If the Ku Klux Klan wished to make self-fulfilling prophecies about black slum children it could not do better than side with the educational and social welfare professionals of the '70s, who said that slum children have a right to their own language and value system and should not be taught white, middle-class values. For then these young people are trained to live their lives in black slums and rendered unable to function anywhere else. Surely the reasonable course, for the remainder of this century and to have something to offer people at the start of the twenty-first century, is to do everything one can, including coercive measures where it is legally possible, to raise black slum children to have the social ethics and character that will make them despise the life—the "value system"—of casual sex and drugs, petty crime, welfare, and a casual or contemptuous attitude toward work. For that is not an "alternative life style," it is just a lousy way to live, and a burden and threat to the larger society.

What is not always understood is that society ought to do everything in its power to prevent children from growing up in certain ways, but that when some children nevertheless grow up that way, they have a perfect right to be what they are and society has no right to torment them. Society's right to socialize children extends to almost every aspect of character and behavior, but shrinks to the domain of the legal and the illegal when these children become adults. We try to instill in children a work ethic, social morality, some degree of sexual restraint, personal virtues, and when we fail the resulting adults are not thought well of, but generally are legally free to be what they are: We try, fail, and live with it. There is no inconsistency in that sequence of attitudes.

We all the more admire someone who grows up to live a successful, ethical, and happy life who came from a single-parent welfare family. These are obstacles, things that increase the odds against a life that is happy and socially responsible, and overcoming them warrants admiration. But it would be crazy to infer that these should be equally valued options to present to children. School and municipal officials should do everything in their power to discourage single-parent families and unmarried pregnancy, because they have to think about average people and the odds against being happy, not about the few who heroically overcome these obstacles.

SIXTEEN

Sanitized Revenge

> The taboo attached to revenge in our culture today is not unlike the illegitimate aura associated with sex in the Victorian world. The personal and social price we pay for the pretense that revenge and justice have nothing to do with each other is as high as the one paid by the Victorians for their conviction that lust was totally alien to the marital love sanctioned by church and state.
>
> —Susan Jacoby

There are a number of reasons why a healthy moral community holds it members personally responsible and blameable for wrongdoing. We partly define a society in terms of its social expectations and institutions, and the rules that safeguard them. And we cannot determine the society's boundaries—not just in the sense of who belongs, but sometimes even geographically—without knowing who are required to observe the rules and are morally criticized for not doing so. Gross violations of the common good, especially serious crimes, not only harm the individual victim but threaten societal identity and affront a way of life. This is especially so if the violators go unpunished.

As we have seen, the moral values crime affronts are attitudes, implying responses that include blame, scolding, shame, punishment, even hatred. In a full-fledged society, accepting its core of social morality and personal virtues implies willingness to censure violators. Teaching social morality to children is not successful unless the grown citizen's reaction to violating the rules includes bad conscience and remorse, a kind of self-judgment. Otherwise the rules do not affect one inwardly, in one's mind and feelings, and are instead mere warnings of danger. Just teaching young people there are prices on certain behavior—"the price for stealing a car is three years in jail (if you are caught)," in the absence of moral censure and attendant punishment, completely fails to put across the ethical basis of a society, and merely teaches the young to be crafty.

Sociologists who pursue causes of crime usually succeed in finding some: poverty, discrimination, unemployment, broken homes, parental rejection, or lack of control—the statistical correlations are there to see. Since, we are told, poverty is the cause and Jones's mugging an old man is the effect, it is tempting to transfer the responsibility from Jones to the cause. As we saw in Chapter Six, doing this would jettison the notion of personal, moral responsibility and replace it with impersonal, causal responsibility. Ought we to follow this line of thought, redefining our notion of a moral community if necessary, and conclude, as have a number of philosophers and social scientists, that no one ever *deserves* punishment or blame? Should we reject the whole idea of desert and retribution? It is now time to meet this issue head on and make the case, if one can, that criminals are personally responsible for their acts and deserve retribution at the hands of society.

Perhaps one reason for the popularity of the utilitarian theory of punishment is that its moral content is simple and minimal. On this theory action by a court, like any action, is right only if it does good, and a criminal punishment is justified only if it is likely to do good in one of three ways: It *incapacitates* (if I am a car thief, I cannot steal cars when I am in jail); it *rehabilitates* (I may be taught a trade, or a way of life, so that I will prefer not to steal cars when I am released); it *deters* (*your* fear of being caught and going to jail like me will outweigh your desire to steal a car). For utilitarians, the past creates no debts and only the future is relevant to what we ought to do.

Since utilitarians look to the future and not the past, criminal punishment is based, in large part, on the likelihood of recidivism. But as Martin Levin points out,

> From what we know about the type of offenders who are most likely to fall into the recidivating group, one clearly could derive the following policy to reduce recidivism: *Incarcerate for the longest terms the youngest offenders, especially if they are black or have a narcotics history.* . . . Conversely, the same findings of social science with regard to reducing recidivism would dictate that judges *incarcerate for the shortest terms possible under the law whites over 40 who have committed murder or sex crimes!*[1]

Levin then observes, "Our penal and judicial systems serve other goals than lowering the rate of recidivism. And the tension among these goals cannot be resolved on utilitarian grounds; one reason is that the punishment of criminals is, in part, a symbolic activity that expresses our ultimate values."[2] We are often told punishment is what criminals deserve, and sometimes told a punishment is correct if it is what the public wants; but Levin calls it a symbolic activity. This is, I believe, an important idea that concerns the rituals by which healthy tribes testify to their cultural integrity and preserve their self-respect.

Those who scorn the idea that a criminal deserves punishment seldom deny, with equal scorn, that people sometimes deserve praise or reward. Could it be that we deserve praise but not blame, rewards but not punishment, and that, somehow, *we* are responsible when we do good things but *society* is responsible when we do bad things? Most of us think heroes deserve their medals, athletes deserve their prizes, and diligent students their good grades. It would indeed be the triumph of sentimentalism over sin to conclude that good Samaritans deserve their praise but rapists do not deserve their punishment. Yet this seems to be what a large number of corrections professionals *have* concluded; unless, perhaps, they are tougher minded than I give them credit for and believe no one ever deserves anything—that it is as wrong to "stigmatize" with praise the person who rescues another from the river as it is to "stigmatize" murderers with blame and punishment. But a whole society that never held its members personally accountable for good or evil, never expressed its collective will through praise and censure, would have at best a weak and inconsequential conception of the difference between members and non-members. Most importantly, it is doubtful they could possess, in a strong, clear way, common values and a common way of life, if they are totally lacking in indignation at affronts to those values and way of life.

This whole way of thinking and acting—of public wrath at injury to the public good, indignation at unfair or predatory behavior, and insistence on personal accountability, is retributive; it is Old Testament, not utilitarian; it is tribal morality. Anyone who reads newspaper accounts of the reactions in court of crime victims, their relatives, or the parents of children whose murderers have been convicted (or acquitted) can have no doubt that the world demands retribution for criminal harm. Not just compensation or restitution, which in any case often is impossible, but retribution. Simply attending to page one of a big city newspaper shows that after every conviction the victims, or their relatives, applaud, or cry with relief, and otherwise indicate that the world could never be right again until the one who hurt them so terribly received his due.

Susan Jacoby has said that "the ability to exact proportional, measured retribution is one way of denying promiscuity to the vindictive drive."[3] All those revengeful rogue cops, tough cops, vigilantes, and enraged parents, in films such as *Death Wish* and television shows such as "The Equalizer," are cheered on by audiences, one cannot help thinking, in proportion to the public's perception that the law lets criminals go free. However, private revenge, at least in fantasy or vicariously in books or on the screen, will be sweet and irresistible to some people no matter how efficient the law is. One need think only of the characters in *The Godfather*, for whom revenge is voluptuous. Indeed, after looking at books such as *Get Even*,[4] it is clear that to some people the harm that justifies revenge is worth it, the whole transaction of being wronged and taking revenge coming out on the plus side: The pleasure of the revenge outweighs the harm that prompted it. But the great majority of us can be socialized to let officials right criminals' wrongs, if they are willing and able.

Is retributive justice, the idea that a criminal "has it coming to him," revenge? There is no doubt about it. Retributive justice is the revenge a society visits on those who seriously harm it or its members. But the desire for retribution does not arise unless the criminal is in some sense one of our own, someone from whom we expect cooperation and group regard; otherwise our thoughts commonly do not go beyond self-defense or quarantine. Moral judgments of transgressions are inseparably bound up with anger and indignation when the transgressor is a member of our society (in many cases just being a member of a non-primitive human society is enough), and retribution is the expression of this indignation. By contrast, those who do not fully belong to our moral community, because they are alien like Nagas or incapable like wild animals and the retarded, are not objects of indignation and anger, except by a kind of emotional momentum or residual animism we usually recognize to be inappropriate as when we scream at infants, kick the car, or when French villagers tried and executed a pig for murder. Members of your family, your church, or your nation have at least some obligations non-members lack, and are held responsible where non-members are not.

For example, consider again our old friends the Nagas. Nagas hunted heads to adorn their huts, which gave them prestige in their village, and not because they had anything against the original owners of the heads. For us, the Nagas are in a sense aliens and not part of our moral community. But only "in a sense" because they are also part of the larger human community to which we all belong. So we condemn their *practice* but at the same time most of us are much less likely to indignant toward *them*, on the ground that head hunting was part of their culture and they "didn't know any better." This was roughly the attitude of the Indian government, which was committed to the elimination of head hunting but withheld the kind of indignation expressed toward ordinary murderers. It is not that our moral reactions are unanimous: At one extreme are those who refuse even to criticize Naga killings, the phrase "it's their culture" excusing all (except, perhaps, when their own American culture is involved). At the other extreme are people who would punish Naga head hunters the same as common murderers. Most of us, however, are inclined to think of head hunting as somewhat like crime by the retarded or the mentally ill: It must be stopped but their personal responsibility is diminished.

Suppose, however, that my neighbor Henry, who lives in apartment 18B, went down to skid row and killed someone in order to get a skull to ornament the corner of the desk in his study. Now our condemnation is not just of his act but also of *him*. Moral indignation, the indignation that demands retributive punishment, now is as appropriate as it would be in a Naga village if one of them killed a fellow villager. For in these latter cases not only is safety and the common good threatened, our expectations of predictable, cooperative behavior from a fellow citizen are betrayed. When we do not punish and demand repentance from criminals, especially youthful ones, we show that we have lost these expectations, we expect nothing from them, and thereby have cast them out morally in a way that is analogous to a tribe's casting someone out physically: We in effect tell them, You are not of us, you are Nagas.

Consider execution, the most dramatic form of retribution. After twenty-five years of arguing against capital punishment I am no longer so sure. The justification of executions, if there is any, is not that it produces a lower murder rate than does life imprisonment, and in any case it is not clear it does. It is probable that sentencing that is swifter and more certain would be equally effective in lowering the murder rate. The merit of execution (again, if there is any) is not even that it tells the murderer and would-be murderers, ritually and persuasively, that murder is wrong. It is that without taking proportional retribution in grave and dreadful cases a society compromises its honor, belittles itself, and undermines public confidence that the society takes itself and its values seriously. If this is at bottom a circuitous utilitarian argument, and it might be, the utility is not necessarily to be measured by safer streets or fewer murders. It has to do with a citizenry's feelings that they are a moral community that defends itself, that they respect and value themselves enough to strike hard at those who violate its most important values. This is a way to make sense of the personal accountability and consequent retribution a healthy society requires, but independently of the issue of capital punishment: To accept retribution is not to accept some particular degree of it; nor do these considerations resolve the difficulties of matching punishments with crimes.

As I said, this might be a way of saying retribution does some roundabout good by increasing general satisfaction with life in one's society and decreasing alienation, even if it doesn't show up in crime rates. Roundabout utility may persuade more people because it reduces such things as "retribution" and "societal self-respect" to people's felt needs for them, thus making a psychological point out of what otherwise may sound obscure and metaphysical. From this subjective perspective, then, let me go on to suggest that not punishing criminals is unkempt and undignified. A society that does not punish its criminals announces something about its self-image, like a person who lets his appearance and personal hygiene go to pot, or a school that abandons its rituals and orderliness and ceases to make repairs. *Punishing* serious crimes (and not just quarantining or curing the perpetrators) is itself one of the rituals, like a bear dance or funerals, that contribute to a society's identity as a self-respecting moral community. Not punishing one's criminals is like not burying one's dead. There is an obvious reason of health for burying the dead, and an obvious reason of safety for jailing criminals. But the respective acts mean more than that. Righting a victim's wrong—taking wrongs seriously, and funerals, like marriages and baptisms, are ways of taking life seriously, and at the same time testifying to the individual's social membership.

Most participants in the capital punishment controversy confine themselves to the simplest utilitarian issue: comparative murder rates in capital punishment and abolitionist states. The retentionists' real reason for supporting capital punishment usually is retribution, but they do not know how to give it a respectable defense, are tired of being called "revengeful" and "atavistic," and hence remain closet retributivists, just as public officials tend to be closet moralists. They argue endlessly past one another, one side quoting statistics to show that executions do not make us safer, the other side attempting to cast doubt on the data but really finding it irrelevant to their conviction that certain murderers *deserve* to die. As James Q. Wilson says,

> Perhaps because we find it hard to argue about first principles, perhaps because our leaders and spokesmen are untrained in the discipline of philosophic discourse, perhaps because we are an increasingly secular and positivist society that has little confidence in its ethical premises, the capital punishment debate has been framed largely in utilitarian terms. Most of the literature, in short, does not explore the moral worth or evil of execution so much as the consequences of executions for other parties, or for society at large.[5]

Can decent people accept the idea that retributive justice is revenge? Or is vengeance by definition barbaric, destroying the morality of anything that partakes of it? The problem is that we cannot have a moral community unless its members are personally accountable for what they do; personal accountability makes no sense unless it means that transgressors deserve punishment—that is, they are owed retribution; and there is no doubt that retribution is revenge, both historically and conceptually. I do not believe that the logic of this chain can be broken—from moral community, to accountability, to retribution, to revenge. Neither do I believe it needs to be. Revenge is not the opposite of justice but part of its anatomy.

The solution to the moral problem lies in seeing that judicial retribution is not mere revenge but "sanitized revenge," revenge over which a moral community assumes stewardship. Simple revenge is retaliation set and carried out by the victims (or their relatives). It is unpredictable from case to case, sometimes gets the wrong person, often cannot be applied because the victim isn't strong enough, and usually is harsher than what non-victims would think is fitting. Personal retaliation also has no built-in mechanism for termination, the result often being an endless feud. Among the Daflas a sense of moral community and common interest did not extend beyond a single long-house of perhaps thirty people. Hence injuries and thefts committed by people outside this extremely narrow circle were personal matters, the only recourse being retaliatory raids. Insecurity, unpredictability, and dependence on personal power and influence characterized "crime control" in the relatively pathetic and chaotic Dafla society.

It is morally and pragmatically superior to have institutionalized revenge—retributive justice—*administered predictably, thoughtfully, impartially, publicly, and relatively effectively by police and judges who are not the criminal's victims or relatives*. It is still society's revenge on its own members who harm and betray it. But retaliation, "getting even," becomes retributive justice when it meets certain conditions. A law that is secret, such as some notorious Nazi laws, imposed unequally for similar offenses, or imposed by vigilantes instead of agents of social institutions, will not be respected. A penalty that is unpredictable will outrage those penalized severely. Punishment by society protects you from your victim's enraged relatives, the fear of which could last forever, and substitutes solemnity and ceremony for their rage, and disgrace for their unpredictable violence. My hypothesis is that when retaliation is "sanitized" in the ways suggested it turns into justice: There is no special ingredient, metaphysical, theological, or uniquely moral that must be superadded.

Fürer-Haimendorf hypothesized the evolution of criminal justice from personal retaliation. The idea is that there is a development from private to public intervention as a society becomes larger and, I would add, develops a sense of a common way of life that needs to be protected. Quarrels and violence come to be seen as threats by third parties, who then enter the retaliatory process giving it consistency and predictability.

The more complex society of the Gonds includes a sense of belonging and social identity among as many as forty or fifty villages. The size of Gond society ruled out personal retaliation as disruptive and threatening to third parties, Gond public opinion demanding arbitration and institutionalized procedure. Perhaps equally importantly, third parties felt it was their business to intervene because quarreling Gonds who were two villages away were still of their kind, members of a single, identifiable community. The sheer size of Gond vis-á-vis Dafla society constituted a threshold in the evolution of criminal justice out of personal retaliation. Nonetheless, Fürer-Haimendorf says,

> All of these sanctions apply only to cases of homicide within the village-community, whereas the killing of a person not belonging to this in-group does not call for legal sanctions but sets in train a sequence of vendettas. Yet, the substitution of the principle of retribution at the hands of kinsmen by a judicial process and the imposition of legal sanctions by the community as a whole, marks a distinct stage in the development of moral and judicial concepts. The role of the kin-group, which avenges the injuries suffered by the members without regard to general principles of justice, is here partly taken over by the territorial group intent on preserving order and upholding justice without appealing to sentiments of personal revenge. . . . This development of a public sense of morality and the assertion on the part of society of a right to intervene in private disputes of individuals has nowhere been a sudden process.[6]

Among the Gonds social control includes an elaborate system of degrees of excommunication from ritual or other forms of social intercourse. If no one will accept food or drink from you or join in ritual activities, life will be very difficult. A tribal council will ask an accused, "Are you a Gond? If you are a Gond you must conform to Gond custom; if you do not want to do that, you are no longer a Gond."[7] The force of threatened ostracism in village life of course depends on the culprit having no gang or sub-culture to which he can flee and be accepted. This is why there must, among the multitude of mini-tribes to which an American can simultaneously belong, be a core of social morality and civility common to them all. One should be able to flee to share an unusual lifestyle, but not to join a sub-society of predators; the predator must be threatened with being outcast, being alone.

In the United States physical banishment is usually but not invariably impractical. We can more profitably consider the emotional and economic consequences of social disgrace in one town or city. We see the different approaches in traditional societies where, again, we can learn from the Gonds.

> While we have seen that Chenchus place physical distance between those who cannot agree, and Nagas may bodily banish an offender from the village . . ., Gonds place *social* distance between tribal society and those who will not abide by its laws. There is a deep conceptual difference between a punishment such as infliction of physical pain, confiscation of property or bodily banishment and the non-violent *désintéressement* in those who flaunt the society's rules.[8]

A mixture of retaliation and proto-justice can be found among the Nagas. These head hunters recognized three degrees of homicide with differing punishments, ranging from accidental killing to killing by stealth, for which one lost his property, was banished, and was called a murderer.[9] Few peoples illustrate more starkly the difference between social morality as an *intra-tribal* phenomenon, and group loyalties—here restricted to a single loyalty to one's tribe—that determine group boundaries and *inter-tribal* relations.

Nowhere, however, did the development of institutionalized justice eliminate the idea of a wrong or sin as something that must be expiated—paid for, confessed, forgiven, wiped clean, or transferred to another (an animal among the Badagas of India as well as among the ancient Hebrews). The notions of punishment, repentance, and restitution seem to be found in almost all the tribes on earth, with the exception of a number of American juvenile justice officials, and function to prevent and deter crime while at the same time allowing the society to maintain its integrity and assure the criminal he still counts as a member of the moral community.

The peculiarities of American culture, for reasons I have discussed and which include race-guilt as well as dubious philosophical assumptions, have made it impossible for some people to accept the existence of moral guilt, or "wickedness" as James Q. Wilson provocatively called it. Karl Menninger responded as follows to the claim that some criminals are wicked:

> Who's wicked? *I'm* wicked, *you're* wicked, *he's* wicked. I'm utterly opposed to such a view, as a psychiatrist, as a scientist, as a Christian—

> ethically, scientifically, morally. Wickedness describes conduct, not people. And most offenders' "wickedness" isn't very wicked. It's stupid, or it's prohibited, or it's irritating, or it's even alarming. . . . Viewing people as wicked or as having a criminal mind justifies their mistreatment; it confirms stereotypes and prejudice.[10]

What is remarkable is that none of the four things Menninger calls criminal behavior—that it is stupid, prohibited, irritating, alarming—has anything to do with morality. The view Menninger expresses here coincides with the criminal's view of the law: arbitrary and prohibitory with no ethical or moral force behind it. The whole point of criminal law, from its earliest forms in clan and tribal councils, is to prohibit what is wrong and hurtful, either to individuals or to the security of the clan itself by the violation of taboos. Only in complex modern societies do you begin to find criminal prohibitions that do not morally stigmatize the perpetrator, these mostly being laws concerning business, mergers, and the like.

To defend retributive punishment it is not necessary to defend capital punishment of the biblical doctrine of "an eye for an eye." Consider, nonetheless, that peculiar expression. The eye-for-an-eye view was actually the position of the "bleeding hearts" of biblical times: One may exact only *one* eye for an eye, only *one* tooth for a tooth. Retribution, as punishment, normally exacts more from the criminal than the criminal took from his victim. Otherwise it would not punish but simply delayed payment. If I steal a bottle of whiskey and the penalty is a bottle of whiskey, I might as well steal it since the worst that can happen to me is that I will be made to buy it.

Considerations of deterrence aside, the fittingness of exacting a greater price from the criminal than he gained from his crime may lie in the fact that the criminal himself typically imposes a price on his victim that is greater than what he gains from the crime. The biblical injunction prohibits this normal ratio in the case of bodily harm, insisting that the costs be equal, presumably on the humanitarian ground that impaired bodily function is permanent and terrible and ought not to enter into judicial calculations in the same way as a criminal's possessions.

Even so, we moved beyond mutilation as a legitimate part of civilized justice, partly because we have jails in which we can deny freedom and leave the body whole. And we kept moving, finally reaching a point at which we are unwilling to shame, humiliate, or even morally censure criminals. Most likely the real reason we prohibit flogging is not its violence, or the risk of mutilation, but the fact that it is a moral ritual, a ceremonial expression of disapprobation and shaming. If so, we ban flogging because of the only thing that was good about it, and lying behind our wrong reason is the fact that we have banned morality from our public life. What the Gonds know and we have forgotten is that passion and indignation are as essential to morality as reason.

I am not suggesting that we should rant at criminals and call them bad names. That would be counterproductive because undignified. A moral community sublimates its indignation and releases it again as solemnity and ceremony: Just as personal revenge gets civilized in the ways described and becomes judicial punishment, moral anger and indignation become solemn ritual and ceremony. For this reason another sympton of the de-moralization of juvenile justice is informality. A judge who sits in black robes, in a setting that is dignified, solemn, and formal, is universally understood to express the moral will of a community. The delinquent knows it is serious and that *he* is taken seriously. A judge or hearing officer who abandons formal ritual and "raps" with a delinquent, trying to be his buddy, abandons his collective identity and is more likely to be viewed with contempt. Juvenile justice officials who think informality and deritualization better enable them to "reach" delinquents probably accomplish the opposite of what they intend and unwittingly sabotage their society's effort to express its moral will.

A judicial proceeding, like a marriage or inauguration, is a ritual, which, world-wide, is how one tells that one's clan or tribe and not just an individual is speaking. Solemn ceremony and judicial punishment replace invective and personal retaliation. A society that of its own accord abandons judicial ceremony and solemnity communicates to observers a sense that the social will no longer speaks but just the individual again.

Many people are utterly opposed to any attempt to rehabilitate the notions of retribution, shame, and humiliation, and what I have said is unlikely to convince them. The sense that it is shameful to shame or humiliate anyone comes, I suspect, from a number of sources. Beginning with the superficial, some people may simply think of teachers gratuitously humiliating pupils, or prudes making young people ashamed of sex, ashamed of their bodies, ashamed of everything, and go from there to an un-thought-out sentiment that shame and humiliation are bad, period.

More thoughtfully, one might say that shame a person naturally feels at breaking his own principles is all right, but imposing shame or humiliation on people is wrong. Apart from the dubious suggestion that the occasions on which we feel shame do not need to be learned, the issue is not just a personal one. People are harmed by crime and delinquency, and shaming and humiliating criminals are morally superior and more effective punishments than just fining them, or beating them, or locking them up. This is because eliciting these emotions, if we can manage to do it, reinforces the tie between delinquents and their moral community and gives them strong motives to regain their honor and acceptance. A fine or beating will not do that. If we just fine someone, or take him out in the yard and shoot him, we are simply disposing of a problem, as we do with a disease or a mad dog. But if, as so many revolutionary tribunals do, we try to elicit confession and contrition, we are seeking a moral transaction with a fellow human being with whom we share at least some principles, even if we then take him out and shoot him.

Most seriously, however, moral and emotional neutrality in the criminal process comes from moral diffidence about our right to judge criminals who are alienated, who appear to reject our values, and who may never have benefitted from society in the first place. I am convinced that this is another way in which slavery and its aftermath have poisoned American society, for the guilt and doubts that begin with our dealings with blacks and black criminals quickly spread to everyone.

One must try somehow to climb out of this state of demoralization. Shame should not be confused with degradation. Much of our criminal processing is degrading precisely because it is impersonal and morally neutral. It is not degrading to hold someone morally responsible for a crime and publicly shame him, for it is appropriate that a shameful act be shamed. It is degrading to treat a person like an animal, *either physically or morally,* and casually abuse him or treat him like a thing, not responsible for his act. But it does not help when criminology books for college students are mainly devoted to the sordid and degrading aspects of processing young criminals. Often little or no attention is paid to the moral dimension of crime and the judicial system is made to look guiltier than the criminal.

It looks as though the social units people can view as *their* moral communities, and which can effectively make claims on them, must be neither too small nor too large. Whether or not it is true that "small is beautiful," it is probable that a society is viable only when strong, small social units are nested here and there within it. It is well to remember that the ancient societies humans evolved to depend on and prize were moderately small ones. Jails are a recent invention and for thousands of generations our ancestors depended (as do many tribes today) wholly on ritualized punishment and the threat of rejection and exile to control criminals. If fear of disgrace and rejection is built into us as one of the primary means by which crime can be controlled, we do well to attend to the *size* of the society within which this mechanism best works, and the kind of socialization by which it is reinforced and channeled, particularly when we are dealing with juvenile crime.

If the police officer who would arrest a teenager lives in his neighborhood and is known by the young person, his family, and neighbors, fear of disgrace is more likely to play a role when he thinks about breaking the law. There are a number of law-enforcement-related activities that might be more localized so as to enhance a sense of community membership. If police spent more time getting to know local teenagers and storekeepers, perhaps even knocked on some doors during slack hours and introduced themselves, they would have better intelligence regarding who was responsible for local crime. The closed, moving police car is an isolating symbol, contributing to an "us" and "them" attitude on all sides. It might be worth the experiment of reviving local precinct stations, and add small-scale courts and jails for minor offenses, staffed wherever possible by people who live in the neighborhood. These sorts of things are tribal surrogates, attempts to recreate in Brooklyn something that shares structural features with a Gond village council. For young delinquents, the difference between an effective moral ritual and mechanical, de-moralized processing may well depend on whether it takes place in their home neighborhood or downtown at the hands of strangers.

The imam of the most important mosque for the Muslim minority of Singapore related to me the following story of crime and rehabilitation. For two months members of the congregation, while at prayer, had had personal possessions disappear. Finally a nineteen-year-old was discovered to be the thief and a policeman in the congregation said, "I will arrest him and take him away." The imam said no, not in his mosque, and if the policeman arrested the young man outside, no member of the congregation would testify. The imam asked to take charge of him. He told the young man, his parents, and the whole congregation, that he must come to prayer twice a week with his parents, make restitution, and if he did not he would turn him over to the policeman. Now a strange thing happened: A number of members of the congregation gave the young man presents. It was a way of wishing him well in his efforts and telling him he still belonged. The story had a happy ending (although the imam told me of other, more serious cases, that ended in failure). Another tribal surrogate. There is something universal about the story: We can understand its psychology, even though the imam's Arab roots and Singaporean environment are pretty distant from American culture. Nonetheless, an American minister, priest, or rabbi is unlikely to reach the first stage, for he is brought up to recoil at the idea of *telling* the whole congregation that the young man was a thief.

Punishment is sanitized revenge. But even understanding revenge is puzzling, because it is useless. Is not revenge as irrational and pointless as retribution itself, for *why* hurt someone if it is too late to do any good? What adaptive purpose is served by the evolution of a universal desire to seek out and harm the one who harmed you?

How far back can we trace the idea of vengeance? Do animals take revenge? The tiger ferociously attacks those who come near its cubs. It is obvious why these rage reactions evolved: They are not protecting their genes in the next generation if they placidly watch you kill and eat their young. But what if you already ate them? Attacking you is counterproductive since the tiger runs some risk of injury. Yet it doesn't break off its attack the instant it sees its cubs are already dead and a retaliatory counterstrike would "do no good." Is it perhaps just not smart enough for that kind of reflection?

Revenge is a sophisticated notion, like selfishness depending on memory and the idea of seeing the same individual again. It is much more than the rage reaction of an animal as you approach its lair or territory. The animal must be smart enough to understand you as a being that continues through time: It must understand a "you" it sees today as the same "you" that killed its young yesterday, and it must continue to care. Revenge depends on a concept of the self as an enduring being; consequently we have the same grounds for doubting that animals can take revenge or exact retribution as we had, in Chapter Nine, for doubting that they can be selfish. We are told that dogs and elephants remember who harmed them and react aggressively toward them. Perhaps this is revenge or borderline revenge and not just rage, if memory and the ability to reidentify the one who did the deed can guide anger that is still alive days or years later.

Begin with the defensive rage of the bear or tiger as you approach its cubs. Could revenge be instinctive rage, continuing by a kind of momentum beyond its original purpose, when the creature is intelligent enough to remember and reidentify individuals? That rage continues after it has ceased to be "useful" is not a mystery: The reason is the familiar one that evolution isn't fine-tuned enough for such sudden cessations of emotion. Pursuing this line, revengeful human thoughts and behavior might be just this emotional momentum in a creature who can reflect about it. If so, revenge, the desire to hurt those who hurt you, is an evolutionary by-product. It is not remarkable that human nature should contain such a trait. But then we must see the retributive punishment of criminals as the civilized management of revenge and not as something that negates and replaces it.

SEVENTEEN

Why There is an Ethics *of Work*

> . . . Imagine those goals [of the philosophers of leisure] achieved. There would be a hundred million adults who have cultured hobbies to occupy their spare time: some expert on the flute, some with do-it-yourself kits, some good at chess and go, some square dancing, some camping out and enjoying nature, and all playing various athletic games. . . . Now even if all these people were indeed getting deep personal satisfaction from these activities, this is a dismaying picture. It doesn't add up to anything. It isn't important. There is no ethical necessity in it, no standard. *One cannot waste a hundred million people that way.* . . .
> —Paul Goodman

> One of the most significant effects of age segregation in our society has been the isolation of children from the world of work. Once children not only saw what their parents did for a living but also shared substantially in the task; now many children have only a vague notion of the parent's job and have had little or no opportunity to observe the parent (or for that matter any other adult) fully engaged in his or her work.
> —Urie Bronfenbrenner

Why can't we just say that we work to eat and work extra hard when ambition drives us? When Adam and Eve were cast out of the Garden of Eden they were condemned to earn their bread by the sweat of their brows: Work was punishment, an imposition and a blemish on the natural life of man rather than something that completes it. What Roman gentleman, watching his slaves toil from the porch of his villa, would consider labor an essential part of the virtuous life? It is not on Aristotle's list of moral or intellectual virtues. Think of the Balinese men on the beach at Sanur who seem to spend their lives flying kites, sailing, and smiling; and of all the accounts of lazy natives. Is it possible that the "work ethic" is just an American, or Protestant, quirk—a sour, dour turn of mind uncharacteristic of the general run of mankind?

Under American capitalism the danger to the work ethic lies not in preaching work but in preaching that work will make you rich. Even if the hardest workers became the richest, which isn't true, an ideology whose reward for work can by definition only be attained by a few can never be the basis for a healthy society. Children who believe becoming *rich* (i.e., having much more money than other people) is the object of work feel betrayed when they see that their hard-working parents are just comfortably off. They may conclude that their parents are dumb plodders and the real money is got by schemes and inside information. Wealth can be attained by luck and unscrupulousness, and if the only point to committed, conscientious work is the attainment of wealth (or under communism, power and privilege) it will, logically enough, not be perceived to have more merit than luck or unscrupulousness.

This is one reason why there has always been an *ethic* of work under both capitalism and communism (where I mean, of course, belief in the merit of honorable labor and not business ethics). But there is a deeper and more important reason. Self-interest has never sufficed, by itself, to create the commitment to hard work that a society requires from its citizens; it is not as though all you need is greed. Most people simply do not want success badly enough. Perhaps in some abstract sense nearly all of us desire riches, but then we are "lazy." Does laziness mean we desire wealth but are imprudent about what we must do to get it, or does it mean that the desire just isn't strong enough? Perhaps these come to the same thing. In any case, ambition and even the mere desire to live comfortably are not strong enough to power a society; something more is needed. The workaholic obviously is moved by more than ambition; less obviously, conscientious mail carriers and secretaries are moved by more than the need to feed themselves. Without an ethical dimension to work our commitment to it can flag to the extent that a satisfying society becomes impossible.

Christopher Lasch has traced the gradual decay of the Puritan work ethic of the seventeenth century, which praised work as a divinely ordained vocation that was good both for our souls and for society. Lasch goes through its various transformations until he finds, today, nothing left besides the idea that work can bring "success" when it is coupled with a marketable image and the ability to manipulate others.

The pursuit of wealth lost the few shreds of moral meaning that still clung to it. Formerly the Protestant virtues appeared to have an independent value of their own. Even when they became purely instrumental, in the second half of the nineteenth century, success itself retained moral and social overtones, by virtue of its contribution to the sum of human comfort and progress. Now success appeared as an end in its own right, the victory over your competitors that alone retained the capacity to instill a sense of self-approval. The latest success manuals differ from earlier ones—even surpassing the cynicism of Dale Carnegie and Peale—in their lack of interest in the substance of success, and in the candor with which they insist that appearances—"winning images"—count for more than performance, ascription for more than achievement.[1]

We saw some of this in the "selfishness manuals" discussed earlier. Yet Lasch's conclusion is too sour. The evidence is that the great majority of Americans rests easy with the idea of a decent job that will never make them rich, which suggests there is a value to a career of work which has to do with neither money nor victory over competitors. Angus Campbell contrasts the intellectuals' analyses of work in America with the reality:

> In light of the numerous tracts that have been written over the years describing the "mindless, hateful, numbing" character of work in this country, one would hardly be surprised to find most American working men in a state of sullen rebellion against their jobs. The fact is that no careful survey that undertook to describe the nation's work force has ever failed to find an impressive majority who say they are satisfied with their jobs. In 1978, four out of five employed men across the country told the Institute for Social Research's interviewers that they were satisfied in some degree with their jobs. One out of three described themselves as "completely satisfied."[2]

What we call the "Protestant work ethic" is a variant of a nearly world-wide trait, clad differently in different cultures and in its transformations in America from the seventeenth century to today: Work is God's will; it improves and preserves the soul; it is honorable because you do your share and are useful; it is the basis for self-respect. A young Moscow philosopher argued for two hours attempting to persuade me that man's essence is his labor. He made a metaphysics of it; the Puritan made it into theology; the late-nineteenth-century American felt it (Lasch says) as a compulsion. The *need* they recognize is the same. It is not greed but something else. Later we shall see that labor indeed is more honored in some times and places than others, but this is because the honor of labor can be contaminated by the social status of the laborers.

Russian workers are inefficient and the consumer goods they produce are often of poor quality. But it would be a mistake to think this is only due to the absence of the profit motive. It is not so simple. It is also caused by job alienation, a condition suffered by many American as well as Russian workers. Alienation and the profit motive relate to the work ethic in very different ways. Alienation is a condition that destroys a person's work ethic, whereas the profit motive or its absence has practically nothing to do with the *ethics* of work. Let me explain.

Making a profit, getting promoted, simply keeping one's job, and ensuring a good career, are all ways it is in our self-interest to work. It is obviously the same in any society that has such things as jobs and promotions. Russian managers, like their American counterparts, can be bypassed for promotion or fired if they perform incompetently. Just before the Moscow Olympics a Russian friend, an administrator at Moscow University, had been charged with preparing a large corps of translators; "I must work very hard, I cannot make any mistakes," he said, as anxious as any American organization man. Self-interest is everywhere a strong motive for competent work and it would be foolish to discuss the ethics of work as though the main reason why people worked was ethics. The work ethic exists *alongside* wanting money, as a distinct motive, but it is more essential where there is less money to be made. The Russian system relies too much on a work ethic, especially for low status jobs, and overloads it as a social motive. Americans recently have placed too much weight on self-interest, consequently corrupting the youth with regard to the honor of work and failing to motivate the quality of work our society requires.

Job alienation is the failure to perceive one's work and workplace as a valued and integral part of one's life, as a partial source of one's identity, and, slightly more idealistically, as an activity useful to a common good one shares with others. Paul Goodman said (in the 1950s) that young people are frustrated by the lack of opportunity for what he called "a manly job," by which he meant dignified and socially useful work.[3] He is right: Doing work that is integrated with the life and ongoing purposes of our moral community is a powerful cause of our sense of belonging to it, and conversely, our sense of belonging gives meaning to our work and makes it part of our lives. What we have lost, particularly among the young and relatively unskilled, is the sense of taking a job as *joining something*, becoming part of a trade or enterprise one is proud to join and which helps to give one an identity. Apprenticeship in the building trades retains this idea, although it has been disgracefully marred by the trade unions' *de facto* virtual exclusion of blacks.

Goodman's sense of the useful is colored by his politics: He does not think advertising and public relations are "manly work." Perhaps we should not even try to define the "useful" and simply encourage commitment to work felt to be useful and important by the workers themselves. One system in which beginning a job is joining something is Japanese industrial paternalism. Like tenured American professors, after a trial period Japanese workers in certain large companies (actually a small minority of the Japanese work force) cannot be fired. More generally, dismissal is the option of last resort, opinions and suggestions are solicited and paid attention to, and company loyalty is high; one consequence is that workers never weld coke bottles into the rocker panels of new cars. Some Americans argued that we are too individualistic and diverse to accept any of the communalistic aspects of Japanese corporate-worker relationships. They forget the communalism of American small town and neighborhood life and they also forget the common social nature of all human beings. In any case, their doubts are belied by the success of Japanese management methods at Honda plants in Ohio. People who insist we are too individualistic for this sort of solution are like people who brag about how drunk they get, making a virtue of the vice and exaggerating it, out of perverse pride, even when they know what it is costing them.

Groceries can be bought in Moscow either from people who sell for profit or from people hired by the state; that is, they can be bought in a farmers' market or *rynok* or in a state food store or *gastronom*. One of the largest gastronoms, on Kalinin Prospect, Nikita Khrushchev's faded modern show street, actually has a self-service "supermarket" on the second floor. You check all your packages and are let in with a small shopping cart. The store has the appearance of a warehouse because a single item, such as quart jars of tomato paste (48 kopecks), cans of Bulgarian beans, or one kind of breakfast food, will fill the shelves from top to bottom for twelve feet of aisle. It has about 2 percent of the variety of American, Western European, or East Asian stores. The downstairs store is crowded and standard Soviet: long, snail-paced lines to buy a small variety of meat and vegetables by the system of check the price, line up and pay the cashier, then back to the clerk with receipt to receive the cabbage. By greatly increasing the time it takes to make a purchase, items in short supply don't sell out as quickly, which makes the supply look larger. The state food stores are not fun; it is a frustrating chore and there is a grim attitude on all sides.

Down Lomonosov Prospect, past Moscow University and the metro station, is a *rynok*, a farmers' market, where they sell what they grow on their private plots, some sellers coming from as far as the

Caucasus. At hundreds of crowded tables in a big cement-floored hall, they sell flowers, fruit, vegetables, meat, mushrooms of every variety. One October day I could buy, if I wanted, pickled garlic, pigs heads, six kinds of pears, and dressed whole rabbits laid out in rows on the old marble counters with the fur left on one hind foot for those who wish to hack off their own lucky charm. The place is thronged and noisy, there is a better quality and variety than in the state food store, and higher prices; the farmers offer samples, importune you to buy, and shout and argue. A well-dressed man set his open briefcase on the marble tabletop and bought pickles. The grizzled peasant behind the table pulled a double handful out of a barrel of brine, set them dripping on his scale, then immediately dumped the pickles, brine pouring out, into the open briefcase. The man didn't bat an eye. Beautiful big pears were five rubles a kilo (about $3.25 a pound), little ones one-third the price and delicious.

The profit motive has a profound and, I think, ultimately pleasing effect on the style of a business transaction. But children cannot come to understand the value of work on the model of the *rynok* any more than they can on the model of the *gastronom*. The lesson is exuberant, single-minded self-interest in the one, sullen, alienated labor in the other; the former is more fun but neither will do as a model for society. Those who serve you enthusiastically for profit are not alienated from their work, but neither are they necessarily social. None of the pure models of the nature of work will do as a template for society. The egoist works with energy and commitment to serve his good, himself; the group egoist works to serve *his* good, the common good of something he identifies with. And the third kind of actor, the alienated, sees no intimate connection between his work and either himself or something with which he identifies.

It is not possible to have a healthy society unless there is a group-egoistic, ethical dimension to work *and* it is in your interest to work. One destructive myth is that work is moral service and the desire for profit or advancement is shameful—"careerist" as the Soviets say. The other destructive myth is that hard work is of value only because it brings you wealth, power, or privilege. There is simply not enough work to go around that is glamorous, or that will make you rich or powerful. This raises another problem. It is easy to preach an ethics of work when you have a nice job. My Moscow philosopher friend said that under communism man's essence is his labor; as we spoke a poorly dressed old woman began sweeping around the trash urns in front of the stores, and true communism seemed as remote from Kalinin Prospect as the second coming of Christ. I wondered if *that* was her "essence," if trash would become interesting, or disappear, when true communism arrives. The slogan sounds smug in America too: Professional people have no trouble finding their essence in their labor; they are proud to identify with their work. "I am a doctor," "I am an engineer," and "I am a carpenter" are ways of acknowledging a self-identity which is at the same time a social identity. But "I am a dishwasher" and "I am a pizza deliverer" usually mean, "I wash dishes (or deliver pizzas), for the moment."

An honest and adequate response to the problem of unglamorous work requires a partial backing off from the claim that man's essence is his labor. Many people, surely the more the better, find their essence and hence a social identity in their labor; many others—the woman sweeping the Moscow sidewalk, the pizza deliverer—hold back from identifying with their work: It is what they do, not what they are. The social component of how they understand their "essence" will come (hopefully) from identification with their neighborhoods, towns, organizations, churches, teams, and other "collectives."

Conceding this does not destroy the possibility of a universal work ethic. Sweeping trash will not become interesting, but steps have been taken in some cities to make trash collecting more glamorous, with good-looking equipment, a trash collectors' formal ball, and apprentice programs it is possible to fail. Much more important is that it can be honorable. And a condition of trash sweeping being honorable is that it is generally perceived to be useful, and respected for that, this being a feature trash sweeping shares with conducting an orchestra. Seeing one's work as honorable allows a weak version of the essentialist view: My essence is labor, not trash sweeping, and this essence I share with the orchestra conductor, the trash aspect being, as the medieval philosophers would put it, "accident" rather than "essence." But this line of argument will be perceived as hocus-pocus if it is all we can say.

Ideally, an ethical dimension to work involves a strong urge, a need, to be useful. When we ask, "Useful for what?", the answer must be that it serves the object of one's group loyalty. This is what useful means—contributing to a *collective* good. When people say they would like a job that is *useful* they do not mean just a job that brings more money, is more interesting, or otherwise benefits them. Useful means useful to society (or to a sub-society within a larger one). At its least articulate this urge presents itself as a "compulsion," but even here the ethical dimension is present. Compulsive workers say they just need to work, they feel itchy and at loose ends when they are not working. So too, people just need to eat, sleep, and find affection. We often call things compulsions in recognition of their universality. Most people, without work that occupies their time and which, hopefully, is perceived to be useful or of significance, simply fester.

The Russians teach the importance of socially useful work, but in practice society as the beneficiary of work is often depersonalized and becomes an abstraction. I mentioned the sullen clerks and the cafeteria workers who "serve food, not people." The old men and women who sweep up cigarette butts around metro stations will sweep it all on your shoes if you get in their path. What has happened, I think, is a quirk of their history and ideology that makes them look even more alienated than they are. In America useful labor serves the good of the community by serving the people in it; but the Russians downplay the human-interactive aspect of useful labor because they have confused it with the master-servant relationship. Our revolution is older and, in this respect, more complete than theirs: We are less self-conscious and uncomfortable about jobs which, in old Europe, carried inferior social status. Perhaps this also partly explains the sullen indifference of Moscow store clerks. They are serving yard goods, not people, serving society, not individuals, and in this cold and abstract way performing their useful labor. It may even be one of the reasons why most Moscow bus drivers are in heavy glass compartments, completely shut off from their passengers: The old terror of a master-servant interaction is blocked, in good Russian fashion, by blocking any interaction at all.

There are grounds for doubting that the emotional need work fulfills is just a matter of culture, the slave-driven culture of ancient Rome and anthropologists' accounts of indolent natives notwithstanding. The value of and personal need for useful work is near universal. We can hypothesize that egoism and group egoism, and the work needed to satisfy the goals of each, increased Darwinian fitness (either individual fitness or inclusive fitness). On this view it is as natural and rational for group egoists to perform work that helps their community survive as it is for egoists to work directly for themselves. Therefore the desire to be useful is as natural, and no more mysterious, than selfishness; for if we evolved to be group egoists *and* egoists, we are naturally disposed to serve both these masters. If this line of explanation is right, the origin of an ethical dimension to socially useful work is not a mystery. Valuing work that benefits our *tribe* is as universal and as much a part of our nature as is valuing work that benefits *oneself.* We value useful work because we value the group loyalty it serves. A life of useful work will coexist with self-interest just because group egoism itself coexists with self-interest.

We may have a strong natural itch to be lazy and avoid taking risks in the hunt—we can easily imagine *that* becoming part of human nature too, back in hominid and early human times—but not too much loafing would be tolerated and I am suggesting that we also have a natural itch to be workers and contributors. It is not obvious that culture alone makes a person feel restless living idly off an inheritance, or diminishes self-respect when living on public welfare, or compels a retiree to seek a new job or at least keep busy in some way. The innate urge perhaps is to keep *busy*, and it is a by-product of the prosperity and complexity of modern society that there are ways to keep busy that are socially useless (nightclubbing on one's inheritance), or boring and insulting to the intelligence (turning a nut on an assembly line like Charlie Chaplin in *Modern Times*). It would have taken considerable imagination for a Pleistocene man or woman to find a way to keep busy that was at the same time as useless or as boring as many modern jobs. That the need for useful work is innate is suggested by some additional findings of Angus Campbell:

> One might imagine, if one took the economic aspects of life to be the main determiners of feelings of well-being, that the most important influence on a worker's evaluation of his job would be how well it pays. Indeed there is a modest tendency for people with higher incomes to feel more satisfied with their work, but the relationship is very weak, largely because so many people with low incomes seem very well pleased with their jobs.[4]

One might expect the lowest level of satisfaction with the dirty, unpleasant, and dangerous jobs the uneducated tend to hold. "But the surprising fact," Campbell says, "is that working men with the least education are most likely to describe themselves as satisfied with their job." Campbell continues,

> As we have seen, most employed men say they would rather work than not work, even if money were not a consideration . . . and we get an additional insight into the meaning of work when we examine the way unemployed men evaluate their life experience. The proportion of unemployed men who describe themselves as "very happy" sinks to one of the lowest levels of any of the groups we will consider, 12 percent in 1971, 10 percent in 1978. . . .

Campbell concludes that "free time, and the leisure activities it makes possible, may be virtually universal values, but work also has value, both instrumental and intrinsic."

We find the most poorly developed work ethic where we find the most welfare, drug addiction, vandalism, and crime. In parts of our urban black slums an ethics of work is largely absent. Why? The deepest, most difficult to eradicate harm done by slavery and the practices in the century that followed slavery was the prevention, in the minds of blacks, of the growth of a sense of common community with the rest of America. Lack of money can be remedied, instantly, by giving money; lack of a job, by providing a job; but the sense of not being part of a community remains in one's soul, and like a birth defect is passed on to the next generation. The mechanisms of discrimination—exclusion from public places and mainstream ritual activities as well as from the opportunity to make money—are exactly what destroy a sense of belonging or, in the case of ex-slaves, block its growth in the first place.

With the opening up of jobs and a national commitment to end discrimination, white people expected blacks from a welfare, slum milieu at once to act like well-socialized whites. A black person hired on the assembly line, in the shop, or in the office, was expected to join the team, work hard and cheerfully, be punctual, and care that things operated well and safely. Many blacks, primarily from the middle class and the stable working class, satisfied these expectations. A considerable number did not; they quit often, came to work late, showed no interest in the purpose of their work, and broke things.

Is it then simply a mistake to think that the emotional need and value of useful work is universal? Are we all "lazy natives," indoctrination and religion here and there creating a thin veneer we call the work ethic? To return to the ancient Roman or Greek, languidly watching his slaves toil, there seems to be no trace of an ethics of work, no more than we find in a welfare dynasty in an American black slum. But there is a common answer to these exceptions: slavery, and its consequences. Tocqueville has a remarkable passage in which he explains how the honor of work, and therefore any possibility of a work ethic, is destroyed equally for slave and master by the institution of slavery:

> When a century had passed since the foundation of the colonies, an extraordinary fact began to strike the attention of everybody. The population of those provinces that had practically no slaves increased in numbers, wealth, and well-being more rapidly than those that had slaves. . . . As time went on, the Anglo-Americans left the Atlantic coast and plunged daily farther into the solitudes of the West. . . . The farther they went, the clearer it became that slavery, so cruel to the slave, was fatal to the master. But the banks of the Ohio provided the final demonstration of this truth. . . . The left bank is called Kentucky; the other takes its name from the river itself. There is only one difference between

the two states: Kentucky allows slaves, but Ohio refuses to have them. So the traveler who lets the current carry him down the Ohio . . . sails, so to say, between freedom and slavery; and he has only to glance around him to see instantly which is best for mankind. On the left bank of the river the population is sparse; from time to time one sees a troop of slaves loitering through half-deserted fields; the primeval forest is constantly reappearing. . . . But on the right bank a confused hum proclaims from afar that men are busily at work; fine crops cover the fields; . . . man appears rich and contented; he works. . . . These contrasting effects of slavery and of freedom are easy to understand; they are enough to explain the differences between ancient civilization and modern.

On the left bank of the Ohio work is connected with the idea of slavery, but on the right with well-being and progress; on the one side it is degrading, but on the other honorable; on the left bank no white laborers are to be found, for they would be afraid of being like the slaves; for work people must rely on the Negroes; but one will never see a man of leisure on the right bank: the white man's intelligent activity is used for work of every sort. Hence those whose task it is in Kentucky to exploit the natural wealth of the soil are neither eager nor instructed, for anyone who might possess those qualities either does nothing or crosses over into Ohio so that he can profit by his industry, and do so without shame.[5]

What degrades work is not inequality, not the fact that some people get rich and some are poor, but the existence of a degraded class of people who do the work: slaves, serfs, or, to a lesser extent, peasants under any kind of feudalism. Slaves and serfs are not degraded because they do physical labor, physical labor is degraded because it is done by slaves and serfs. Not only is labor contaminated by the status of the laborers, but particular kinds of jobs have been thought of as contaminated because they were traditionally done by blacks, or itinerants, or women. At one time (from my recollection) garbage collectors were black and the men who drove the trucks always white. When driving the truck was exclusive, like an exclusive neighborhood it had more status than it deserved, and working the truck had less status than it deserved because "only X's do it" (as distinct from "only Y's *may* do it"). Being a garbage collector—"sanitation worker"—is a more respected job than it used to be because black sanitation workers can advance to supervisory positions and some whites can be found working the trucks.

In the USSR the same causes are at work. Waiters and store clerks cannot cheerfully and solicitously help their customers for the same reason that a Kentucky farmer in Tocqueville's time could not get down on his knees and pull weeds. The Kentuckian would be like a slave, the Russians like servants before the revolution, whom Soviets are taught were obsequious and deprived of dignity. This is purely a matter of local culture. In Bali, servants and chauffers tend to do their jobs cheerfully as your equals, without servililty, obsequiousness, or surliness, whereas this is less often the case across the strait in Muslim Java.

Hunter-gatherers are virtually immune to alienated labor, guaranteeing the integrity of their work ethic. This is because their work is so intimately and continuously a part of clan life, is interwoven with their rituals, and the young, unlike American suburban youngsters or youngsters in slum families on welfare, grow up watching and gradually being initiated into the work of adults. Moreover, with the significant exception of women's work, the society of hunter-gatherers isn't large or powerful enough to keep a subclass that taints a certain kind of work.

Much of what we call laziness, and a careless, desultory, exploitive attitude toward one's job, are the outer expressions of alienation, of a sense of tribal non-membership, sensed either in society at large or in the mini-tribe of the workplace. Commitment, belonging, esprit, are tribal emotions; and because they are matters of a person's character and spirit they do not automatically come into being with a change in a law or a paycheck. Consequently, coming to possess a strong work ethic, for that part of the black slum population and other sub-populations lacking it, probably is at best a generational change. Being a law-abiding, hard-working, well-functioning American is as much the result of the correct molding of a whole life, from infancy on, as is being a well-functioning Arapesh or Gond.

This is a pessimistic view because it tells us that some people, once raised in a certain environment, are ruined, and that the consequences of our history will be a long time in the undoing. But it also tells us that our social policies can help or exacerbate the situation; and that intelligent and morally self-confident socialization will awaken the innate sociality and sense of community of slum dwellers, if they are young enough and if we are not paralyzed by guilt or misled by sentimentalism or ideology. No human being is alienated by nature and there is not a shred of evidence that the absence of communal identity and a work ethic are inherited racial traits. The suggestion, in the face of our tribal, hunter-gatherer, evolutionary history, that in some races but not others people are innately disposed to work for the good of their clans, would be preposterous. In the 1980s and 1990s, the problem of the black urban underclass is a matter of social class inertia and the solution is strong, thorough intervention by every institution of mainstream society.

However, creating "belonging" is not just a matter of ceremony and socialization. There needs to be a real possibility of that "manly job" Paul Goodman mentioned for youths who are on the bottom of the social ladder and who, for the next generation at least, will disproportionately be black youths. The Soviets have discovered the solution to the problem of unemployment: Inefficiency. We should not be too quick to despise it. If four or even six people do what two could do, there obviously isn't going to be unemployment. In Moscow about 10 percent of the work force seems to be employed just watching and guarding things: Old women and men sit by doors, stairways, entrances, escalators, elevators, halls, and so on, waiting to say "nyet" if you wander off course or where you don't belong. In one mid-sized Moscow hotel two old men watched the front door, two more 15 feet away sat on stools and watched the narrow entrance to the elevator lobby, and in the lobby three women at a time were employed to watch the self-service elevators. These people earned 80 rubles a month. "Key ladies" on each floor of a hotel have desks or little offices from which they watch elevators and hallways. My own sixth floor Watcher (pay: 125 rubles a month) sold tea in the evening and wrote down in a big ledger the hour and minute each guest left or entered his room.

If people who have respect for their work-lives are given make-work jobs, their only recourse is to make something of the jobs—to create for themselves functions that earn their dollars or rubles. It is a mark of our own plight, of the alienation of those in a make-work job, that they often make nothing of it, accepting the pay and treating the job with contempt. It depends, of course, on whether the person has been brought up with an inner need to have work one takes seriously, and on whether he or she identifies with the society in which the make-work job is embedded. We can draw another analogy between egoism and group egoism: Perhaps job or community alienation is lack of *"collective* respect" and a vitiating defect of one's group egoism, that is on all fours with lack of *self*-respect as a debilitation of egoism. Low self-esteem is diminished or damaged self-love, alienation is diminished or damaged group loyalty.

I most admired the creativity of Moscow elevator watchers since, on the surface, there is nothing whatever for even one of these women to do, let alone three. But they ingeniously created functions: When the elevator door is open they tell you to go in, when it is closed they tell you not to go in. When everybody is waiting in front of elevator #3 an elevator watcher will unlock a little box on the wall and turn off #3, turn on #1, and shoo everyone over to the new door. Another watcher will count the people entering and stand in front with her arms spread when she thinks there are enough. The third elevator watcher gives advice to the first two.

How does one tell the difference between control, simple inefficiency, and welfare? The thousands of watchers and nyet-sayers in Moscow are mostly old people incapable of more strenuous and productive labor. They have jobs, they receive pay, and if they didn't they would be on "pure" welfare or become a burden to the relatives with whom most of them live (80 rubles a month, then about 120 dollars, is not enough to live on by oneself). They can say, "We earn our keep." But only the Russians would think of making an army of Watchers. Assuming that Americans were willing to pay the bill for nearly full employment, surely we could think of better things for people to do. In the face of greatly increased rates of crime and vandalism it would be worthwhile to look again at estimates of the costs of near full employment compared with savings in law enforcement, juvenile justice and corrections personnel, victimization, insurance, welfare, and depressed property values in dangerous neighborhoods.

Public work projects are not the only avenue to near full employment. Others are incentives to private employers and national service. Youth unemployment would be minimal if at any given time 20 percent of the youth between eighteen and twenty-two were doing one year of compulsory national service, a national service that could range from the completely military through various mixes to the completely nonmilitary. In addition to taking millions of young people off the job market each year, a totally compulsory, truly universal, national service would be a tribal ritual. It would be a community and citizenship-building performance, and an implicit national acknowledgment that the way to make young people love their society is to demand their time, labor, and commitment. A universal national service requirement tells young people they owe something to the collective good, they are needed, and they belong. A society must have moral self-confidence to say this to youth; it cannot feel completely ashamed of itself or be run by people whose primary social emotion is guilt. Youths at loose ends with themselves will not believe that the moral community within whose boundaries and institutions they pursue happiness has a claim on them, needs their useful labor, and constitutes their community, unless the community demonstrates its claims and needs by appropriate action.

EIGHTEEN

Alienation and De-Alienation

> Where do the roots of alienation lie? . . . Over the past three decades literally thousands of investigations . . . point to an almost omnipresent overriding factor: family disorganization. . . . The same research shows that family disorganization arises from its external environment, the way of life imposed on it by . . . circumstances, not from internal forces.
> —Urie Bronfenbrenner

If I am "alienated" from a thing—my neighborhood, my country, my work—I lack a sense of possession and identity with it in a situation in which it is reasonably to be expected of me. This is the meaning that was implicit in the preceding chapters. As a social sickness that can afflict both free market and communist societies, we need to understand it better, if we can, as well as continue the search for causes. What is the secret of community, and what exactly *is* alienation? Successful people who write about their youth in urban slums such as New York's Lower East Side frequently are wistful about the sense of community they had then and lack now. Must we, for example, have a slum?

I have argued that whether I view my community as my own, and hence want to be proud of it (and, ideally, want *it* to be proud of me), or instead am alienated, depends on a great many causes. It depends to an unappreciated degree on a community's *physical* organization—its size, ready identifiability, complexity, and features that make it look pleasing, safe, grand, fun, private, sheltering, or unique. It depends on features that individuate it, on whether it shows visible signs of care and maintenance, on aesthetics, symbols, rituals, traditions, and on the frequency and nature of social encounters. It also depends vitally on public evidence that citizens are needed and are held personally accountable for the good or ill they do their community.

While it initially seemed implausible that there could be a "formula" for determining what alienates or instead creates group loyalty in a community, I suggested one anyway in terms of what I called our Secret Pleistocene Inheritance and a revisionary notion of the "state of nature." Since our first 200,000 years had a far greater effect on the human biogram than the few thousands of years we have lived in modern societies, the formula is to look for qualities of modern societies and sub-societies which are *analogues* of the most common qualities of primitive tribal life and, by extrapolation, life during the past 200,000 years.

The point, at once social and biological, is that social institutions and practices that worked during those years of hard selective pressure almost certainly left their mark on our emotional/valuational makeup; deviations from them are likely to make us anxious, threatened, unhappy, hostile, and what we call alienated. Sociobiologists, such as Hamilton, Trivers, Wilson, and Dawkins, talked about biology and society from a limited perspective that probably was yet another expression of American individualist mentality. They focused too narrowly an altruism and egoism, essentially a matter of behavior in one-on-one, individual transactions, and did not speculate enough about humans as tribal and communal animals.

Attending to human nature as evolutionary history redresses an imbalance in our thinking about American society: While the past 2,000 years of political history are important to what we are, we can make little sense of it except in conjunction with the past 200,000 (or 2,000,000) of biological history. No one can prove that a particular human response is so-many-percent innate, however cross-cultural and unconnected with poverty or powerlessness it may be, and I would be the last to make such a claim. But the recipes for social policy during the past twenty years have been so off the wall and have had such poor results, that it is time to take seriously biologically based hypotheses about the collectivist, communitarian side of human beings.

We may begin by once more picking up the theme of aesthetics and consider public housing. Most low-rent public housing is built according to very strict safety standards of design and materials. Construction cost per square foot is considerably higher than for comparable private housing and higher than for many luxury apartments. Usually, however, not a cent is spent to make the building appeal to the eye or for decoration or embellishment of any kind. This is understandable: Taxpayers are footing a large part of the bill and they are, presumably, duty bound to pay for buildings that are structurally sound but think it preposterous to pay for frills or luxuries. In many projects vandalism is anticipated: Lights and heaters are enclosed in heavy metal grills and lobby walls are of glazed ceramic tile to make it easier to remove graffiti. Typically, each apartment is like every other and each building is like the others in its cluster.

A building like this enters into a dialogue with its tenants. It says to them, "You are welfare. We are special buildings for people like you." And the tenants answer the building by smashing it to pieces, urinating in its elevators, and taking no interest whatever in its maintenance. This is alienation. The tenants are alienated from the building because it lacks individuality and visual appeal, and because it anticipates destructiveness from them instead of care and pride. This is not to say that welfare clients are bound to take good care of clean, handsome attractive buildings; vandalism and neglect have multiple causes, but buildings that are alienating in the ways described exacerbate whatever impetus for vandalism already exists. The tenants also are likely to be alienated from the surrounding community because, like pythons in a zoo, they have housing which is structurally safe, relatively secure from internal (but not necessarily from external) attack, and which would satisfy the aesthetic, spiritual, and social aspirations of pythons.

As an alternative to new construction and to gentrification that prices the original residents out of the neighborhood, it is almost always less alienating to patch up existing housing and stores. Modest restoration preserves the old and the familiar and assures diversity, saves the architectural embellishment made before labor became expensive, and can be arranged to generate jobs for local workers. In the 1980s the cost of new housing is a serendipitous benefit to neighborhood integrity. Fewer people can afford the price or interest rates and since the late 1970s many more people remodeled instead of moving, thus adding to the physical and financial causes of community commitment.

The idea of alienation is intuitively judgmental, the object of judgment, among people who write on the topic, almost invariably being society or the political system. If alienation were a descriptive, "value free" notion, we should be able to pick out alienated people by differences in the ways they feel, behave, and in what causes their feelings and behavior. But I don't think we can. For example, a worker may say, "I just work here," and have no sense of fulfillment or loyalty, not because he is alienated but because he chose the wrong kind of job or is mentally ill. Or a worker may behave carelessly and be frequently drunk or absent, not because he is alienated but because he was never socialized to be careful and responsible, or because he wants to hurt the company for a personal or political reason. I am not necessarily alienated when I have no loyalty to my job or neighborhood because I am enslaved, sick, if it's full of cobras and tsetse flies, if I am regularly shot at, or if in certain objective ways the job or neighborhood is simply no good.

Marxists define alienated work in terms of objective, descriptive features of the economy and political system. I may sell my labor under working conditions of the sort accepted by American labor unions but nonetheless make a product over whose price, quality, and distribution I have no say. This fits the Marxist conception of alienation because it is a situation in which the conditions of work and the product of one's labor are determined by market forces and acquire, as it were, a life of their own: My labor and the products of my labor are estranged from me. And insofar as my essence is my labor, I am estranged from myself. Marxists define alienation in terms of objective features of the capitalist mode of production, and downgrade identifying alienation by means of "subjective" motives and feelings.

The inferiority of the Marxist idea lies in its abstractness, its lack of empirical connection with what satisfies and dissatisfies us. Workers are alienated if certain theoretical conditions obtain, regardless whether or not their work is poor or they are dissatisfied. According to the Marxist view a worker might be efficient, well paid, secure, happy in his work, and alienated. But unless our goals are purely political, and alienation defined in whatever way serves those goals, we should insist that when workers or citizens are alienated something has *gone wrong*, something hurts or doesn't work right. Otherwise, we only have a piece of jargon and not a usable concept for social diagnosis and criticism. On the other hand, the examples I gave at the start show that just appealing to feelings and behavior doesn't get us what we want.

Throughout, I have implicitly defined alienation as missing community: People are alienated from their workplace, company, neighborhood, or school, if, in a situation in which it would be expected of them to view it as "theirs" and have a sense of community, they do not. I am alienated if I am never willing to sacrifice for the good of my community, if I vandalize it, or at least, never express pride or shame over its condition, reject all solicitations for my time or money, care nothing about how it is zoned, respond to serious community problems by moving away, and so on. Now, for such behavior really to evidence alienation, we have to understand when—in the deliberately ambiguous phrase I chose—committed labor and good citizenship is "to be expected of someone."

I'm not expected to feel commitment to Chicago if I just visit the city; in Moscow I felt alien, not alienated. In neither case do we "expect" group loyalty, as we might from a life-long resident, and just because of that I was not alienated from Moscow. Neither do we expect commitment from life-long residents who are mentally retarded, or so totally engrossed in their work, or in drinking, that they care about nothing else. Nonetheless, while in some cases we may not *expect* commitment, we may at the same time feel it *is expected of them*. Hence there has to be more to alienation than disappointed expectation of good citizenship.

The main problem with the disappointed expectation view is that there always is *some* explanation why a person doesn't care about his community, and if we know the explanation we no more expect loyalty from him than we do from an infant. If we rule out alienation whenever we know what makes him uncaring, it seems that calling him alienated is just an expression of our ignorance. This is a familiar kind of deterministic argument, which makes the difference between the alien and the alienated depend only on whether we know what makes them behave as they do. Saying criminals are not responsible for their actions when we can give psychiatric or social causes of their behavior, and that otherwise they are responsible, confronts the same difficulty. The notion of responsibility seems indefensible if the only difference lies in us, not in the criminals, insofar as we blame criminals when we are ignorant of what causes their behavior and we excuse them when we think we know what caused it.

The point is that slovenly, uncaring, or hostile behavior *counts as alienation only in normal and "appropriate" people*, not in visitors, aliens, the retarded, professional criminals, dedicated political enemies, people who would have serious character defects in any society, and others. Alienation is a defect we attribute only to reasonably normal members of our moral community, and not to people in the above categories. The teachers and students in school A can be alienated from school A, but not the pigeons on the roof, a Naga tribesman, or the teachers and students from school B. The same is true of our workplaces and nation. Behavior counts as alienated only among appropriate people and "appropriate" makes sense only when it is understood in terms of the *demands* the school, job, or nation can make on its people but not on Nagas or the pigeons on the roof.

Even to be a candidate for alienation you must in some sense belong. And part of the idea of belonging, and of the importance we attach to it, is that citizens *ought* to be committed to their societies, and when they instead are alienated something has gone wrong with them. *Unless*, of course, what makes them poor workers or poor citizens is, so to speak, *too good a reason*, and we say instead that they are sick and excused; or simply alien and we have no claim on them; or they are disloyal or predators, and our enemies.

In everyday use "alienation" often implies criticism of the alienated individual: Something is wrong that reflects poorly on you if you are alienated from your job, family, or neighborhood. To most writers on alienation, on the other hand, the alienated individual is 100 percent a victim and society or the political system is entirely to blame: Alienation is a kind of oppression. Two reasons for the popularity of this view are contemporary social scientists' inclinations to blame society and not individuals for failings of any kind, and Marxists' use of "alienation" as an overall criticism of non-Marxist political/economic systems. However, the "pure victim" theory will not help us understand particular alienating and non-alienating practices in a mixed economy such as the United States.

When we call someone alienated we usually imply a failure of loyalty or commitment, a pulling back from collective involvement, an emotional withdrawal from the group, a retreat from "us" to "me." There is overall a tone of moral failing, not in the sense of gross violation of duty or principle, but of default on one's owed emotional contribution to a collective enterprise. Alienated people are not just victims. Healthy societies *demand* loyalty from members who are adult, sane, and normal in certain other respects. The uncaring businessperson and the barfly *ought* to care about their community; they lack the excuses of infants, the retarded, aliens, and the socially ostracized.

But at the same time, when people are alienated something has gone wrong with the causal machinery that we think it both desirable and possible should operate in our society: It is not "wickedness" but a failure in their socialization or in their social environment. It is vitally important that we be able to distinguish the alienated—who may commit criminal acts that can be traced to their alienation—from predatory criminals. We need to search for social policies that reduce alienation. But what reduces alienation may not have the slightest effect on the predatory criminal.

We lay varying degrees of responsibility on those we call alienated and who care nothing for—or harm—their own schools, towns, neighborhoods, or countries, and we *also* admit there are identifiable causes of their behavior. It is not different in the case of crime: It would be mad to deny that crime has causes and equally mad to deny that sane, adult criminals are personally responsible for their crimes. A good society's citizens care about it, and when they do not we try to discover what changes will make them care and no longer be bad citizens.

There are three important differences between the Marxist view of alienation as an intrinsic defect of a political system and my suggestion that alienation is an avoidable *malaise* found here and there in mixed economies (as well as here and there in socialist societies).

First, on the Marxist view alienated individuals are 100 percent victims. Second, those who, like myself, are interested in piecemeal de-alienation think of alienating practices as deviations from attainable normal functioning, whereas alienating causes according to the Marxists are an essential part of the capitalist system. Finally, alienation as a necessary consequence of capitalism tends to be independent of psychology and non-empirical, whereas local, behavioral alienation does not require that one consult an ideology before we know we have it: It is immediately and painfully evident.

"Practical" American social planners usually ignore alienation as too vague or too mixed up with Karl Marx, and instead think only of what is useful: good sewer lines, highways, and welfare checks delivered on time. What is useful people accept, but it does not create the sense of possession and commitment on which society depends. I have argued that all too often we are anti-historical, boring utilitarians who think that ritual, ceremony and symbol, even a sense of style, are useless nonsense best left to dictators and witch-doctors. So we offer each other nourishing cold porridge. We actually think of *mailing* diplomas to college graduates, and General Motors would never dream of making its employees dance (nor would the United Auto Workers look kindly on the idea). But the New Guinea tribe makes its "employees" dance, the Japanese corporation makes them sing, and each reaps a much deeper commitment.

We have forgotten, in our cities and in our factories, how essential to collective commitment is the "useless"—the ornaments, the rituals and ceremonies, attention to the past, and the things which are expensive and relatively functionless but grand. We alienate delinquents and misbehaving students by not holding them personally responsible, by dispensing with formal solemnity in judicial proceedings, and by bringing up the young feeling at bay from society rather than enmeshed in it. In all these respects street gangs and jungle tribes are wiser than our educators, urban planners, and juvenile justice professionals. We need to look for things which, today, strike the right chord and create in us a sense of belonging and communal value because they remind us of "home," evolutionarily speaking—of the ancient, intimately social, communal life within which, like moths in our cocoons, over the millennia our minds and bodies changed from beast to man. When we translate ignorance of our history—our evolutionary history, not just our recent political history—into social policies, the result is insecure, alienated, hostile people who don't give a damn about anything, often not even about themselves.

Surely, it will be objected, the educational and social problems I have been discussing are caused by poverty, powerlessness, and racial discrimination, and are marginally related, at best, to ceremonies and park statuary. If someone is deprived of the basic protections and opportunities of his society he will reject it; he will be alienated and it will be unreasonable to expect good citizenship. I would like to pin down when this rejection response comes, but one thing is certain: There is ample evidence that poverty, political despotism, and insecurity have little to do with it. History is replete with groups and subgroups who have lived with far less freedom and prosperity than the residents of the worst American slums and yet live relatively fulfilled and law-abiding lives because of a strong sense of community and group identity. Conversely, wealth and political representation are by no means a guarantee of good citizenship. The social/political system I have been defending—what we might call small-scale, free market collectivism—does not ensure economic equality or equality of political power, but it does attend to what preserves community and minimizes alienation.

What invites explanation is why people will put up with grinding poverty and insecurity but explode with indignation at what they believe is unfairness. What is so special about unfairness? Unfair treatment usually does less physical harm than poverty and insecurity and yet people who believe they are treated unjustly can be counted on least to be good citizens. Philosophers and social scientists accept, without puzzlement, the white-hot anger unfairness produces; or else they merely say it shows the power or authority of our sense of justice, which doesn't explain anything.

What human docility under all conditions except gross unfairness shows, I suggest, is that unfairness is clan rejection and clan rejection is what we have evolved over the past million years to fear and hate more than anything. I tried to show earlier that group egoism or tribal morality sets the boundary on our willingness to make universal ethical judgments: It distinguishes insiders from outsiders, establishing a domain within which we are concerned to treat equals equally. Unfairness treats insiders like outsiders (and therefore alienates them provided they remain insiders). If a parent provides something to each of her children, say, an allowance, but excludes one of them apparently just because she likes him less, the child will feel much more hurt, insecure, and perhaps outraged than if no one got an allowance. Nor would a neighbor's child be hurt, outraged, or alienated by not receiving an allowance from this parent, for he doesn't belong to the family in the first place. The special sting of unfairness is in-group rejection: By some obvious criterion you *belong*—sometimes it is just being human—but you are treated as though you did not.

We evolved to need and value group belonging because starvation and the leopards waited beyond the campfire. Unfair treatment awakens in us the ancient emotions one felt at the threat of banishment, of separation from the clan. Poverty and insecurity have been man's lot throughout history; it is something we put up with. But unfairness is being treated worse than the rest of your community for no good reason. It is the opposite of formal punishment, which is a reassurance of belonging. Systematic unfairness, as in racial discrimination, is the ultimate alienator because it treats social animals who can only live in clans as though they are not members, or not full-fledged members, of their clans.

Someone who thinks he is not getting a fair share of whatever benefits his society has to offer cannot be counted on for law-abiding citizenship. From this we can develop a second sense of "alienation" and call people who suffer from it "radically alienated." But when, exactly, does radical alienation arise and how do we distinguish such a person from a predator? I wish to conclude with an analogy that partly draws on the Prisoner's Dilemma situations discussed in Chapter Eight. Compare very badly off slum dwellers with people in a movie line (waiting for a benefit, the movie), with an eye to finding a way to predict when each will "give up on the system." Each is being asked to pay a certain price: The slum dweller (minimally) to obey the law, the moviegoer to wait his turn in the line. Recall that the "Good/Good" world of mutual concession was assumed to be the best world, but also the one in which the individual is second best off: He is better off if he is a free-rider within a cooperative system, and worse off if he lives in a world in which everyone tries to be a free-rider.

Now, we are willing to stand in line, even if we know we would be better off jumping the line at the ticket booth (assume the other people in line will merely grouch at us, if that). I had asked *why we stay in line*, assuming that pure selfishness tells us not to. Sense of fairness was one answer: Others are waiting their turn and we are no different from them. We may add childhood socialization that reinforces or helps create a sense of fairness. We know we are better off in a world of wait-your-turn than in a world of push-and-shove; but we also know, if the argument of Chapter Eight is correct, that this awareness does not give us a *selfish* reason to wait our turn, it only gives us a reason of fairness.

What happens when we see line jumpers ahead of us? We are indignant: the natural response of a moral community toward members who receive its benefits without paying their share. But most of us remain in the line unless the free-riders become too numerous. *What is "too numerous?"* At what point, in the gradual corruption of an orderly movie line by line jumpers up ahead, do you quit the line and join the game of push-and-shove? The hope is that we can learn something about when a person quits on his moral community and

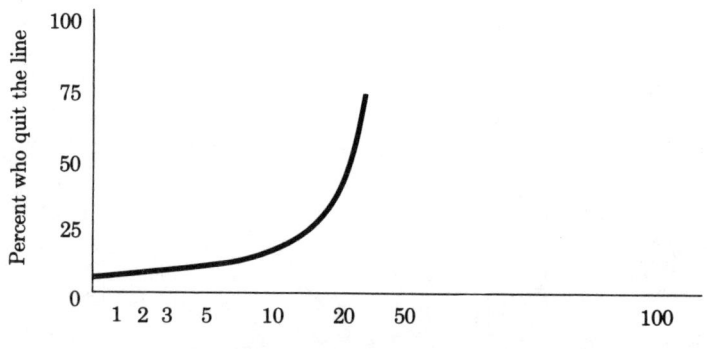

FIGURE 16. The Movie Line

When do we give up on a system of rules? The diagram is meant to show the *structure* of radical alienation and the idea of a subjective threshold beyond which most of us will give up on following the rules of a social system. But the numbers are mere guesses—their real values could be determined by a sufficiently clever experiment.

instead goes all out for himself. The answer I suggest is that we quit the line when "it doesn't pay," when "we might as well push and shove with the others or forget the movie." This answer is not as obvious as it sounds.

We obviously quit if so many parasites are jumping the line that we don't move forward at all. *But there is another point, short of this, at which we decide waiting in the line "doesn't pay." It is when we feel that we are not better off waiting in the line than we are likely to be in the game of push-and-shove. In other words, we are willing to make sacrifices as members of a rule-guided social system—for example, we don't join a small number of line jumpers—but we expect as a result to be better off than we would be in the state of nature.* This is the payoff that will be insisted on. We do not insist that rules of fairness and restraint make us *best* off, like the egoist in a world of altruists, but we do insist that they make us *better off* than we would be in a world without rules of fairness and restraint.

This is the grain of truth in the individualist, contractarian conception of society. Members of a moral community are willing to pay a real price to live in a civilized society, but they expect to receive the benefits of civilization in return: To be better off than they would be in a world in which *nobody* paid that price. This is why it is absurd to expect a slave to follow the social morality of the slave masters, for he is not better off for it. I am not for an instant denying that slum youths

Alienation and De-Alienation / 249

have the same obligations as the rest of us not to be free-riders. But if someone sees himself in society as in a movie line that has no advantage over a system of push-and-shove, he is no more likely to feel obliged to follow that society's rules than to wait in such a line. Perhaps many street youths in slums *believe* they personally are not better off in the "2/2" world of mutual concession than they would be in the "3/3" world of dog-eat-dog. Many confusedly believe they already live in a "3/3" society, that the whole world is "3/3".

If youths in slums are minimally socialized, or not socialized at all, then they are very likely doubly lost. For if they *believe* they are not better off obeying the rules than living in a world without rules, they are radically alienated. And if they are not socialized, they will be unsuited to live anywhere but the slum, if even there. They will lack the social morality and personal virtues that enable one to flourish in society, and will lack the group loyalties that motivate one to obey the rules—which means their belief they are not better off will be true, although not for the reasons they think.

The eighteenth-century moral psychologist Joseph Butler said self-love does not create or motivate social morality, but self-love does, when certain limits are reached, exercise a veto power over it.[1] Civilized society depends on most people following rules which require small to moderate sacrifices of self-interest. If the demands become too large, the mass of the citizenry cannot be counted on: Social morality cannot be made too expensive or self-love will exercise its veto. So, too, regarding the prediction of radical alienation: Society asks its members to be willing to restrain self-interest, follow rules, and hence be "second best off." This we are willing to do; but we will not make this sacrifice unless we sense that we *are* second best off, that is, better off on the whole than we would be in a world of dog-eat-dog. If we have this sense enough of us will follow the rules and not take unfair advantage, but if not, rational selfishness exercises the veto: We will not wait in pointless lines.

Earlier, a number of things were described that ruin sense-of-community, ranging from foolish educational and juvenile justice policies to cloned neighborhoods. Unfortunately, there is, additionally, an attitude or state of mind that can totally destroy societal affiliation. People who have this attitude accuse their society of false advertising: They aren't better off than they would be in a Hobbesian state of nature. So they become *radically alienated* and either have no tribal identity whatever, which will make them miserable and unpredictable, or join street gangs whose rules, they hope, do *not* constitute false advertising.

It is difficult, however, to see how we can employ the idea of radical alienation in particular cases. This is because it is nearly impossible, in a particular case, to distinguish someone who is radically alienated from a predator. Sissela Bok has noticed the distinction between predators and people I call radically alienated. Speaking of liars, she says,

> At times, liars operate as if they believed that such a free-rider status is theirs and that it excuses them. At other times, on the contrary, it is the very fact that others *do* lie that excuses their deceptive stance in their own eyes. It is crucial to see the distinction between the free-loading liar and the liar whose deception is a strategy for survival in a corrupt society. . . . While different, the two are closely linked. If enough persons adopt the free-rider strategy for lying, the time will come when all will feel pressed to lie to survive."[2]

The theoretical distinction is clear: Predators know they are better off in a world in which people follow a social ethics than in a world in which they do not. They just want to be best off, not second best off. Predators elect to be piranhas in a tank of guppies, whereas people who are radically alienated think they might as well be piranhas since they are not better off than they would be if the tank were full of piranhas. Radical alienation is a different sense of alienation from the alienation-as-loss-of-community with which I began. It is more a matter of angry rejection than a matter of uncaring and is more closely linked with the traditional notion of the alienated as social victim.

But which of these persons is Mr. Jones, who has just robbed a gas station? Of course, it is in the interest of people who do not believe in criminal responsibility to label him "alienated" instead of "predator," since it appears to provide an excuse. My suggestion is that we react to the idea of radical alienation only on the level of large-scale social and economic policy and not on the level of how one treats individual criminals. For if it is true that the integrity of a moral community requires holding its delinquents personally responsible for what they do, true that radical alienation destroys a society's shared common good, and true in any case that we cannot easily tell predators from the alienated, the only rational option is to punish criminals and enact policies that minimize alienation.

Notes

CHAPTER ONE

First lead quote: Alexis de Tocqueville, *Democracy in America*, trans. by George Lawrence, J. P. Mayer, ed. (Garden City, New York: Anchor Books; Doubleday & Company, Inc., 1969), p. 429.
Second lead quote: *Crime and Public Policy*, James Q. Wilson, ed. (San Francisco: ICS Press, 1983), p. xi.
    1. Christopher Lasch, *The Culture of Narcissism* (New York: W. W. Norton and Company, 1978).
    2. Emile Durkheim, *Suicide,* translated by John A. Spaulding and George Simpson (New York: The Free Press, 1951), pp. 373–374.
    3. Edward Wynne, "Facts About the Character of Young Americans," *Character,* November 1979.
    4. "Remorse and Repentance," *The Wall Street Journal,* 22 September 1980.
    5. Jethro Koller Lieberman, *The Litigious Society* (New York: Basic Books, 1981), p. 15.

CHAPTER TWO

First lead quote: Mary Midgley, *Beast and Man* (Ithaca, New York: Cornell University Press, 1978), p. 166.
Second lead quote: Frithjof Bergmann, personal communication.
    1. Tocqueville, *Democracy in America,* pp. 506–507.
    2. Thomas Hobbes, *Leviathan,* Part 1, Chapter 13.
    3. John Locke, *Two Treatises on Government,* Book 2, Chapter 1.
    4. Colin Turnbull, *The Mountain People* (New York: Simon and Schuster, 1972).

CHAPTER THREE

Lead Quote: Diane Ravitch, "Educational Policies that Frustrate Character Development," *Character,* July 1980.
    1. Yvonne L. Wharton, "List of Hypotheses Advanced to Explain the SAT Score Decline," report to the College Entrance Examination Board, February 1976 (ERIC document 148 885—006 775).
    2. "Private-School Boom," *U.S. News and World Report,* August 13, 1979.
    3. Fred Reed, "The Color of Education," *Harpers,* January 1981.
    4. *Statistical Abstracts of the United States, 1981* (Washington: U.S. Department of Commerce, 1981).

5. Gilbert T. Sewall, *Necessary Lessons: Decline and Renewal in American Schools* (New York: The Free Press, 1983), p. 99.
6. Ibid., p. 96.
7. Sidney Suslow, "Grade Inflation: End of a Trend?" *Change*, March 1977.
8. Ibid.
9. William F. Lasner, "Memorandum on Grade Trends," The University of Texas at Austin: Office of Institutional Studies, 1981.
10. These grades were in the spring of 1977. "Report of the Faculty Senate Committee on Grade Inflation," The University of Texas at Austin, 1978.
11. "Annual Report of the Registrar," The Ohio State University, 1980.
12. Ravitch, "Educational Policies."
13. Worthy Ward, "Classroom Crisis in Science and Math," *Chemical and Engineering News* (July 19, 1982).
14. Ravitch, "Educational Policies."
15. Michael Young, Survey, The Ohio State University, 1981.
16. "Memorandum on Student Flow by Ethnic Group," The University of Texas at Austin: Office of Institutional Studies, 1980.

CHAPTER FOUR

First lead quote: Horace Mann, *The Republic and the School*, ed. Lawrence A. Cremin (New York: Teachers College, Columbia University, 1957), p. 98.
Second lead quote: Christoph von Fürer-Haimendorf, *Morals and Merit* (Chicago: The University of Chicago Press, 1967), p. 11.

1. Sidney Simon, Merrill Harmon, and Lewis Raths, *Values and Teaching* (Columbus, Ohio: Charles Merrill Co., 1967).
2. Lawrence Kohlberg, *The Unstudied Curriculum* (Washington, D.C.: Association for Supervision and Curriculum Development, 1970).
3. Alexander S. Neill, *Summerhill: A Radical Approach to Child Rearing* (New York: Hart Publishing Co., 1960), p. 4, my italics.
4. Melville Herskovits, *Cultural Relativism: Perspectives in Cultural pluralism* (New York: Random House, 1972).
5. Fürer-Haimendorf, *Morals and Merit*, p. 11.
6. *The ABC's of Moral Education* [in Russian] (Moscow, 1979), passage translated by James Scanlon.
7. Paul Hollander, *Soviet and American Society: A Comparison* (New York: Oxford University Press, 1973), p. 142.
8. *Pravda*, July 24, 1968.
9. Urie Bronfenbrenner, *Two Worlds of Childhood* (New York: Russell Sage Foundation, 1970).

CHAPTER FIVE

First lead quote: George Will, *Newsweek*, September 15, 1982.
Second lead quote: Urie Bronfenbrenner, *Two Worlds of Childhood*, p. 156.

1. *Violent Schools, Safe Schools*, National Institute of Education, 1981, Appendix A, pp. A6–A7.
2. Joel Kupperman, "Inhibition," *Oxford Review of Education*, 1978.
3. Raymond Firth, *Elements of Social Organization* (London: Watts, 1951), p. 213.

4. Ruth Benedict, *Patterns of Culture* (Boston: Houghton Mifflin Co., 1959), pp. 21–22.
5. Fürer-Haimendorf, *Morals and Merit*, pp. 10, 114.
6. Bronfenbrenner, *Two Worlds of Childhood*, p. 115.
7. Ibid., pp. 79–80.
8. Ibid., pp. 116–117.

CHAPTER SIX

First lead quote: James Q. Wilson, *Thinking About Crime* (New York: Random House, Inc., 1977), p. 23.
Second lead quote: Oliver Wendell Holmes, "The Path of the Law," in *Collected Legal Papers* (New York: Harcourt, Brace and Co., 1921), p. 170.
1. Wilson, *Thinking About Crime*, pp. 53 and 223.
2. Urie Bronfenbrenner's research shows a strong connection between family stability and satisfaction and objective, external social institutions. Cf. "On the Origins of Alienation," *Scientific American*, August 1974.
3. Denis Szabo, "Sociological Criminology and Models of Juvenile Delinquency and Maladjustment," *The Annals of the American Academy of Political and Social Science*, November 1977.
4. Michael Philipson, *Sociological Aspects of Crime and Delinquency* (London: Routledge and Kegan Paul, 1971).
5. Wilson, *Thinking About Crime*, p. xiii.
6. George Feiffer, *Justice in Moscow* (New York: Simon and Schuster, 1964).
7. Wilson, *Thinking About Crime*, p. 230.
8. Fürer-Haimendorf, *Morals and Merit*, pp. 132–133.
9. Ibid., p. 91.
10. Ibid., p. 23.
11. Ibid., p. 27.
12. Ibid., p. 31.
13. Wesley G. Skogan and Michael G. Maxfield, *Coping With Crime* (Beverly Hills: Sage Publications, 1981), p. 13.
14. Fürer-Haimendorf, p. 117.
15. Wilson, *Thinking About Crime*, pp. 26–28.
16. Skogan and Maxfield, *Coping with Crime*, pp. 91–96.

CHAPTER SEVEN

First lead quote: Plato, *The Republic*, Book 2.
Second lead quote: Ogden Nash, "Kind of an Ode to Duty."
1. Ayn Rand, *The Virtue of Selfishness* (New York: The New American Library and *The Objectivist Newsletter*, Inc., 1961), p. viii.
2. Hobbes, *Leviathan*, Part 1, Chapter 13, and Part 2, Chapter 17.
3. Robert Hogan and David Schroeder, "The Joy of Sex for Children and Other Modern Fables," *Character*, August, 1980.
4. Harold Sherman, *The New TNT* (Englewood Cliffs, New Jersey: Prentice-Hall, 1966) pp. 173, 189.
5. David Seabury, *The Art of Selfishness* (New York: J. Messner, Inc., 1937), pp. 55, 49.
6. Robert L. Shook, *Winning Images* (New York: Pocket Books, 1977), from the jacket blurb.

7. Plato, *The Republic*, Book 2.

CHAPTER EIGHT

Lead quote: Tocqueville, p. 526.
    1. Donald T. Campbell, "On the Conflicts Between Biological and Social Evolution and Between Psychology and Moral Traditions," *American Psychologist*, December 1975, p. 1120.
    2. Robert Axelrod, *The Evolution of Cooperation* (New York: Basic Books, 1984), and also described by Douglas R. Hofstadter, "Metamagical Themas," *Scientific American*, May 1983.
    3. David Hume, *A Treatise of Human Nature*, Book III.
    4. Plato, *Republic*, Book II.

CHAPTER NINE

Lead quote: Durkheim, *Suicide*, p. 389.
    1. Alvin Toffler, *Future Shock* (New York: Random House, 1970).

CHAPTER TEN

Lead quote: Alexander Hamilton, *The Federalist*, No. xvii.
    1. Fürer-Haimendorf, pp. 112, 109.
    2. Ibid., p. 110.
    3. Tocqueville, p. 235.
    4. Ibid., p. 236.
    5. John Agresto, "The American Founders and the Character of Citizens," *Character*, February 1981.

CHAPTER ELEVEN

Lead quote: Midgley, *Beast and Man*, p. xiii.
    1. Thomas Henry Huxley, "Evolution and Ethics," The Romanes Lecture of 1893.
    2. William Graham Sumner, *What Social Classes Owe to Each Other* (New York: Harper and Bros., 1883), p. 101.
    3. Herbert Spencer, *Social Statics* (New York: D. Appleton and Co., 1864), pp. 414–415.
    4. Quoted by Philip Appleman in *Darwin* (New York: W.W. Norton and Co., 1970), p. 487, and attributed to the year 1915.
    5. William D. Hamilton, "The Genetical Evolution of Social Behavior, I," *Journal of Theoretical Biology*, 1964.
    6. Robert Trivers, "The Evolution of Reciprocal Altruism," *Quarterly Review of Biology*, 1971.
    7. See Richard Dawkins, *The Selfish Gene* (London: Oxford University Press, 1976), and Edward O. Wilson, *Sociobiology: The New Synthesis* (Cambridge: Belknap Press of Harvard University Press, 1975).
    8. Richard Dawkins, *The Selfish Gene*, p. 95.
    9. Wilson, *Sociobiology: The New Synthesis*, p. 3.
    10. Peter Singer, *The Expanding Circle* (New York: Farrar, Straus, & Giroux, 1981), p. 77.

11. Ibid., p. 78.
12. Ibid.

CHAPTER TWELVE

Lead quote: Peter Singer, *The Expanding Circle*, pp. 3–4.
1. Hobbes, *Leviathan*, Part 2.
2. John Rawls, *A Theory of Justice* (Cambridge, Mass.: Belknap Press of Harvard University Press, 1971), Chapter 1, Section 3.
3. Ibid., Chapter 2, Section 12.
4. Robert Nozick, *Anarchy, State, and Utopia* (New York: Basic Books, 1974), p. 88.
5. William A. Schambra, "The Roots of the American Public Philosophy," *The Public Interest*, Spring 1982.
6. Edward O. Wilson, *On Human Nature* (Cambridge, Mass.: Harvard University Press, 1978), p. 84.
7. Don Martindale, *Community, Character, and Civilization* (New York: The Free Press, 1963), p. 3.
8. Robert Hogan and Nicholas Emler, "The Biases in Contemporary Social Psychology," *Social Research*, Autumn 1978.
9. Martin Hoffman, "Altruistic Motivation," *Developmental Psychology*, September 1975.
10. Daniel Batson, Bruce D. Duncan, Paula Ackerman, Terese Buckley, Kimberly Birch, "Is Empathetic Emotion a Source of Altruistic Motivation?", *Journal of Personality and Social Psychology*, February 1981.
11. Midgley, p. 47.
12. Ibid., pp. 167–168.
13. Jean Jacques Rousseau, *The Social Contract*, Book 2, Ch. 3.
14. Fürer-Haimendorf, p. 15.

CHAPTER THIRTEEN

First lead quote: Midgley, p. 286.
Second lead quote: Conrad Lorenz, *On Aggression*, trans. by Marjorie Kerr Wilson (New York: Harcourt, Brace and World, Inc., 1966), pp. 264–265.
1. Carl Sagan, *The Dragons of Eden* (New York: Random House, 1977), p. 60.
2. Fürer-Haimendorf, p. 16.
3. Ibid., pp. 66–67.
4. Franz Boas, *The Mind of Primitive Man* (New York: The Macmillan Co., 1938), p. 234.
5. Ibid., pp. 237, 239.
6. Richard Lewontin, "The Corpse in the Elevator," *The New York Review of Books*, January 20, 1983.
7. Ibid.
8. Midgley, pp. xx–xxi, xviii.
9. Richard Alexander, *Darwinism and Human Affairs* (Seattle and London: University of Washington Press, 1979), pp. 192–193.
10. Joseph Shepher, "Mate Selection Among Second Generation Kibbutz Adolescents and Adults: Incest Avoidance and Negative Imprinting," *Archives of Sexual Behavior*, 1971.

11. Iris Murdoch, *A Word Child* (New York, The Viking Press, 1975), p. 3.
12. A point made by Robert Hogan and David Schroeder in "The Joy of Sex for Children and Other Modern Fables," *Character*, 1980.
13. Midgley, pp. 287, 298.

CHAPTER FOURTEEN

First lead quote: Urie Bronfenbrenner, "On Making Human Beings Human," *Character*, December 8, 1980.
Second lead quote: Edward Shils, *Tradition* (Chicago: University of Chicago Press, 1981), p. 329.
1. Conrad Lorenz, *King Solomon's Ring*, trans. by Marjorie Kerr Wilson (New York: Crowell Publishing Co., 1952).
2. Urie Bronfenbrenner, "The Origins of Alienation," *Scientific American*, August 1974, p. 61.
3. Durkheim, p. 385.
4. *The Columbus Dispatch*, 5 October 1980.
5. Robert Audrey, *The Territorial Imperative* (New York: Atheneum, 1970), p. 102.
6. Hervé Varenne, "Symbolizing American Culture in Schools," *Character*, April 1981.
7. Ibid.
8. Ibid.
9. Ralph Ross, *Symbols and Civilization: Science, Morals, Religion, Art* (San Diego and New York: Harcourt, Brace, Jovanovich, Inc., 1963).
10. Taeko Helen Ishida, Dissertation, University of California at Berkeley, 1978.
11. Varenne, "Symbolizing American Culture."
12. I. M. Lewis, *Social Anthropology in Perspective* (New York: Penguin Books, 1976), pp. 136–137.
13. Yoram Roman, Michael and Gay Pinto, R. George, "Rites of Passage: A Ritual of Detoxification," *Journal of Altered States of Consciousness*, 1973, pp. 81–92.
14. Irenaus Eibl-Eibesfeldt, *Love and Hate*, trans. by Geoffrey Strachan (New York: Holt, Rinehart and Winston, 1972), pp. 123–124.

CHAPTER FIFTEEN

First lead quote: Tocqueville, p. 340.
Second lead quote: Kenneth T. Clark, *The Declining Significance of Race?: A Dialogue Among Black and White Social Scientists*, ed. Joseph R. Washington, Jr. (Joseph R. Washington, Jr., 1979), pp. 125–126.
1. Tocqueville, pp. 317, 319.
2. Ibid., p. 319.
3. Ibid., p. 318.
4. Ann Hulbert, "Children as Parents," *The New Republic*, September 1984.
5. William Julius Wilson, *The Declining Significance of Race?: A Dialogue Among Black and White Social Scientists*, pp. 4, 111–112.
6. James Q. Wilson, *Thinking About Crime*, p. 32.
7. Kenneth T. Clark and others, *The Declining Significance of Race?: A*

Dialogue Among Black and White Social Scientists, pp. 104–105.
  8. Bronfenbrenner, *Two Worlds of Childhood*, pp. 104, 71.

CHAPTER SIXTEEN

Lead quote: Susan Jacoby, *Wild Justice: The Evolution of Revenge* (New York: Harper and Row, 1983), p. 12.
  1. Martin A. Levin, "Crime and Punishment and Social Science," *The Public Interest*, Spring 1972.
  2. Ibid.
  3. Jacoby, p. 182.
  4. George Hayduke, *Get Even: The Complete Book of Dirty Tricks* (Cornville, Arizona: Desert Publications, 1979).
  5. James Q. Wilson, *Thinking About Crime*.
  6. Fürer-Haimendorf, p. 105.
  7. Ibid., p. 124.
  8. Ibid., p. 126.
  9. Ibid., pp. 104–105.
  10. Daniel Goleman, "Proud to be a Bleeding Heart, an Interview with Karl Menninger," *Psychology Today*, June 1978.

CHAPTER SEVENTEEN

First lead quote: Paul Goodman, *Growing up Absurd* (New York: Vintage Books, 1956), pp. 234–235.
Second lead quote: Bronfenbrenner, *Two Worlds of Childhood*, p. 57.
  1. Christopher Lasch, *The Culture of Narcissism* (New York: Norton, 1978), pp. 58–59.
  2. Angus Campbell, *The Sense of Well-Being in America* (New York: McGraw-Hill Book Company, 1981), pp. 117–118, 120.
  3. Paul Goodman, *Growing Up Absurd*.
  4. Campbell, p. 127.
  5. Tocqueville, pp. 344–346.

CHAPTER EIGHTEEN

Lead quote: Bronfenbrenner, "The Origins of Alienation," *Scientific American*, August 1974.
  1. Joseph Butler, Sermon Eleven from *Fifteen Sermons Preached at the Rolls Chapel*.
  2. Sissela Bok, *Lying: Moral Choice in Public and Private Life* (New York: Pantheon Books, 1978), p. 23.

Index

ABC's of Moral Education, The, 52
Adolescents, 204. See also Teenagers; Youth
Aesthetics, 188
Affective education, 35
Age segregation, 66
Agresto, John, 139
Alienation, 239–250; defined, 243; Ik and, 19; radical, 247, 249–250; work and, 228, 236, 237, 241–242
Altruism, 88; egoists and, 100–102; reciprocal, 104, 145–147, 182
Ambition, 226
Analysis of Textbooks in Relation to Declining SAT Scores, An (Chall), 36
Andamanese, 81
Anger, 61
Animals, 116–117, 223
Anthropology, 6
Apprenticeship, 228
Arapesh, 183
Aristotle, 58, 60, 225
Art, 190–191
Art of Selfishness, The (Seabury), 93
Audrey, Robert, 191
Axelrod, Robert, 103, 104, 146

Bali, 236
Batson, Daniel, 159
Behavioral selfishness, 116, 146–147
Belonging, 72; alienation and, 243; work and, 237
Benedict, Ruth, 63
Bergmann, Frithjof, 15
Births, out of wedlock, 201
Black English, 43
Blacks, 198–209. See also Race
Boas, Franz, 169, 170
Bok, Sissela, 250
Bronfenbrenner, Urie, 53, 57, 65, 66, 180, 183, 204, 225, 239
Buildings, abandoned, 83–84
Butler, Joseph, 249

Campbell, Angus, 227, 233
Campbell, Donald, 100
Capitalism, 25, 26; alienation and, 245; late, 5; utopian, 88; work and, 226
Capital punishment, 214, 219
Carcinogens, 174
Carnegie, Andrew, 142
Carnegie, Dale, 227
Causation, inviting, 151
Ceremony: human nature and, 186, 191–196; justice and, 220
Chall, Jeanne, 36
Chaplin, Charlie, 233
Chemicals, 174
Chenchus, 80, 218
China, 21
Chomsky, Noam, 12
Christianity, 107, 159
Cities, 83, 182–183
Civic loyalty, 128
Civility, 59
Clan rejection, 246
Clark, Kenneth T., 198
Closet morality, 58
Cognitive education, 35, 36
Collectivism: individualism and, 20–29; as organism, 148
Commission stores, 25
Commitment, 193
Communism, 230–231
Community, 22–24; breakdown of, 71; moral, 9, 10, 59, 62
Compulsions, 231–232
Conflictual model of delinquency, 72–73
Conformer genes, 170
Conformity, 170, 172–173
Conscious selfishness, 116
Consensual model of delinquency, 72
Conservatism, 26–27
Cooperation, 103–104, 105
Core morality, 54, 55
Corporations, 187
Cosmic Philosophy (Fiske), 142

259

Courage, 55–56
Crime, 64, 67–86; alienation and, 244; causes of, 211; de-moralization of, 76–77; race and, 201; revenge and, 210–224; signs of, 83–84
Culture of Narcissism, The (Lasch), 5
Curfews, 208

Daflas, 82, 168–169, 216
Darwin, Charles, 141, 143, 145
Dawkins, Richard, 147, 148, 240
De-alienation, 239–250
Death Wish, 213
Degradation, 221
Delinquency, 69, 71; control of, 13; models of, 72–73
Democracy, 54
Depression, 8
Determinism, 155
Dewey, John, 88
Discourse on Inequality (Rousseau), 161
Discrimination, 202; historical, 200; work ethic and, 234
Dragons of Eden (Sagan), 167
Drugs, 84
Durkheim, Emile, 113, 184

Economics, 25–26, 155
Education: affective, 35; cognitive, 35, 36; moral, 45–56; trashing of, 30–44
Edwards, Jonathan, 88
Egalitarianism, 157
Egoism, 15–16, 87; altruism and, 100–102; group, 9, 114–115; rational, 89–90, 104–105, 155; self and, 120–121; social contract and, 154–155. *See also* Group loyalty; Selfishness
Eibl-Eibesfeldt, Irenaus, 196
Elevator watchers, 237–238
Emler, Nicholas, 159
Emotions, 61–62, 162–163, 167
Ethically neutered society, 57–66
Ethical relativism, 50–51
Ethics: of evolution, 141–152; of parts and wholes, 127–140; of work, 225–238
Evolution, 141–152; of cooperation, 104, 105; social, 12
Evolutionary biology, 6
Execution, 214, 219
Existentialism, 17
Expectation, disappointed, 243
Exploitation, 103–104

Factions, 139
Facts, 37
Fairness, 247

Family: black, 203–204; loyalty to, 120; rituals of, 195–196
Fanatic, 138
Fascism, 23
Father absence, 204–205
Fear, 82
Feiffer, George, 75
Feudalism, 16
Firth, Raymond, 62
Fiske, John, 142
Fitness, 145, 149
Flogging, 219–220
Flynt, Larry, 10
Friedman, Milton, 89
Fürer-Haimendorf, Christoph von, 45, 80, 81, 133, 164, 217
Future, 118
Future Shock (Toffler), 125

Gangs, 14
Gemeinschaft, 14
Genetics, 162–163, 170, 171; altruism and, 147–150; crime and, 85–86
Genovese, Kitty, 64
George Washington University Medical Center, 195
Gesellschaft, 14
Get Even: The Complete Book of Dirty Tricks (Hayduke), 213
Godfather, The, 213
Golden Rule, 120
Gonds, 77, 183; justice and, 217, 220, 222; work and, 236
Goodall, Jane, 176
Goodman, Paul, 225, 228–229, 237
Gospel of Wealth, The (Carnegie), 142
Grades, 34
Graffiti, 84, 188–189
Group loyalty, 9, 114–115, 231; genetics and, 169; motives for, 105; self and, 120–121, 122–124
Guilt, 58; crime and, 76, 218–219; slavery and, 221

Haight-Ashbury Free Medical Clinic, 195
Hamilton, Alexander, 127
Hamilton, William D., 145, 149, 240
Harrington, Michael, 125
Hatred, 61
Hayduke, George, 213
Head-hunters, 79–80, 213–214, 218
Hegel, Georg Wilhelm Friedrich, 22
Heinz dilemma, 48
Herskovits, Melville, 51
Historical discrimination, 200
Hitler, Adolph, 51, 61

Hobbes, Thomas, 15, 16, 17, 89, 95, 99, 109, 113, 122, 146, 148, 154, 158, 160, 161, 163, 168
Hoffman, Martin, 159
Hogan, Robert, 92, 159
Hollander, Paul, 53
Holmes, Oliver Wendell, 67, 76
Homicide, 68
Homosexuality, 177–179
Hooliganism, 74–75
Housing, public, 240–241
Hulbert, Ann, 201
Humanity, loyalty to, 133
Human nature, 11–12; social contract and, 153–165; society and, 180–197
Hume, David, 90, 107
Hunter-gatherers, 236
Huxley, 141

Ideas, 33
Ik, 18, 19–20, 28
Impartial patriotism, 135
Imprudence, 117
Inclusive fitness, 145, 149
Indians, 199–200
Individualism, 15–29; education and, 33; ritual and, 192; selfishness and, 89
Individualistic society, 122
Inefficiency, 237
Infants, 196
Initiation, 186
Innocence, 62, 63
Intelligence, 203
Interest group, 23–24
Internalized morality, 60
Isolation, 184

Japanese, 9, 10, 229
Java, 236
Jesus, 132
Justice, 156, 210–224

Kalingas, 133
Kant, Immanuel, 62, 63, 90, 91
Khrushchev, Nikita, 229
Kin-altruism, 129, 146, 148
Kohlberg, Lawrence, 12, 46, 48, 49
Kropotkin, Peter, 142, 143, 144
Ku Klux Klan, 208
Kupperman, Joel, 60

Lao Tzu, 167
Lasch, Christopher, 5, 226, 227
Late capitalism, 5
Latham, Emma, 73
Law of non-contradiction, 34

Learning, 181–182
Levin, Martin, 211
Lewis, I. M., 195
Lewontin, Richard, 170, 171
Liars, 250
Liberalism, 27, 156
Libertarians, 27
Lieberman, Jethro, 11
Locke, John, 16, 17, 113, 148, 154
Lorenz, Conrad, 166, 181, 191
Love, 132, 196–197
Loyalty: civic, 128; family, 121; group, 9, 114–115, 231. *See also* Group loyalty
Loyalty patriotism, 135–136, 137
Lysenkoism, 74

Majority rule, 17
Man as Part of Nature (Huxley), 141
Mann, Horace, 45
Manson, Charles, 62, 95
Martindale, Don, 158, 159
Marx, Karl, 161, 245
Marxism, 24, 25; alienation and, 242, 244–245; individualism and, 17
Mather, Cotton, 88
Maxfield, Michael, 82, 83
Menninger, Karl, 218–219
Metaphysics, 113–126
Midgley, Mary, 15, 141, 160, 161, 166, 171, 179
Mill, John Stuart, 17, 99, 148, 161
Moore, George Edward, 150
Moral community, 9, 10, 59, 62
Moral core, 54, 55
Moral education, 45–56
Morality, 62; closet, 58; internalized, 60; philosophy of, 151–152; stages of, 46, 47–49; tribal, 132–133
Moscow, 189, 229
Mother Earth News, 94
Mother Teresa, 132
Movie line, 247–248
Murdoch, Iris, 176
Muslim, 222–223
Mussolini, Benito, 22
Mutilation, 219
Mutual Aid (Kropotkin), 143

Nagas, 79–80, 133; human nature and, 183; retribution and, 213–214, 218
Nash, Ogden, 87
National Education Association, 58
National Institute of Education, 58
Natural state, 163

Nature, human, 11–12. *See also* Human nature
Naylor, Kenneth, 43
Neighborhood loyalty, 128
Neill, A. S., 49
New Deal, 157
New TNT, The (Sherman), 92
New York, 190
Nietzsche, Friedrich Wilhelm, 88, 89, 107, 108, 112
Non-contradiction, law of, 34
Nonsocial self, 119
Nozick, Robert, 122, 155, 156

Objectivity, 61–62
Ohio State University, 35, 39
Oppression, 244
Original position, 155

Pair bonding, 176, 196
Parental love, 196
Parts and wholes, 127–140
Paternalism, 205
Patriotism, 134–137
Peale, Norman Vincent, 227
Peer intervention, 65
Personal virtues, 54, 55
Philipson, Michael, 72
Philosophy: moral, 151–152; social, 6
Piaget, Jean, 12, 47
Plato, 58, 87, 90, 94, 111
Pleasure-pain mechanisms, 116, 117–118
Pleistocene inheritance, 163, 166–179
Poisons, 174
Police, 222
Population biology, 145
Poverty, 85, 211
Pravda, 53
Predators, 250
Pregnancy, teenaged, 206–208
Prejudice, 202
Present, 118
Pressure, 8–9
Pride, 115
Prisoner's Dilemma, 102–103, 247
Private education, 41–42
Profit, 228, 230
Psychology, 159
Public housing, 240–241
Public work projects, 238
Punishment, 147, 210–224
Puritan work ethic, 226–227

Race, 198–209; crime and, 76; education and, 32, 38–41; work ethic and, 234
Raj Gonds, 82–83

Rand, Ayn, 15, 87–88, 89, 90, 91, 99, 114, 122
Rational egoism, 89–90, 104–105, 155
Ravitch, Diane, 36, 37
Rawls, John, 151, 154, 155, 156, 158
Recidivism, 211
Reciprocal altruism, 104, 145–147, 182
Rejection, 246
Relativism, 50–51
Religion, 160
Republic (Plato), 94, 111
Respect, 59–60, 237
Responsibility, 73, 75
Restoration, 241
Retribution, 210–224
Revenge, 147, 210–224
Ritual: human nature and, 186, 191–196; justice and, 220
Rockefeller, John D., 142
Romantic love, 196–197
Ross, Ralph, 194
Rousseau, Jean Jacques, 17, 88, 154, 160, 161, 162
Rules, 11
Russell, Bertrand, 150

Sacrifice, 88
Sagan, Carl, 167
SAT. *See* Scholastic Aptitude Test
Schambra, William, 156, 157
Scholastic Aptitude Test (SAT), 30
Schroeder, David, 92
Seabury, David, 93
Self, 113–126; nonsocial, 119; social, 119
Self-esteem, 35–36, 37–38, 249
Selfishness: animals and, 116–117; behavioral, 116; conscious, 116; failure of, 99–112; selling of, 87–95. *See also* Egoism
Self-respect, 237
Self-sacrifice, 88
Sewall, G. T., 32
Sex, 175–179, 196–197
Shame, 115, 220–221
Shepher, Joseph, 176
Sherman, Harold, 92, 93
Shikita, Mr., 9
Shils, Edward, 180
Shook, Robert, 94
Shoplifting, 110
Singapore, 222–223
Singer, Peter, 150, 151, 153
Skogan, Wesley, 82, 83
Slavery, 221, 234–235
Social contract, 153–165
Social Darwinism, 142

Social determinism, 155
Socialization, 85–86
Social philosophy, 6
Social self, 119
Society, 113–126; fully developed, 121–122; individualistic, 122; suicidal, 5, 7, 135, 198
Sociobiology (Wilson), 150
Solzhenitsyn, Aleksandr, 20
Sovereign, 16
Soviet Union, 20–21; crime in, 73–75; economics of, 25–26; farming in, 191; moral education in, 51–54; subways in, 189; trust in, 111; work in, 228, 229–231, 232, 235–236, 237–238
Spencer, Herbert, 141, 142
Sports patriotism, 136–137
State, 16
Stigma, 76–77, 78, 232
Stoics, 167
Stores, 110, 229–230
Subjectivity, 119
Subways, 189–190
Success, 226–227
Suicidal society, 5, 7, 135, 198
Suicide, 7, 8, 68
Summerhill School, 49
Sumner, William Graham, 142
Survival literature, 94–95
Suslow, Sidney, 34
Szabo, Denis, 72

Taoists, 166, 167
Tax credits, 41, 42
Teenagers: father and, 204–205; pregnancy and, 206–207; unsupervised, 84. *See also* Youth
Temptation, 118
Territoriality, 191
Tit-for-Tat, 104
Tocqueville, Alexis de, 3, 15, 16, 23, 24, 99, 134, 135, 192, 198, 199, 234
Toffler, Alvin, 125
Toleration, 177
Tönnies, Ferdinand, 14
Tribal morality, 132–133
Tribal surrogates, 13, 180
Trivers, Robert, 104, 145, 146, 240
Truman, Harry, 187

Trust, 10–11, 110
Tuition tax credits, 41–42
Turnbull, Colin, 18, 28
Two Worlds of Childhood (Bronfenbrenner), 53

Unemployment, 85
Unfairness, 246–247
University of Michigan, 103
University of Texas at Austin, 34, 39
Uproar effect, 65–66
Urban problem, 83, 182–183
Utilitarians, 131, 132, 133, 211
Utopias, 14, 88

Values, 118–119
Values clarification, 46–47, 49–51
Values and Teaching (Simon, Harmon, and Raths), 47
Vandalism, 84, 240–241
Varenne, Hervé, 192, 194, 195
Violence, 67–86
Violent Schools, Safe Schools, 58–59
Virtues, 54, 55

Wad-Ja-Get?—The Grading Game in America, 34
Wall Street Journal, 9
Weakness, 118
Wealth, 226–227
West Germany, 183
Wharton, Yvonne L., 30
Wholes and parts, 127–140
Wickedness, 218–219, 244
Will, George, 57
Wilson, Edward O., 147, 148, 150, 151, 170, 171, 240
Wilson, James Q., 3, 67, 69, 70, 71, 72, 73, 76, 202, 215, 218
Wilson, William Julius, 200, 201, 202, 203
Wittgenstein, Ludwig, 20, 150
Wollaston, William H., 90
Women, 184
Work: alienation and, 228, 236, 237, 241–242; ethics of, 225–238
Wynne, Edward, 8

Youth: crime and, 13, 69, 71, 72–73; employment of, 238. *See also* Teenagers

ANDREW OLDENQUIST, Professor of Philosophy and member of the Mershon Center Senior Faculty at The Ohio State University, is the author of Normative Behavior, *a textbook and anthology in ethics, as well as numerous articles on ethics, education, and policy-oriented social philosophy.*